book, bath, table, and time

Other books in the series

Practicing Discernment with Youth:
A Transformative Youth Ministry Approach

by David F. White

Branded:
Adolescents Converting from Consumer Faith

by Katherine Turpin

Lives to Offer:
Accompanying Youth on Their Vocational Quests

by Dori Grinenko Baker and Joyce Ann Mercer

book, bath, table, and time

*christian worship as source
and resource for youth ministry*

fred p. edie

THE
PILGRIM
PRESS
Cleveland

This book is dedicated to my parents,
George and Connie,
who have gone on to glory ahead of the rest of us

The Pilgrim Press
700 Prospect Avenue
Cleveland, Ohio 44115-1100
thepilgrimpress.com

© 2007 by Fred P. Edie

Scripture quotations unless otherwise noted are from the New Revised Standard Version Bible, copyright © 1989 by the Division of Christian Education of the National Council of the Churches of Christ in the U.S.A.

11   5

Library of Congress Cataloging-in-Publication Data
Edie, Fred P., 1960-
    Book, bath, table, and time : Christian worship as source and resource for youth ministry / Fred P. Edie.
        p.   cm. – (Youth ministry alternatives)
    Includes bibliographical references and index.
    ISBN 978-0-8298-1744-7 (alk. paper)
    1. Church work with youth – Catholic Church. 2. Public worship – Catholic Church. I. Title. II. Title: Book, bath, table, and time.
BX2347.8.Y7E43 2007
264.00835 – dc22
                                        2007020983

Contents

Foreword

For three decades the task of conceptualizing youth ministry has largely been left to independent commercial enterprises that have failed to recognize the importance of denomination, theology, ethnicity, class, and other cultural particularities for shaping Christian discipleship. In addition, youth ministry as it has evolved over these decades lacks significant critique of the shift in the social roles of young people in the second half of the twentieth century and into the twenty-first century, in which youth are increasingly ghettoized as passive consumers rather than treated as agents of faith influencing the common good.

Decades of domestication, marginalization, and trivialization of youth ministry by theology schools, denominations, and publishing houses have distorted our imagination of what counts as youth ministry. The image of youth ministry as trivial or pragmatic has left many hungry for youth ministry approaches that include social critique and engagement, theological sophistication, faith formation, and a genuine knowledge of and respect for the unique youth of today. The Youth Ministry ALTERNATIVES series has been jointly conceived by The Pilgrim Press and David F. White and Faith Kirkham Hawkins to address that hunger.

The Youth Ministry ALTERNATIVES series aims to clearly articulate approaches to youth ministry that embody social awareness and theological reflection and foster the distinctive gifts of youth for the church and the world. The series will highlight approaches to youth ministry that embody the following commitments:

1. **Dialogue with Living Communities.** This series will highlight approaches for fostering dynamic dialogue between the Christian traditions and youth and adults in living communities of faith.

2. **Deeper Understanding.** This series will engage this dialogue to deepen understanding of youth, theology, and youth ministry. Of particular interest is the wisdom emerging from a variety of underexplored sources that will be identified and interpreted, including the following:

   - the wisdom of youth
   - the wisdom of communities engaged in youth ministry
   - the contexts of youth, including their inner landscapes, communities, cultures, and physical environments
   - the resources of Christian tradition

3. **Transformative Practices.** From these conversations and the wisdom gleaned from youth, communities, and their contexts, this series will especially highlight a range of practices for engaging youth in ministry, such as:

   - doing theology and ministry with youth
   - taking youth seriously — their wounds, blessings, and gifts
   - mobilizing and enhancing youth agency and vocation
   - enhancing formation and transformation of youth as they journey in faith
   - articulating clear approaches to youth ministry
   - discerning a congregation's unique youth ministry

In *Book, Bath, Table, and Time: Christian Worship as Source and Resource for Youth Ministry,* Fred Edie elaborates his thesis that liturgical holy things provide the church with an ecology of practices that form Christian youth by offering experiences of God's presence, by identifying God rightly, and by compelling them to take up their baptismal vocations before God and for the world. In this book, Fred draws on ancient emphases regarding the centrality of worship, especially as it is being reclaimed by the contemporary liturgical renewal movement. Yet it would be a mistake to imagine that these emphases are anachronistic; instead they are especially relevant in a postmodern consumer world in which Christians and youth ministers are trying to find their bearings.

While it comes as no surprise in a market driven culture that many North American congregations are adapting the methods and products of the marketplace to their own practices of ministry — staging worship with the panache of a TV variety special or the amped-up intensity of a rock concert — thoughtful youth workers question these methods and their results. *Book, Bath, Table, and Time* offers pastors, youth ministry practitioners, and theorizers one way out of this morass. It does so, however, with the assistance of an unlikely source and resource: the Christian *ordo*, the name given to the pattern of the ancient church's life "ordered" around its liturgical "holy things" — bath (Baptism); book (Scriptures); table (Eucharist); and the prayerful patterning of time (Calendar) (Gordon Lathrop, *Holy Things: A Liturgical Theology,* Fortress, 1993). This *ordo* constitutes a living ecology that initiates persons into Christian faith and communal life through baptism and continues to nurture them in faithfulness to their baptismal vocations through deep participation in book, table, and Christian timekeeping. Thus, *Book, Bath, Table, and Time* describes this faithful, if neglected, way of being *church*; a way that recognizes and practices through the *ordo* the church's unique identity as Christ's Body for the world; and a way that offers youth engaged in such a community the means to be formed into that identity as well. Of course, the irony here is that the book's approach to renewing youth ministry utilizes "fossils" from church tradition. It is anything but cutting-edge innovative and cannot be assimilated to consumer/entertainment culture. Clearly, *Book, Bath, Table, and Time* disputes the conventional wisdom that assumes that youth ministry must be hipper than yesterday and otherwise disguise its affiliation with the church in order to be vital.

The ideas presented in this book were not forged in a professor's office, but have been tested by the Duke Youth Academy for Christian Formation, of which Fred Edie is the founding director. DYA stands as a living testimony to the theological and formational accounts of an *ordo*-based approach to youth ministry. DYA is a temporary community of high school students and adults that takes up residence together at Duke University's Divinity School for two weeks each summer. The Academy teaches, lives, and reflects upon the *ordo* as the basis of communal life. Thus DYA practices what this book preaches. Readers will find fulsome descriptions of this community — what the *ordo* looks like walking around in T-shirts and flip flops, for example — to help them imagine how it may be appropriated in their own ministry settings. DYA is not the church, nor does it claim to be. It does, however, take up the *church's* holy things with gusto, something many "real" churches have forgotten how to do. It intends, therefore, to be a sign or a parable of the church and to remind its students, staff, and, indirectly, the *church* of the church's own distinctive identity and vocation.

We are proud to present *Book, Bath, Table, and Time: Christian Worship as Source and Resource for Youth Ministry* in this series. It represents a lively and well-crafted interpretation of an important movement in Christian formation and youth ministry.

DAVID F. WHITE AND FAITH KIRKHAM HAWKINS
Series editors, Youth Ministry Alternatives

Series editors David F. White and Faith Kirkham Hawkins are respectively the C. Ellis and Nancy Gribble Nelson Associate Professor of Christian Education at Austin Presbyterian Theological Seminary in Austin, Texas, and Director of the Youth Theological Initiative and Assistant Professor of Youth and Education at Candler School of Theology at Emory University in Atlanta, Georgia.

Acknowledgments

It takes a village to raise an author. In my case the primary village is the small community of Isle of Hope just east of Savannah, Georgia. Isle of Hope is an increasingly rare phenomenon — an authentic community. The community evolved naturally over two hundred years, nestling itself amidst the contours of river and marsh. It is a place where people know one another and one another's children, where children walk or ride their bikes to church or school, where tree surgeons live next door to heart surgeons. Isle of Hope was for me, to borrow the lyrical phrase of my friend Mary McClintock Fulkerson, "a place to appear." The entire community cheered my successes, nurtured my becoming, and disciplined my excesses, including especially my tendencies to imagine myself as too clever by half.

It also takes a church to raise a Christian. What modest Christian character I manage to display is the gift of multiple teachers, choir members, pastors, youth workers, and other caring peers and adults in the congregations of my upbringing. Lynn Drake, Rob Grotheer, and Rick Monroe were vital mentors to me during my own adolescence. They befriended me, nurtured my gifts for ministry, and kept company with me through the ups and downs of that season.

I am deeply thankful for ministry apprenticeships under Dan Benedict and Helen Rogers. Dan's profound Christian character and deep spirituality is clearly the result of a lifetime of grace-filled formation through the liturgy. Under his tutelage I discovered a way to be faithful that curbed (some of) my arrogance and reclaimed the vital presence of God over against my suspicions of shallow emotional manipulation. Helen taught me much of what I know about the practice of educational ministry. She demonstrated how through hard work and vision it is possible to transform a congregation's educational culture.

To the two different generations of youth with whom I served in South Georgia, Nashville, and southern California I say "thanks." From you I learned what it means for youth to struggle for their own places to appear and to serve in the name of Christ. You are all adults now, some of you with teens of your own, and I wish you God's peace.

My principal teachers at Emory — James Fowler, Rod Hunter, Don Saliers, Charles Foster, Richard Bondi, and Roberta Bondi — witness to the grace-filled character that emerges from "the love of learning and the desire for God." Their breadth of scholarship and generosity of spirit are unmatched in my experience. In addition, Charles Foster served as pastor, priest, and prophet to me through those years.

During those lean graduate school years church friends and neighbors from Isle of Hope supported our family through prayer, gifts of money, help with carpooling, and other practices essential to maintaining family sanity. I've never fully understood what to make of this. I was not particularly deserving. I've come to believe that their gifts were expressions of God's dreams for all of God's people. I am especially indebted to the extended Barnes clan — Bee and Pop, Carole and Fred, Betsy and Geoff — who took turns housing me, feeding me, employing me, funding me, and lending me tools out of that amazing garage.

Thanks also to Greg Jones, dean, Willie Jennings, academic dean, and Janice Virtue, associate dean for continuing education here at Duke Divinity School. This trinity of bosses never fails to encourage me and continues to nurture my development as a scholar and a person. That Duke has become for me another village and a place to appear is partly the result of their persistence and patience.

The Duke Youth Academy for Christian Formation stands as a backdrop to this book. DYA and its peer programs grew out of the vision of Craig Dykstra and the generous funding of the Lilly Endowment, Inc. This vision was also nurtured by Chris Coble, also of Lilly, and Carol Lytch, who worked through the Fund for Theological Education to shepherd DYA and its peer ministries through their early years. I am grateful for their mentoring and advice.

A sister institution, Candler School of Theology, paved the way for the many theological initiatives with high school youth including DYA through its own Youth Theology Initiative. My thanks to Faith Kirkham Hawkins and David White, whose present and past association with YTI inspires the rest of us and whose Youth Ministry Alternatives series with The Pilgrim Press provides me this forum.

My thanks also to past and present DYA assistant directors Cindy Monteith, Brian Jones, and Elizabeth Ingram Schindler. Cindy undertook the Herculean task of getting DYA off the ground, Brian brought discipline, theological insight and a joie de vivre to the ministry, and Elizabeth brings unmatched skills for leadership, administration, and the authentic practice of ministry. Elizabeth's competence made it possible for me to find the time to write. She has also offered critical insights on multiple manuscript drafts.

The staff and students of DYA are remarkable for their faithfulness and their hope. From where I sit, the coming Reign of God is appearing in our midst! May Christ's baptismal waters continue to bear you toward that Promised Land.

Thanks to Ulrike Guthrie, my editor at Pilgrim, who was throughout this process unfailingly professional and encouraging.

Finally, I wish to express gratitude to my family. My wife, Alison, regularly plants my feet back on earth and testifies daily through her own extraordinary gifts for compassion and the arts to the reality of incarnation. My children, Stewart and Rebekah, are two of God's richest blessings in my own life. I pray they will continue to find deepened identity *en Christo*.

One

Christian worship as the generative context for youth ministry[1]

Present-day challenges to youth ministry

Over the last few years I've had the good fortune of being invited to teach theology to youth workers at an annual week-long school loosely affiliated with a denominational seminary. I teach in this school gladly because of its mission to equip youth workers for ministry over the long haul. One day, however, a chance encounter awakened me to challenges to youth ministry that until then I had not entirely comprehended. The occasion was a community lunch hosted by a local travel agency. It was an opportunity for the company owner to say "thank you" to youth workers from his part of the country for booking, in his words, "many thousands" of youth group ski packages through his agency. His expressions of thanks were met with a standing ovation. Apparently he delivered excellent service. But there was more. He was that day announcing a dynamic new "product" to youth workers: all inclusive youth "mission trip packages." To sum it up, he said, "We want to be your first contact in the missions business!" More enthusiastic applause.

Now I am more pinheaded than most, but this spiel and the response it occasioned vexed me. On the one hand, a nice Christian businessman laid out some serious cash to feed three hundred folks, so gratitude was the order of the day. On the other hand, I was perturbed that no one else seemed to be troubled by the man's rhetoric

1. Portions of this chapter appear in my essay "Cultivating Baptismal Spirituality in High School Youth," *Doxology* 19 (2002): 85–107, and are reprinted with permission.

and what it implied about the church and its ministries with youth. He received multiple ovations, and he and his staff were besieged afterward by youth workers anxious to inquire further into the details of the company's services.

Less than happily, I sat at the empty table and pondered questions like these: When did ski trips become a requirement for the church's ministry with youth? Is skiing now a "mark" of the church? Or has "ski trip" become part of the Christian year, sandwiched between Epiphany and Lent to assure excellent powder? Do students read Bonhoeffer's *Life Together* while riding up the lifts? More fundamentally, do we Christians believe any longer that our spiritual convictions manifest themselves in distinctive or even countercultural ways of living in the world? Or, are our claims to use ski trips as a chance to love teens for Jesus or bring teens to Jesus actually simply denial of the fact that what we are really doing is entertaining them?

As for the "missions business": when did the church get out of missions and into subcontracting? What happens when a practice so risky, messy, and unpredictable as taking Christ to and meeting Christ in places away from home becomes a comfortable religious field trip with every contingency covered for a small fee?

That leaders of the church may come to view a travel agency as part and parcel of the "ministry business" or that Christian missions may be characterized without a trace of irony as one more product to be marketed and sold to religious consumers is compelling evidence that our churches' ministries have capitulated to such dominant North American cultural marketplace values as individualism, consumption, and the pursuit of entertaining experiences. Whether these values snuck into the church like Trojan horses without our realizing what was going on or have been adopted strategically ("If we take them skiing they'll learn how much Jesus loves them!"), the results are the same: a Gospel so distorted and church ministries so domesticated that they are nearly indistinguishable from the culture at large.

Where does this leave our youth? For one thing, it ensures that North American Christian teens and their parents continue to fall prey to the destructive influences of individualism, consumption, and entertainment. For another, as these values come to dominate the mind-set and practices of church ministries, they cloud and distort the meanings and lived implications of Christianity for professing Christians.

The suggestion that Christians in general and Christian youth in particular do not know who they are as members of the Body of Christ comes from some sobering conversations. In my youth ministry courses at Duke Divinity School, I assign students a series of three extensive interviews with churchgoing high school students. Consistently, these interviews demonstrate that even young people professedly committed to Christ and the church do not know their scriptures, do not understand the significance of their participation in the church's worship and sacramental life, do not engage in Christian practices with any regularity or depth, and cannot imagine what being Christian means for their present and future vocations. The sociologist of religion Christian Smith has recently provided compelling evidence consistent with my students' informal findings. After interviews conducted with thousands of North American teens, Smith contends that most churchgoing teens like their congregations and feel welcome and at home in them.[2] Many know almost nothing, however, about Christian theological convictions. Smith characterizes these students as "moralistic, therapeutic, deists."[3] As Smith sees it, these students believe that Christian faith exists to help them do what is right and avoid what is wrong (personally, that is, for they would not want to impose their particular morality upon others). In addition, God is to them an emotionally available life coach who sanctions whatever they happen to be feeling at any given moment but otherwise remains uninvolved in the historic, social, or political affairs of the world.

Smith suggests that his findings may be interpreted either as a strong indication that the church is failing to teach and form its young into orthodox Christian life or it may be seen as evidence that the content of orthodoxy itself is devolving to a syrupy therapeutic prop to

2. Christian Smith, *Soul Searching: The Religious and Spiritual Lives of American Teens* (New York: Oxford University Press, 2005), 266.

3. Ibid., 163.

underwrite North Americans' overriding goal of feeling good all the time.[4] Put slightly differently, my students' findings and those of Smith suggest that even Christian youth believe they are self-constructed autonomous individuals who need Christianity to feel close to God so that they may feel good about themselves and their purpose in life, which often seems as if it is to consume.

Looking to the church at worship for clues to faithful youth ministry

Given the almost Orwellian cast to this introduction so far, readers may be expecting an angry exposé, one that seeks to unmask these dark powers vying for our minds, bodies, hearts, and souls and those of our youth. Yet I am more interested in suggesting how the church may practice creative and faithful ministry that also happens to be resistant, responsive, and transformational to a culture espousing individualism, consumption, and experience for its own sake.[5] This book is not one more collection of "dynamic, life-changing, easy-to-teach, youth ministry programs guaranteed to fire your kids up for Jesus or your money back." No. The commodifying of youth ministry, congregations, the culture, and youth themselves is at the heart of the problem. Instead of market-driven youth ministry products or youth ministry service providers (including travel agents), I look to the *church itself* (including its history, theology, ministry, and mission) for clues to faithful youth ministry. That such a strategy may strike some as ironic or surprising or novel or even doomed to failure is itself testimony to how far youth ministry has drifted from its moorings.

In particular, I look to the church at worship. If the fundamental gift and call to Christ's Body in the world is the love of God and

---

4. Ibid., 171.
5. Refer to David F. White, *Practicing Discernment with Youth: A Transformative Youth Ministry Approach* (Cleveland: Pilgrim, 2005). In chapters 1 and 2 White provides an astute historical-critical reading of adolescence and the cultural forces operating on teenagers and youth ministry.

the love of neighbor, then worship will ever be the primary and principal practice of Christian life. Theologically speaking, the church's faith that the triune God creates, redeems, and sustains all life always prompts its grace-engendered responses of praise and gratitude — of worship. In and through this worshipful communion with God, we also learn to draw upon the Spirit's gifts and power for loving ourselves and our neighbors. Thus, from a theological perspective worship must be at the heart of the church's ministry and mission, including its youth ministry. I am, in fact, more apt to use the term "liturgy" than worship in this account. For liturgy, meaning "work of the people," captures well the sense of communal, participative, and embodied worship into which I hope to see youth formed.

You may quite rightly be asking whether present-day corporate worship in the churches isn't shot through with the values of individualism, consumerism, and self-interested experience that I protest so vigorously above. Whether strategically or unwittingly, many communities have indeed come to emulate the entertainment industry in their worship practice. Worship "guests" are offered worship "performances" targeted to their specific demographic tastes and designed to feed their desire for entertaining experiences. Thus, as a youth worker at a large church once told me, his staff offered "hymns and the pipe organ" to the older folks at an early service, "praise band and 'Cat's in the Cradle'" to the baby boomers at another, and "sacraments and Taizé chants to the Gen-X'ers" at a third "because they're into the really old stuff." Worship in this view qualifies as whatever satisfies my individual preferences for an entertaining worshipful experience. In the process, God and neighbor are bumped to the balcony to make room for me front and center.

Even congregations that have for various reasons not chosen to practice entertainment worship or demographically driven worship can be fairly sure that their members are so thoroughly formed as consumers of entertainment that they are likely interpreting and judging the significance of worship through those marketplace lenses.

Unlike ski trips and mission packages, the church's worship fortunately has a history that predates the rise of North American media and consumer-driven Christianity. We have two millennia of accounts, prescriptions, and communal inspiration and wisdom about Christian worship — a veritable treasure trove of liturgical patterns and practices that can redirect our present infatuation with ourselves and our own amusement. This liturgical treasure trove is a means by which youth can be recreated, free from the disproportionate influence of individualism, and through which their attentions and passions can be redirected to resist the unfettered consumption of goods and experiences designed for personal amusement.

But it won't be easy. It will require that youth, their leaders, and their congregations begin much more transparently to think and act theologically. It will require that the church look to historic practices of worship in order to recover its distinctive identity as Christ's body before God and for the world. It will require working overtime to break down the divisions that typically fence off youth ministry from the rest of congregational life, including especially its worship life. It will challenge congregations to shed the cultural consumerist skin and to wash themselves afresh in Christ's living waters. It will require sustained rethinking of how to incorporate youth in the life of the church, and years of work — more years, in fact, than the tenure of a typical youth worker.

The liturgical ordo
and the reconceiving of youth ministry

I propose that much of this long-term work can center on the church's worshiping tradition, or *ordo*. The meaning of *ordo* is at once pedestrian and profound. First, it is a generic name for ancient Christian communities' collections of worship instructions which some traditions today refer to as their order of worship — what's printed in their bulletin or found in their book of worship.[6] This *ordo* "ordered" or

---

6. Gordon W. Lathrop, *Holy Things: A Liturgical Theology* (Minneapolis: Fortress, 1993). See chapters 2 and 3 for detailed discussions of the *ordo*. I am heavily indebted to Lathrop's groundbreaking work in liturgical theology. My sense of the content and meaning of the *ordo* as well as my use of the phrase "holy things" draws primarily upon his work. I am also drawing upon the insights of the Greek

set out liturgical practices, particularly with regard to the holy things: bath (baptism), book (scriptures), table (Holy Communion or Eucharist), and the patterning of temporal rhythms in light of the triune God (Christian timekeeping).[7] For example, community *ordos* tended to such mundane matters as what the Sunday assembly should consist of and how it should proceed; how and when to baptize; where to stand when reading the scriptures, who should read them, and which ones should be read; how to set the table for Eucharist, and so on. At first pass, we might think of the *ordo* as simply a liturgical how-to manual.

More broadly, the word *ordo* also came to describe the patterned communal way of life shaped around the practice of these holy things. Understood this way, the *ordo* constitutes a living communal ecology: one that included initiating persons into Christian faith through baptism (bath), then continued to nurture them in faithfulness to their baptismal callings through sustained participation in the book (Bible), table (Eucharist), and Christian timekeeping. Thus, the *ordo* "ordered" not only worship life on Sundays but the entirety of the church's life before God. Patterns for worshiping became the patterns for communal living. Early Christians self-consciously undertook baptismal, Eucharistic, temporally patterned, and Word en-fleshed lives. Such patterning is what spurs Don Saliers to describe worship as a "...characterizing activity. When worship occurs," he writes, "people are characterized, given their life and fundamental location and orientation in the world."[8] Worship by way of the *ordo*'s book,

Orthodox liturgical theologian Alexander Schmemann's *Introduction to Liturgical Theology* (Crestwood, NY: St. Vladimir's Seminary Press, 1986) and *For the Life of the World: Sacraments and Orthodoxy* (Crestwood, NY: St. Vladimir's Seminary Press, 1973), as well as my teacher Don Saliers's *Worship as Theology: Foretaste of Glory Divine* (Nashville: Abingdon, 1994) and *The Soul in Paraphrase: Prayer and the Religious Affections* (New York: Seabury, 1980).

7. Lathrop, *Holy Things*. See Part 2 for descriptions of holy things. I adopt Lathrop's phenomenological language because it reiterates the ordinary, earthy, everyday quality of God's grace-filled means of revelatory self-disclosure and because it is readily allied with the bodily practices of formation I envision for youth ministry.

8. Don Saliers, "Liturgy and Ethics: Some New Beginnings" in *Liturgy and the Moral Self: Humanity at Full Stretch before God*, ed. E. Byran Anderson and Bruce T. Morrill (Collegeville, MN: Liturgical Press, 1998), 17.

bath, table, and time came to characterize Christians as a people distinct from other peoples in part because it patterned all of their communal life around these holy things.

At still another level, the *ordo*'s implications are nothing less than cosmic. The church recognized that to enter into the *ordo* was to join together with God in spinning the universe on its ear. Through its liturgical practices of book, bath, table, and time the worshiping assembly wasn't merely reminding itself of or imitating or pretending about God's activity. Rather, it understood itself to be actively participating in and joining with God through these things in God's own saving action of re-membering, reordering, recreating, and redeeming the cosmos. For the church to enact this *ordo* meant being swept up in the triune God's theological big bang: the creation (past, present, and future) of all that exists; the redemption of this existence by way of covenant with Israel and the life, death, and resurrection of Jesus Christ; and the community's continuing journey with the Spirit to the fullness of God's Reign. To get involved with the liturgical *ordo* was to become part and parcel of God's work of salvation — nothing less!

Together these descriptions and explanations of the *ordo* point to a church animated by a different sensibility than the church of our day. First, worship was less about individual enrichment and more about communal engagement for and with God. It is unlikely, for example, that worship in the third century prompted comments like "I just didn't get much out of church today." Christians were too busy worshipfully entering into the presence and practice of God's Reign on Earth to dwell on how they felt about it or whether it was meeting their needs. Second, there was little distinction between the church engaged in worship and the church engaged in ministry. Evangelism was organic to the practice of baptism. Hospitality took its cue from Eucharist. Justice was practiced because of and by way of a common bath, shared cup, and a preference for Sabbath rest over pursuit of personal empire. In other words, the liturgy of the church's worship was understood to be organically linked to the liturgy of the church's life together with God and for the world. The church's life and vision, its vocation, flowed into and out of its *ordo*.

Such a way of life envisioned and practiced through the holy things of the *ordo* can be instructive for us. It offers the church the possibility of renewed vision and renewed practice of ministry that is resistant to current cultural ills including misplaced esteem for personal fulfillment as the supreme end of life. It offers a way of reclaiming worship, evangelism, formation, and servant ministry as interdependent pieces in a living ecology rather than boutique services offered by a religious shopping mall. Its emphasis on organic relationship between the liturgical and extra-liturgical practices of church bears the promise of clearer congregational identity and purpose.[9]

But what about youth ministry? My hope is that by exploring the nature of the church as it is known through this *ordo,* the liturgies of the holy things (book, bath, table, and time) that it prescribes, the communal way of life it fashions, and the reordering of the universe that it enacts, those of us involved in youth ministry will be reminded

---

9. Since I am endeavoring to describe a liturgical youth ministry and not simply a liturgical theology, I cannot fully develop an apology for worship as I describe it or for the normative status I ascribe to the *ordo*. I do acknowledge that not every congregation or every denomination practices worship through the *ordo*. In light of the crisis of youth's Christian identity, however, it is critical to differentiate between those traditions that do not practice the *ordo* out of principled or historic objection to it and those that have simply forgotten it. With respect to the former, such liturgical "iconoclasm" often arose out of what a tradition's founders judged to be distorted practices of holy things on the part of church forbears. Such distortions, as in the case of private masses, for example, are undeniable. Nevertheless, for the Quakers — to cite one tradition of dissent — to practice asacramental worship requires the continued existence of the liturgical *ordo* in the wider church in order for their dissent to make sense. In another case, many African American communities have historically deemphasized holy things because the legacy of slavery once prevented them from sharing the baptism or Holy Communion with their white masters. My own contention is that the solution to corrupt or distorted practice of the *ordo* is not to abandon it, but to become cognizant of how the ecology of book, bath, table, and time is itself capable of critiquing those who would domesticate it. I seek to demonstrate this prophetic capacity of the *ordo* throughout my account. On a slightly different tack, it may surprise some readers to learn that wide consensus already exists around normative claims for the *ordo* in traditions ranging from Catholicism to the Protestant left. See, for example, *Baptism, Eucharist, and Ministry* (World Council of Churches, 1982). Finally, even though principled and historic objections are real, I nonetheless contend that the primary reason for neglect of the *ordo* in most congregations is bad memory, lack of theological imagination, and colonization by consumer culture.

that we are already in possession of extraordinary and grace-filled means to recover faithful and vital ministry with youth. In other words, we don't need to go shopping elsewhere or call in the travel agents. To that end, chapters 5 and 8 focus primarily on the bath in relation to youth ministry, chapters 2 and 4 on the book, chapters 2 and 7 on the table, and chapter 6 on the patterning of time. Chapter 3, while not taking up any single one of the holy things, attempts to explain the requisite ways of knowing critical to liturgical youth ministry.

The ordo's formative dynamics

Besides being a theological type, I am also a church educator and youth worker. So in addition to recalling and reclaiming the theological significance of the *ordo* itself as the ground for the church's worship and ministry, I propose in these pages that we pay attention to how practicing the *ordo* may shape us into authentic Christian faith and life. What is it about the *ordo,* in other words, that may form youth into Christians?

Ministry as formation

Formation is an ancient term and way of conceiving ministry best known to our Catholic brothers and sisters but lately finding a place within Protestantism as well. Its roots are biblical. Genesis 2 testifies to God's artful formation of the human being from the dust of the earth. God then breathes into (in-spires) that human being with the animating energy of life (Gen. 2:7). Thus, formation as a practice of Christian ministry should be understood in light of God's own creative activity. To practice the ministry of Christian formation is to participate with the Spirit in the renewal or restoration of God-likeness or God-"lifeness" in human beings. In other words, formation of Christian youth means restoring or deepening within them the *imago Dei,* the image of God. At least two additional insights critical to my account follow from this brief description of formation.

First, as Genesis 2 illustrates, God forms *bodies* and not merely spirits. Thus, the earthiness, the soma, the "humus" of human beings matters essentially to the equation of formation. Some youth and youth workers imagine that Christian faith is a purely spiritual affair, but the Genesis account reminds us that body and spirit are not separate entities. Youth are "in-spirited" bodies or embodied spirits. In addition to intellectual capacities for reasoned reflection, youth possess and are possessed by passionate desire and other bodily dispositions. To engage with youth in ministries of formation, therefore, is to attend to youthful bodies and to animate these bodies through bodily and affectively laden gestures, practices, and motions consistent with the Spirit's redemptive activity in the world. Though I will develop this argument further in subsequent chapters, I contend that the (appropriate) renewed focus on youth as embodied beings also supports the reconceiving of ministry through ritually embodied and affectively laden practices around book, bath, table, and time.

The language of formation offers a second potential insight to youth ministry. It rightly emphasizes living a faithful life instead of merely thinking deep spiritual thoughts. As Aristotle points out, theoretical knowledge does not exhaust all forms of human knowing. He champions practical knowing (*praxis*), a kind of knowing characterized by thinking-informed action or active reflection. These dimensions of action and reflection are best conceived as two sides of the same coin. In contrast to the passively contemplative nature of theoretical knowledge this practical knowledge is oriented to doing, to living.[10] Moreover, this kind of knowing requires cultivation of virtues, bodily habitual dispositions that assist persons toward acting consistent with a community's vision of the good life. Of primary importance to my account, Aristotle contends that persons (usually youth in his day) are formed into this life of virtue not by sitting in school and contemplating theoretical knowledge but by following around and imitating virtuous persons — in short, by practicing the good life.

---

10. Aristotle, *Nicomachean Ethics*, trans. Terence Irwin (Indianapolis: Hackett, 1985), 40.

The language of formation holds the potential to remind us all that following Jesus requires forming youths' bodies perhaps as much as and perhaps more than it does filling their minds. Repenting, for example, *turning around,* is a bodily gesture and a disposition of the heart not fulfilled solely by contemplating contrition. Learning to approach the God we worship with fear, awe, and gratitude is a matter of learning to kneel in humility or to stretch arms heavenward. Welcoming strangers with hospitality and compassion requires expunging bodily passions of fear or "obliviousness" and replacing them with compassion and loving engagement.[11] Such formation requires practice by way of apprenticeship to exemplary Christians.

To reiterate, the language of Christian formation, in contrast to the more conventional language of Christian education, refocuses attention on the need for youth ministry to attend to the bodies of young persons by inviting youth into the practice of a faithful way of life as a means to become faithful. Such formational ministry does not exclude theoretical knowledge; indeed, it requires such knowledge for proper reflection on practices. But living the Christian life, more than just thinking about living the Christian life is formational ministry's goal.

Three dynamics of formation through the ordo

Formation through the *ordo* displays three overlapping dynamics: (1) practicing the *ordo* is a means by which youth experience the presence of the living God; (2) practicing the *ordo* reveals the identity of God; and (3) practicing the *ordo* invites youth to practice and further discern their vocation before God and for the world.[12]

---

11. Saliers, *The Soul in Paraphrase.* Saliers considers how worship may form persons into an affective "grammar" of praise and lament, awe and holy fear, and more. In addition, I am borrowing Mary McClintock-Fulkerson's term "obliviousness." She uses it to describe a human habitual disposition of "not seeing," particularly with respect to the failure of persons of privilege to "see" or "make space for" "marginal" persons. Her use of postmodern place theory in *Places of Redemption: Theology for a Worldly Church* (Oxford: Oxford University Press, forthcoming) serves as a strong reminder of the bodily character of Christian faith in local communities.

12. I am indebted here to Henry Knight, *The Presence of God in the Christian Life: John Wesley and the Means of Grace* (Metuchen, NJ: Scarecrow, 1992) for

1. Experiencing the presence of God

First, practicing the *ordo*'s holy things (book, bath, table, and time) offers a vital means to experience the presence of the living God. Historically, at least, worship by way of the *ordo* was anything but dead. The church knew its liturgical rites to be heart-pounding contexts for encountering the power of holy Mystery. For example, early church theologians described the rites of baptismal initiation as "awesome."[13] And participants in weekly Word and Table worship on Sunday (the Lord's Day) showed up expecting to encounter the *risen, living* Christ, not some mildewed memory. No one doubted the presence of the Spirit of God in the *ordo*-grounded assembly. God was experienced as alive and powerfully present in this worshiping life ordered around book, bath, table, and time.

From the standpoint of formation, contexts for encountering the presence of the living God matter tremendously. As the scriptures suggest, when God "speaks" God's incarnational Word, that Word does not return to God empty (Isa. 55:11). The Christian God is not a deist sort who sits and watches. No, the Christian God is a player/coach, actively involved in the affairs of creation. And it is precisely God's grace-filled presence with creation, revealed through the life, death, and resurrection of Jesus Christ that offers the power to accomplish creation's redemption. Thus, to enter God's presence is to enter a zone of holy formation and transformation. One does not truly encounter God and remain unmoved.

The Roman Catholic liturgical theologian Aidan Kavanagh describes the worshiping assembly's encounter with God as the occasion for an "adjustment" in the life of the assembly.[14] Adjustment means change here: formative and perhaps transformative change in

---

much of the descriptive language of the first two dynamics. The third is the result of my explorations in baptismal theology.

13. Chrysostom is one of several church fathers who employ this descriptor. See Edward Yarnold, S.J., *The Awe-Inspiring Rites of Initiation: The Origins of the R.C.I.A.* (Collegeville, MN: Liturgical Press, 1994), 57.

14. Aidan Kavanagh, *On Liturgical Theology* (Collegeville, MN: Liturgical Press, 1984), 74.

response to God's presence. The assembly's adjustment may be dramatic and immediately discernible — or not — but it is real. For when people experience God's living presence, formation happens. Moreover, persons who meet God over a lifetime of Sundays may hope for and expect ever deeper adjustment (formation) into their character as little brothers and sisters of Christ. Abiding in the presence of the living God has that effect! Thus, the *ordo* is critical to the equation of formation because it ushers persons into the presence of a God who is continually making all things new.

How do human beings experience God's presence? Awareness of encounter with God's living presence requires more than human thinking or reason. It is a knowing that also stirs the hearts, bodies, imaginations, and spirits of believers. Sometimes it is beyond language. We feel it in our bones. Not coincidentally, practicing worship through the *ordo*'s holy things positively requires the engagement of the hearts, bodies, imaginations, and spirits of the assembly's participants. Indeed, one might even claim that human beings are created by God with hearts, bodies, imaginations, and spirits (and intellects) precisely for the purpose of encountering God, communing with God, and experiencing God's living presence in worship through holy things so that they may formed and transformed consistent with God's loving intent.

Many researchers in the field of adolescence have noted the profound deepening of teens' epistemological capacities as they grow toward adulthood.[15] More recently, we are learning from scientists investigating the adolescent brain how teens' deepening *affective* capacities are as important as their cognitive ones.[16] In light of these insights, Kenda Dean suggests that youth tend primarily to discern with and lead from their hearts.[17] From a purely biological

---

15. See James W. Fowler, *Stages of Faith: The Psychology of Human Development and the Quest for Meaning* (San Francisco: Harper, 1995), especially chapter 18. See also Robert Kegan, *In Over Our Heads: The Mental Demands of Modern Life* (Cambridge, MA: Harvard, 1994), especially chapter 1.

16. See Barbara Strauch, *The Primal Teen: What the New Discoveries about the Teenage Brain Tell Us about Our Kids* (New York: Doubleday, 2003).

17. Kenda Creasy Dean, *Practicing Passion: Youth and the Quest for a Passionate Church* (Grand Rapids: Eerdmans, 2004), chapters 1 and 2.

perspective, learning to give and receive love or to feel what another is feeling assists persons in the tasks of recruiting mates and in caring for offspring. New parents must develop bodily and emotionally mediated means of communicating with infants, for example, if these children are to flourish.[18] From a formational perspective, however, the emergence of the adolescent heart also makes teens emergently capable of passionate encounters with the mysterious presence of a loving God in and through worship. They are better able to perceive and receive God's grace-filled loving presence, and then to give themselves to others in the loving spirit of that presence.

The claim that youth may be transformed through the worshipful encounter with God may strike some as simple common sense. What may be less self-evident is that worship *through holy things* is critical to authentic encounter with God and, therefore, to authentic formation. In other words, not just any form of worship goes. Christian worship that neglects book, bath, table, and time does not do it. Admittedly, many persons languish in congregations where the practice of the *ordo*'s ancient holy things is minimized, apologized for, truncated, edited, hurried, convoluted, or completely eliminated, or where liturgical leaders are theologically inept, aesthetically blind, ritually ham-handed, rhetorically stupor-inducing, or just plain bad. In those cases it's understandable why youth and their leaders may conclude that the holy things of the *ordo* are spiritually dead and to be avoided like the plague.

Abandoning holy things is not the answer, however. Bath, book, table, and time have persisted for two millennia because when robustly practiced and strongly interpreted they have proven themselves to be essential and trustworthy ingredients of the church's worshipful encounter with God. Our present neglect of holy things signals not their spiritual irrelevance but the church's forgetfulness. Therefore, in the chapters that follow, I will seek to demonstrate how youth may yet be worshipfully engaged in the *ordo*'s holy things rightly practiced

---

18. See James W. Jones, *Contemporary Psychoanalysis and Religion: Transference and Transcendence* (New Haven: Yale University Press, 1991), especially the sections on D. W. Winnicott, pp. 57–62, and Daniel Stern, pp. 96–99.

and strongly interpreted, and through this engagement may hope and expect to encounter the awesome presence of grace-filled Mystery.

But there is still another important reason for reclaiming the *ordo* as crucial to mediating God's presence, and that is that we're living in a culture infatuated not only with products but with *experiences*. Cars are no longer four wheels and two pedals that take you places: they are driving *experiences*. Tiny electronic devices wired with ear buds sell by the millions not because they are clever boxes but because they deliver media *experiences*. Adventure travel is so popular these days because it offers challenging yet fulfilling *experiences*. I daresay that even the present attractiveness of spirituality is its promise of unique self-fulfillment *experiences*.

Equating experience with feeling good, however, threatens to distort authentic *Christian* experience of God's living presence in at least three ways.

First, in many cases, congregations have too uncritically adopted the culture's tools of and appreciation for the production of experience. I've already noted the convergence of adventure travel with youth ministry strategies. Then there's the transition of published curricular resources from straightforward religious instruction to infotainment. Why else would a vacation Bible school curriculum be titled *Lava Lava Island?*[19] The assumption at work in such a title is that the only way to appeal to children and their parents is by promising that vacation Bible school will produce enjoyable experiences. In many cases churches have also adopted the culture's tools for producing positive experience as an aid to their worship. Especially in fast-growing congregations with youthful membership, worship is aided by audio and video technologies and takes on the feel and pace of a well-produced TV variety show. Their mantra becomes in effect, "Worship must sizzle so the church won't fizzle."

The operative assumption is that such experiential productions are benign delivery systems for the Gospel. If, however, the wider cultural

---

19. Group Publishing's very popular vacation Bible school curriculum for 2004 was titled *Lava Lava Island: Where Jesus' Love Flows*. Group Publishing's Website (*www.groupvbs.com/2004*) cited this curriculum as "The Hottest VBS Around" and "The Easy VBS."

agenda is to use the production and consumption of entertaining experiences to form us into docile, navel-gazing consumers, then we must ask ourselves critically and often, "Are these cultural means we employ capable of forming a community of cross-bearers? Will they, for example, form youth capable of compassionate response to Christ's presence in a neighbor's suffering, or will they form youth capable only of continuing to seek out and maximize their own pleasure?"

Second, planners of worship may be tempted to forget or delete holy things because practices as commonplace as reading from a book, ritual bathing, eating together, or taking the time to attend to time do not lend themselves well to an environment of polished production. But absent these distinctive Christian worship practices, how are worshipers to discern whether they are encountering the presence of the living God or the calculated experiential buzz of a well-produced show?

Third, we in the churches would do well to pay attention to the kinds of experiences the culture produces for our consumption. In general, the experiences that sell best are stimulating, entertaining, and self-satisfying. To what extent does this wider cultural preference for "positive" experiences shape or color our own engagement with worship? To what extent does a satisfying experience equate with an authentic encounter with the living God? Entering God's presence requires and evokes more than benign happiness and an occasional goose bump after a rousing praise band piece. Real encounter with God also evokes awe, holy fear, lament, and cries for mercy along with the easy ecstasies of praise.[20] Many of these forms of experience are absent from the commercial culture's production of experience because they may not make us feel particularly good and therefore do not sell particularly well. Worship through book, bath, table, and time helps ensure an authentic encounter with God (and not just a feel-good experience) because it attends as readily to suffering, despair, and longing for what has not yet come to pass as it does to what is praiseworthy and delightful. Christian worship that attends

---

20. See Job 42:1–6, Isa. 6:1–5, Ps. 51, and Acts 3:1–10 for examples.

to human struggle and suffering may hope to form youthful bodies capable of the same.

We tend to ask, "How can we make worship more appealing to our youth?" rather than, "How can we ensure that youth will encounter the fullness of the presence of the living God in worship?" One question is framed by the market, the other by the theological tradition. One thinks first about the needs of young consumers and how to produce experiences to satisfy those needs. The other recognizes that God's presence is the gift (freely and graciously given, not for sale, no marketing required) of the incarnation mediated through book, bath, table, and time. One question implicitly supports a world ordered around consumption; the other explicitly renounces it and instead names and enacts a Reign of grace, justice, and peace.

Don't misunderstand me. I do not intend to imply that worship is authentic only when it makes persons feel bad. Pastors and youth workers are absolutely on target when they seek to engage youth in the passionate and ultimately joyous worship of God. I am simply suggesting, first, that the church's *ordo* provides youth an essential context for this passionate encounter, and, second, that in a culture rife with experience, not every powerful experience adds up to God. The authentic experience of God's presence in worship makes space, as Saliers says, for both the "ethos" of God and the "pathos" of human suffering.[21]

2. Discovering the identity of God

Practicing the *ordo* is also critical to the formation of Christian youth because it offers them keys to discovering the identity of God. At first blush, God would seem the least likely of beings to have an identity problem. God is, after all, well, *God*. What else needs saying? Who doesn't know God? God is God; end of discussion. Unfortunately, the scriptures and our own experience testify to the sinful propensity to make God over into whatever kind of being best suits human interests. In North America these days God appears, at different turns, as

---

21. See Saliers, *Worship as Theology* (Nashville: Abingdon, 1994), chapter 1.

a flag-waving patriot, a nonjudgmental therapist, a warm and affirming friend, a crusader for gay rights, a preserver of traditional values, and so on.

Yet this confusion over God's identity surely mirrors our confusion about our own identities or even the possibility of possessing an identity. That is partly because we live in a culture that imagines identity to be a personal choice. After all, that is what freedom means in a culture of consumerist individualism, isn't it? I am my own creator. Indeed, even well-meaning parents of youth affirm this conventional wisdom every time they tell their children "you can be anything you set your mind to." Only there exists a bewildering array of choices. Which me shall I be? And for how long shall I be this me? Confusion over God's identity is more understandable in a culture where human identity is up for grabs.

God does not have an identity problem; it is we Christians who have a problem identifying God. As youth workers and pastors have long suspected and as the sociologist Christian Smith suggests, most youth and their parents do not know with any precision the church's insights into God's identity.[22] They do not know the biblical stories of God's saving past or of God's promised future. They do not understand such bedrock theological keys to God as Trinity or Incarnation or Resurrection or God's Reign. They do not possess a sufficiently large stash of biblical metaphors for exploring the identity of God. Indeed, many lack even the appreciation for the power (or limits) of metaphorical language for identifying God in the first place. God may literally be for many youth (and adults) an old man with a white beard—a really, *really* powerful Gandalf.

This level of ignorance, perhaps unprecedented in the history of the North American church, persists at the same time that biblical and theological resources are widely available to youth. Or so it would seem. There are Bibles written in youthful vernacular. There are Bibles featuring interpretive aids in their margins to assist teens' biblical understanding. Ironically, however, these resources may be part of the problem. One Bible I know of is targeted to teenage girls.

---

22. See Smith, *Soul Searching*, particularly chapter 4.

It has the look and feel of a *Seventeen* magazine. It includes multiple full-color photographs of extremely attractive adolescent girls and boys. It offers interest-catching quizzes with titles like "Are You an Introvert or an Extrovert?" and "Are You Dating a Godly Guy?" plus collections of helpful tips like "How to Get Along with Your Mom."[23]

The effect of this "biblical" commentary is to portray God as the *girlfriends' Girlfriend* or, maybe slightly more charitably, as Wonderful (Clinical) Counselor. By way of what educators call "the implicit curriculum,"[24] this Bible's therapeutic "midrash" or interpretation is substantially distorting God's identity for teens in the very book where they might otherwise expect to find reliable information on this God. We reduce God to an instrumental prop for the therapeutic self-fulfilling lifestyle the culture espouses.

Ministry grounded in book, bath, table, and time offers the hope of overcoming some of the pitfalls described above. For example, from early in the history of the church there are descriptions of worship services that included readings from the Old Testament, Psalms, Epistles, and Gospels. And not just one or two verses either. The texts were read in large chunks so that hearers could gain a sense of their sweep. This regular practice of extensive public, aural, and communal reading from the scriptures in the worshiping assembly and then interpreting their meaning suggests that the church viewed this task as critical for providing believers with a wide and deep understanding of God's identity and their own in relation to God.

Such a claim would seem self-evident. Of course Christians use the Bible in worship. Except that many don't, or at least haven't always. It wasn't until after the Second Vatican Council in the 1960s that scriptures were widely recovered in the vernacular in the Roman Catholic mass. Even Protestants who profess to know the value of the book don't have the best of track records in actually using it. The

---

23. See *Revolve 2007: The Complete New Testament*, NCV (Nashville: Thomas Nelson, 2003).

24. Elliot W. Eisner, *The Educational Imagination: On the Design and Evaluation of School Programs* (New York: Macmillan, 1979), chapter 4.

late James F. White, the United Methodist worship scholar, once commented that worship in his tradition had succeeded where Marcion the heretic had failed: it had silenced the Old Testament and removed it from the community's conscious memory.[25]

Who is the God the *ordo*'s book invites us to meet? It is first and foremost a storied God. This God has a storied past and is acting toward a storied future. The story begins with the creation of all that is and includes covenant making and renewal with the people Israel. When those same people were enslaved in Egypt, they cried out. God heard their cries and delivered them out of Pharaoh's hand. After a generation of wilderness wandering, God led them into the Promised Land. Being a 'stiff-necked" people, they soon found themselves in trouble again and in need of God's deliverance. This continuing story of redemption is incarnated most vividly in Jesus Christ, but also includes the gift of the Spirited Church and the promise, well begun in Christ, of a future Reign of justice and peace. Specifically, the book describes the man Jesus who is also God. Jesus was born to human parents, baptized by John, undertook a ministry that declared and revealed the coming of God's Reign. He fellowshipped with sinners and persons on the margins of society, he healed the sick, he preached words of judgment and grace. His ministry threatened the powerful and all of us who are tainted by sin, so he was crucified. God raised him from the dead, however, as a sign that God's loving dream for creation will not be thwarted. Jesus has promised to return in the fulfillment of God's Reign. In the interim his Spirit abides with the church. This is the God that the scriptures identify.

Within such stories, youth may discover God's identity as One who is radically for and with them, but that is because God is incarnate in Christ and not because God is a nice "godly guy," easy to talk to, emotionally available, and an extrovert. To put the matter differently, the stories that the *ordo* bears for youth are also fraught with theological implications. Thus, the *ordo*'s book also serves as a springboard

---

25. James F. White, "Our Apostasy in Worship," *The Christian Century,* September 28, 1977, 842.

into youth's consideration of such bedrock theological themes as creation, the crisis of sin, covenant, Christology, the Spirit-born church, human calling in response to God, and God's coming Reign. Further, only by way of discovering God's identity are youth provided with critical information for making sense of their own identities. Specifically, the *ordo* reveals to those who are baptized "in Christ" how they are to bear the vocation of the one into whom their identities have been sealed.

Proclaiming the stories from the book is not the only means the *ordo* offers for forming youth into the identity of God. These stories are also enacted as living dramas, and worshipers become participants in them every time they attend to the practices of bath, table, and time. These ritual symbolic gestures re-present the stories of God's saving action and re-member worshipers into that action. We might say that the *ordo* calls worshipers to perform the stories of God in ways that invite them over time to embody God's identity within their own bodies. We might also say that enacting the book re-members the one Body.

3. Practicing vocation before God and for the world

There is a third way that practicing the *ordo* participates in the dynamics of formation. The *ordo* offers youth and congregations not only a pattern for worship and thus the hope of encountering the presence of God and discovering the identity of God but also a pattern for practicing and further discerning their vocations in community before God and for the world. Vocation is still another word finding its way back into the Christian lexicon these days. The root of vocation is the Latin *vocare*, "to call." For Christians to speak again of vocation is to recover the legacy of scriptures and tradition that testifies to persons' hearing and responding to God's call on their lives to be or do something for God's sake. Abraham and Sarah hear and respond to God's call to go to a new land (Gen. 12). Moses hears and responds to God's call to deliver Israel from bondage (Exod. 3–4). Jeremiah says "yes" to God's call despite misgivings over his own youthfulness (Jer. 1:4–8). In broad terms, persons take up Christian vocations as a response to God's loving claim upon them and to get involved with what God is doing in the world. It is the opposite of imagining themselves as self-motivated and self-created.

Faith has increasingly become a private, interior matter intentionally kept out of the messiness of North American public life. This privatization makes possible politicians' sincere declarations that they are at once devoted to and uninfluenced by their Christian faith when making decisions affecting the wider public. Further, in the church of recent times, the possibility of vocation was increasingly limited to professional religious types. Only persons who wore robes and collars could be called; everyone else volunteered. Vocation has slipped out of the parlance of the wider culture as well. The notion that a source or cause outside the autonomous self might dictate the shape and trajectory of a life came to be regarded as quaint or even laughable. Not surprisingly, therefore, Christian youth rarely hear about, much less take up, Christian vocations. Instead they learn the wider cultural curriculum, one that in North America is mostly about striving, effort, and competition, all oriented to "success." This success is correlated with the ability to purchase the goods and experiences that are the markers of high status and personal enjoyment. It seems that all that makes Christians different is that they don't gloat about their success.

In this account, I hope to show how the *ordo* may function for youth as a context for vocational living and continued shaping of their vocational imaginations. The premise is simple: the *ordo* invites persons into the essential practices of Christian life. Thus, the *ordo* shapes youth's capacities to imagine, understand, and receive the gift of Christian vocation as their own futures with God unfold.

Consider the gesture of "sharing Christ's peace" in worship preliminary to receiving the Eucharistic bread and cup. Worshippers usually speak to one another words something like these: "The Peace of the Lord be with you," which prompts the response, "And also with you." In addition they may shake hands or hug as well. Through this small ritual, worshipers are invited to practice peace and reconciliation. Now admittedly, this is the humblest of gestures. It lasts only moments. And it is possible for individual worshipers to participate in passing the peace without meaning what the gesture intends for and from them. But the public intention remains — reconciliation and peacemaking — and congregations that pass the peace regularly consistently practice this public intention.

I have noticed that many congregations do not pass the peace (a gesture rooted in the scriptures, by the way). Apparently judging the ritual to be too stuffy or too presumptuous or just too "ritually," they opt for one like this: "Hi, how are you?" "I'm good, and you?" One exchange intends and practices a communal way of life framed by Christ's peace; indeed, it seeks to offer Christ and to build a bridge to the neighbor. The other intends and practices a life framed by bounded individuals wishing to retain these boundaries while being nice to each other.

Humble though it may be, passing the peace and other practices like it rooted in the *ordo* are at the heart of imagining then practicing the radical nature of Christian vocation. What else are Christians called to be if not a reconciled, reconciling, peaceful, and peacemaking people? The possibility of imagining and practicing such authentic vocation begins in authentic Christian worship.

Meanwhile, out there in the tough world, I recently read about a school district that banned its high school athletes from lining up to shake hands after games.[26] It seems that this ritual had become an occasion to spit at, curse, and even fight with opponents. Might it have turned out differently if all the Christian players were being properly formed into their vocations as peacemakers at Sunday worship? Might youthful bodies formed by expressions of Christ's peace in the liturgy be capable of resisting sinful inversions of this practice elsewhere? Subsequent chapters will ponder in more detail the "broad stroke" vocational implications of this and other practices of the *ordo*.

---

26. See Lawrence Latane III, "Northern Neck District to Keep Handshake Ban," *Richmond Times-Dispatch*, November 8, 2005, sec. B, 2, or Phillip Matier and Andrew Ross, "S.F. Girls Soccer Team Run-Ins Prompt Ban on Post-Match High Fives," *San Francisco Chronicle*, March 23, 2005, sec. B, 1.

With respect to vocation, adolescence is a season of forward imagining. Youth wonder about who they are becoming and how they will make their way in life. These are pregnant moments for youth and for the church. Given this opening, we dare not bore them with vague pronouncements about being nice, becoming successful, and feeling good. That message is already pulsing through their headphones. By recovering its holy things, the church may offer to youth hopeful resources for radically re-forming their imaginations and practices toward the way of life that Christ calls abundant. In the process, youth may also hope and expect to discern, cultivate, and offer their own distinctive gifts in service of God's Reign.[27]

The ordo *as an ecology of formation*

Worship through the practices of book, bath, table, and time offers the church the promise of transformative encounter with the presence of the living God, deepened awareness of who this God is and what this God intends for creation, plus the means to practice and imagine faithful life as God's people. Though I have described these formative dynamics separately, they are interrelated and interdependent. We

---

27. Similar to the cautionary note sounded at the end of the section describing the *ordo*, I add this caveat on formation. Admittedly, some faith communities do not practice the *ordo* yet manage to form their young into exemplary Christians. I do not wish to explain away their success in order to salvage my account. I do offer the following observations. First, obviously God is not limited to my own or any other strategy for formational ministry. At the same time, exceptions do not automatically disprove two millennia of church wisdom and tradition on issues of formation. The fact that a small minority of North American traditions do manage to form Christian youth effectively while explicitly disavowing the *ordo* does not mean that the vast majority of congregations for whom the *ordo* is (at least historically) significant should also disavow it. The exception does not disprove the rule. Claiming otherwise is analogous to claiming that the quick entry into paradise by the thief on the cross negates any significance that baptism may have played in forming millions of persons over the past two millennia into the identity of Christ. Second, non-*ordo*-grounded worshiping communities often do a remarkable job of inviting their youth to practice what I call in chapter 7 "*ordo*-nary" things, practices including hospitality, stewardship, peacemaking, and more that extend beyond the worshiping assembly but are also integral to it. In other words, I'm suggesting that, despite their liturgical iconoclasm, these communities practice a way of life that embodies remarkably well the holy things of the *ordo*.

could say they form an ecology. Youth's vital encounters with God's presence are linked to and dependent upon their knowledge of God's identity which, in turn, is linked to and dependent upon their practice and discernment of Christian vocation. In the case of the table, for example, youth are invited into Christ's resurrection presence, reminded of God's identity as both guest and host of the communal meal, and beckoned to participate in the Christian vocation for hospitality.

In addition, just as the formative dynamics of holy things are ecologically linked, the same is true for the *ordo*'s holy things themselves. For example, book and table require one another for providing mutual interpretation and grace-filled evocation. Bath is strengthened immeasurably by attention to the patterning of time, as, for example, when baptisms are scheduled for Easter dawn. And table finds its deep significance when rightly understood as the meal that nourishes the baptized toward their vocations. Without this ecological appreciation for holy things they become hollow shells with shallow meanings. When practiced by communities as a living ecology, however, they spiral outward and upward in relation to one another and in ever-unfolding grace-filled evocation. Though the chapters that follow tend to focus on one of the holy things at a time, I also make efforts to describe their essential and organic relationships with one another. While it may seem logical to conceive of *ordo*-based ministry as first offering youth the Word of Life, then baptizing them into that life, then sustaining them in that life through participation in Eucharist and distinctive temporal rhythms, that linear approach is not all I envision. Instead, consistent with the *ordo* itself, this book proposes an ecological approach to youth ministry. It invites youth into an *ordo*-inspired web of content, experience, and transformational practice. It is a matrix of sorts, or a full-court press. It seeks to immerse youth in a total way of life inclusive of practices related to book, bath, table, and time, then to practice these practices ecologically in relation to one another and to the lives, sufferings, and dreams of youth. My hope is that through immersion in this way of life youth may discover the Way and the Life. Chapter 7 in particular attends to the ecology at work.

From theory to practice: A description of one ordo-grounded youth ministry

Such theorizing about youth ministry may seem hopelessly idealistic, if not anachronistic.

Well, maybe not. It is already happening at Duke Divinity School's Duke Youth Academy for Christian Formation. DYA exists as testimony to the theological and formational accounts of an *ordo*-based approach to youth ministry as described above. No doubt, this form of ministry also is occurring in many other faith communities. We don't claim to have invented it. But Duke's Youth Academy is the context I know best.

DYA is a temporary community of high school students and adults that takes up residence at Duke University's Divinity School for two weeks each summer. The academy teaches, lives, and reflects upon the liturgical *ordo* as the basis of communal life. Thus DYA practices what this book preaches and may, therefore, stand as a practical backdrop for this book's theorizing. Considering what the *ordo* looks like walking around in T-shirts and flip-flops can also help us imagine how it may be appropriated in our own ministry settings. Student experiences and reflections are therefore included along the way in this book.

A day in the life of DYA

So what is it that we do at the DYA?

The DYA community gathers each morning in the chancel of Duke Chapel for morning prayer. This service follows a traditional pattern of scripture reading, antiphonal chanting of Psalms, corporate and meditative prayer, and singing. Students and adults share leadership responsibilities.

After breakfast, the community reconvenes for a two-hour theological plenary session led by a member of the Divinity School faculty. These sessions develop themes of baptismal theology. Their purpose is to provide theological and conceptual language for making sense of the life in which the community is immersed. Generally, students delight in discovering this new language and in wrestling with its ideas as well as its practical force.

Following a midmorning break, the community divides into pairs of covenant groups — small groups of seven students and two adult mentors — for an hour and fifteen minutes devoted to learning about, planning for, and reflecting on community worship. Since the academy assembles for "Word and Table" worship each evening, these morning sessions are designed to address a variety of issues related to the evening assembly. The sessions include three movements: First, they teach about the theological and ritual symbolic significance of holy things. Second, youth and their mentors are engaged in the process of planning a service of worship and then preparing and practicing for leadership in communal worship. Third, after offering this leadership, youth and mentors gather to reflect on the work they did together.

At the noon meal, our community is hosted on six occasions by churches of a variety of traditions and ethnicities from the surrounding area. Members of the academy community come from all over the country; thus these meals are often their first tastes of soul food, authentic (non–Taco Bell) Central and South American food, or even deep-fried Southern cholesterol food. Tables are set with cloths, simple centerpieces, and real china, glass, and utensils. Hosts and guests serve one another family style and eat together. As the academy progresses, persons find themselves *lingering* in these periods of shared hospitality, enjoying the food and the unrushed conversation. In addition, the Eucharistic overtones of such gatherings become food for subsequent small group reflection as well as ritual enactment in worship. Further, through its encounter with these different faith communities, our own temporary community is reminded repeatedly of the enduring baptismal unity of the church in all its diversity of expression.

Academy afternoons follow different paths on different days. Some are spent in the "Arts Village." Here, students and adults rotate through sessions with a variety of theologically trained media and performing artists. Past academies have featured potters, musicians, photographers, writers, dancers, dramatists, and storytellers. The

Arts Village exemplifies the academy's commitment to forming youth bodily. If the mornings are mostly devoted to intellectual engagement with the theological tradition, the afternoons seek to get involved with it bodily. By tailoring their sessions to the theological themes of the day, artists also invite students to participate in the poetic and aesthetic dimensions of the theological tradition they are exploring. We also judge the Arts Village as essential to assisting students and adults in cultivating imaginative capacities for worshipful engagement with holy things.

Other afternoons find the community serving meals at shelters, caring for hospitalized children, hanging sheetrock, or conversing over dinner with AIDS patients. Our intent is to provide multiple opportunities to hug, sweat, speak, and hammer in the name of Christ. Inevitably, members of the community discover that Christ is already present in the situations where some had imagined they were delivering him. This dynamic also complicates and deepens the meaning and object of baptismal ministries of reconciliation. Some students wonder aloud, "Who exactly needs reconciling here, them or us?" and, "Is this we/they division even a helpful one?"

On still other afternoons, the academy works hard at doing nothing. This is a self-conscious effort to repent of the Martha syndrome: the notion that productivity equals value. Doing nothing also creates space for our mentoring process to work. A distinctive feature of the youth academy is the strong ratio of adult mentors to students, approximately one to three. That we are so adult-heavy is testimony to our conviction that that the young become Christian and then more deeply Christian through their association with experienced, exemplary Christians. Our leadership constitutes an embarrassment of riches. They are seminarians and graduate students, ministry professionals, and talented laity representing a wide spectrum of ethnicity, giftedness, and denominational identity. But mentors are more *chosen* than assigned; students must be able to see something of themselves in their mentors and therefore something of the hopeful possibility of what their lives may become by the grace of God. By practicing doing nothing, we create space for students to seek out such mentoring relationships of their own choosing free from the disciplined agenda we impose on them elsewhere.

Each evening after dinner the entire community assembles for worship. As noted above, students share responsibilities in concert with adult staff for planning and leading worship. Consistent with the teaching and learning of the morning sessions, worship strives to "play" heartily with book, bath, table, and time. We employ a lectionary (a pre-appointed collection of daily scripture readings including Old Testament, Psalms, Epistle, and Gospel) based on a given day's baptismal theological theme. The means for proclaiming the scriptures may include anything from song to simple reading, liturgical dance, or dramatic performance. Preaching is grounded in these scriptures, oriented to the day's theme, and anticipates the sharing of Eucharist. Eucharistic celebrants "take, bless, break, and share" with vigor, witnessing to the many grace-filled possibilities of the ritual meal. They also invite students to contribute imagery or phrases to prayers of thanksgiving and to share in the serving of the meal to the community. The symbol of water is always powerfully present in communal worship as well and is often ritualized in creative ways.

Academy leadership is well aware of the debate between proponents of "contemporary" and "traditional" worship forms. However, we do not accept the assertion that often accompanies such a debate that the former is "spiritual" and "full of feeling" ("Dude, this rocks!") and that the latter is "boring" or "dead" ("Dude, this sucks!"). By working to cultivate the poetic and symbolic theological imaginations of our community members, and by practicing robustly our holy things in worship, students discover there is life in them yet. Indeed, one of the most exciting findings of our academy research is students' professed deepened appreciation for these ancient treasures (an appreciation that returns with them to their home churches), and their sense of loving encounter with God through them.

By highlighting our effort to cultivate deepened sensibility around ancient liturgical symbols, I do not wish to convey an image of monastics' mumbling monotones. Communal worship creatively juxtaposes old with new as well as inviting a variety of worship styles from Anglican to African American, Hispanic to Pentecostal. Contemporary music finds a place alongside of hymnody, chanted Psalms next to canted hip-hop, and meditative silence offers counterpoint to shouted praise. Through it all, youthful enthusiasm inevitably injects a huge dose of vitality into the assembly's proceedings. Indeed, another example of the academy's attempt at an end run on the contemporary/traditional debate is the fact that we are not afraid of powerfully expressed emotion as a vital means to encounter and be moved by the One who meets us in mystery and in love. Yet we are not in the business of modulating experience for its own sake. Academy worship attempts to be open to the presence of the triune God (and not merely to the god of experience) and to attend to the nature of this one true God.

The final structured event of a typical day features the gathering of persons into covenant groups. Mentors follow a flexible curriculum that invites reflection on the themes and experiences of the day and the cumulative experiences of the community's life together. This is another setting where students are invited to connect what they have learned about the significance of the *ordo* and their life in the *ordo* by way of the baptismal covenant with their practices of living together. For example, mentors may ask, "What connection have you sensed between our sharing in Eucharist together and our preparing the meal and eating at the shelter this evening?" Inevitably, these groups also become a setting for working through conflict toward reconciliation and for dealing with the pressing issues students bring with them from home. It is also a context where persons are invited to discern God's calling on their present lives and their unfolding futures. Covenant groups conclude with evening prayer.

Weekends follow a different pattern. Saturdays are spent gleaning agricultural produce for area food banks and shelters. Sundays are devoted to Sabbath-keeping: worship, rest, then dinner together in the evening.

What does DYA offer the church?

Some may wonder whether DYA's ministry practices may, in fact, translate to congregations. A temporary community without the typical baggage of congregational histories, leadership structures, and relationships may seem less relevant to the "real world" of church youth ministry. Admittedly, DYA is not the church, nor does it claim to be. It does, however, take up the church's holy things with gusto, something many "real" churches have forgotten how to do. It intends, therefore, to be a sign or a parable of the church and to remind its students, adults, and, indirectly, the *church* of the church's own distinctive identity, vocation, and mediation of grace-filled Presence.

A liturgical youth ministry necessarily begins with worship. In the next chapter, I explore problems and possibilities in contemporary youth worship and consider in some detail practices related to table as a means to deepen and enliven youthful liturgical practice. I also begin the task of demonstrating how the patterns of worship may undergird and animate the patterns of faithful youth ministry as well as how different holy things may form youth into God's presence, God's identity, and their own vocations.

Two

Finding themselves at the table

Youth practice God's presence, identity, and their own vocations through Eucharistic worship[28]

On a cold winter night approximately two hundred teenagers from a variety of congregations gather with their adult leaders along with staff members of a popular retreat center who are presiding over worship. The service commences when the college-aged leader of the staff rock-and-roll band declares, "Come on y'all, let's get up and rock the Lord!"

The congregation responds to this call to worship with approximately twenty minutes of dancing, clapping, and singing along with the band. Christian song lyrics are projected on an overhead screen. The band's volume mutes congregational singing, but no one seems to mind. Gradually the music becomes more subdued, the lights are dimmed, and the congregation mellows.

As if on cue, a lay speaker is introduced — an earnest if inexperienced college student. Her message includes stories of struggles in high school and descriptions of crises weathered through her faith in Christ. She does not read from the Bible or overtly cite the scriptures. She concludes with an invitation for students to walk to the front of the worship space where they may invite Christ into their lives, rededicate their lives to Christ, or simply pray for themselves or others. Staff persons make themselves available for prayerful conversation with those who venture forward. About 20 students, some in tears, do so. Gentle acoustic guitar music accompanies this informal

---

28. This chapter expands upon my essay "Uncovering Eucharistic Vitality in High School Youth: Who Knew?" *Doxology* 21 (2004): 92–110.

33

processional. The rest of the congregation sits quietly; some seem to be praying.

When it appears that all who felt the need to respond publicly to this invitation have done so, the worship/band leader bounces up again and declares, "All right y'all, let's give it up to God!" Instantly, high voltage guitar chords, wailing Bono-esque vocals, and dancing in the aisles by the less inhibited members of the congregation break the meditative silence. I notice several students who'd tearfully trouped forward moments earlier now dancing with abandon. The service concludes in climactic chordal conflagration, guitarists jumping in unison, arms furiously windmilling their instruments, drummer whipping around his kit, lights pulsing, and congregation standing and screaming.

And then it is over. My middle-aged ears are ringing. A friend says, "Man, talk about bringin' 'em up, takin' 'em down, and bringin' 'em back up again!" We leave a little shell-shocked.

But not surprised. Having worked in youth ministry for many of the past twenty years, I found this experience a familiar one. Though the musical styles (and intensity of production) have changed, the basic pattern of youth worship has not. It includes a gathering period of informal praise music, a talk typically delivered in the vernacular of youth and for the purpose of inviting youth to accept God's offer of salvation in Jesus Christ, and an invitation to respond publicly to that offer. In fact, the pattern is rooted more deeply than its recent incarnations in youth ministry settings. This "hipper than thou" youth service was actually a contemporary version of the nineteenth-century camp meeting but with an extra infusion of amped-up seeker aesthetic. More specifically, as L. Edward Phillips notes, it is an example of the "three-fold revivalist pattern": one that includes "preliminaries, message, and altar call."[29] Such a pattern, born out of the revivalist movements and refined by evangelist Charles Finney

---

29. As Phillips notes, contemporary seeker worship is also an example of this revivalist pattern and carries the same intention: conversion of the unchurched. See his "How Shall We Worship?" in *Worship Matters: A United Methodist Guide to Worship*, ed. E. Byron Anderson (Nashville: Discipleship Resources, 1999), 24. Though I write out of the tradition of Methodism, I have seen this pattern employed in other

as a strategy and technique for winning souls to Christ, has proven effective for the purpose for which it was designed.

But is it Christian worship?

Daniel Benedict, past head of the United Methodist Church's Center for Worship Resourcing, uses a sports metaphor to make a distinction between the church "playing away" for the sake of its evangelical mission and "playing at home" for the sake of the assembly's right worship of God.[30] Benedict believes that problems arise when the church's "away" strategies and practices (i.e., the revivalist pattern) replace its "at home" worship *at home*. Or, as Stanley Hauerwas puts it, when "the revivalists' 'tent' has been set up in the sanctuary."[31] Benedict cites a crucial difference between these forms. The evangelistic strategy, he claims, is primarily "self-referential" — meaning that the self and its sinful state before God are the consistent focus. On the other hand, Christian worship, according to Benedict, is what might be called "God-referential." The "true Self," the "Holy One, the Holy Three" are the consistent focus.[32] This is not to disparage the church's evangelical mission or its strategies to convict persons of sin and to offer them new life in Jesus Christ, but to suggest that these strategies are being confused with and substituted for the practices of orthodox Christian worship. One result is the loss of the *ordo*'s liturgical holy things: book, bath, table, and time.

But allow me to make a more provocative claim. I suggest there is a relationship, a conceptual and imaginative one if not a causal one, between the ways Christians worship and the ways they live (or fail to live) faithfully before God and for the world. Given this premise, and by way of making clear my bias, I find the revivalist practice

---

denominations including free church traditions, but, more surprisingly, in Episcopal, Lutheran, and Roman Catholic ones as well.

30. Daniel T. Benedict, "The Basic Pattern of Worship: Is Your Church 'Playing' at Home and Away?" *Worship Arts* (November–December 2004): 8–12.

31. Stanley M. Hauerwas, "Worship, Evangelism, Ethics: On Eliminating the 'And,'" in *Liturgy and the Moral Self: Humanity at Full Stretch Before God*, ed. E. Byron Anderson and Bruce T. Morrill (Collegeville, MN: Liturgical Press, 1998), 95.

32. Benedict, "The Basic Pattern of Worship," 9.

fundamentally inadequate as a pattern for youth worship. I am convinced that the cumulative effect of revivalist/entertainment worship for youth is the rough equivalent of a long-term diet of Doritos and Mountain Dew: the spiritual buzz may be immediate and gratifying, but the enduring formative implications for the personal and corporate Body are malnutrition and decay.

At the outset, such a critique may seem elitist and unfair. After all, the Spirit of God seems to have moved in youthful lives through this service despite my misgivings. From a different perspective, however, I believe the criticism is justified. I live and minister in a denomination struggling to provide its people a distinctive Christian identity and vocation. Its children and youth do not know their scriptures, let alone the sweep of the church's salvation story; their capacities for engagement with Holy Mystery through metaphor, symbol, ritual, and sacrament go unnurtured; they have precious few opportunities for engaging in communities of vital Christian practice; and they are not taught to reflect theologically on the tension between their Christian convictions and the culture of North American consumerist individualism.

Despite good intentions, Doritos and Dew worship practices only play into such ignorance. Though they are powerfully experiential, they do not provide youth the formative dimensions related to the identity of God or to faithful vocation before God and for the world. As a result, one wonders to what extent youth are invited to worship God through such worship and to what extent they are invited to worship experience itself.

Always and everywhere teens are conditioned to seek out powerful experience, and many churches are pulling out all the stops in order to offer these customers what they want. Such "worship," however, may only hook teens on a spiritualized religiosity devoid of any lived vocational implications for their lives. Nor are they cultivated in imaginative encounters with holy things where they might otherwise discern such implications. They remain junk-food junkies: unacquainted with and never even given a chance to develop a taste for wine or bread or the Life-giving waters, always snacking and never growing, denied access to the grown-up table where they might find the food to grow strong and deep in the Word made Flesh. "Give us *more!*" the teens cry, "and make it *pop!* If you don't, we'll dump you and your lame church and go watch videos." Can you blame them, when we've never shown them a better way?

And so this chapter offers an alternative possibility for youth worship, one that, over time, may also hope to overcome the malnutrition described above. One alternative to the revivalist pattern is what has come to be called a pattern of "Word and Table" because of the co-centrality of the Bible, and the practice variously named the Lord's Supper or Holy Communion or Eucharist. Such a proposal may seem impractical or even fantastic to persons in traditions that historically have not emphasized sacramentality. I hope to show that regardless of specific doctrines of Christological presence (or absence) in the ritual meal, ritual symbolic engagement of the kind found in Eucharist is a critical piece for the formation of distinctly Christian identity in the young. In contrast, such a proposal may seem *under*whelming to persons rooted in traditions that historically have adhered to Word and Table practice. To this constituency I gently suggest that familiarity is not automatically the equivalent of full appreciation for formative efficacy. Youth must also be provided contexts and settings to reflect on the significance of Eucharist and to practice living eucharistically.

Thus, this chapter has three goals. Its primary focus is on the table in the ecology of holy things. Thus, with the help of liturgical scholars it briefly revisits the theological significance of Eucharist within the context of Word and Table, harvesting treasures of grace long forgotten by some faith communities or never discovered by others. Here I will suggest how Eucharistic worship provides vital keys to the identity of God, to youths' vocation before God, and, perhaps surprisingly, to experiencing the presence of God.

Second, I describe contexts and associated supportive pedagogical practices where Eucharistic worship may gain traction with youth. These include occasions for teaching and learning and for reflective practice. I also consider how we may best cultivate distinctive capacities for youths' full engagement with Eucharist in worship. Such engagement requires a different way of knowing from the kind most students practice in school. In turn, such a way of knowing may also offer the creative means to cultivating distinctly Christian identity in the world.

Third, I employ this alternative pattern of worship and its attending pedagogical structures of support to ask some broader critical questions of the church in relation to youth ministry.

My approach is influenced not only by growing misgivings about youth worship gatherings like the one described above, but also by the results of my stimulating work as faculty director of the Duke Youth Academy for Christian Formation. With regard to worship, the Academy takes a contrarian approach. We are as interested in youth recovering the vitality of ancient tradition as we are in innovation. We question the assumption that for youth "cutting edge" means younger than yesterday. We also do not accept the cliché that youth have no interest in tradition and that ritual action for them is automatically qualified by the word "empty." And so we train students at the youth academy in worship planning and worship leadership, and they take an active role in both. Scripture appears in large storied portions in our worship at the academy. We use a lectionary of sorts that narrates the great sweep of salvation history from creation to the life, death, and resurrection of Jesus Christ, on to the eschatological hope for the fullness of the Reign of God. Eucharist as the nourishing meal of the baptized is celebrated daily: fourteen times over two weeks. For most of our students (save the overachieving Episcopalians) this is more Eucharist than they've received in a year or three years or their entire lives! We enjoy a variety of musical styles, and the feel of worship can range from African American Baptist to Anglo-Catholicism. Whatever the particulars, undergirding all this stylistic variety is the Word and Table pattern.

Theological and formational reasons for frequent Eucharistic practice

The youth academy is indebted to insights from liturgical theology that are helping the entire church to recover and revalue the grace-filled treasures of its sometimes neglected worshiping practices.

Nevertheless, most youth I talk to still describe the holy meal in reductionist sound-bite fashion as a "reminder of what Jesus did for me."
Such a response is on the right track but woefully inadequate. As
Lawrence Stookey notes, in addition to communicating the essential
truth of Christ's self-giving death and life (" ... what Jesus *did* ... "),
Eucharist also reveals the goodness of God's creation, the church as
Christ's Body in the world, and our vocation to live as a hospitable
people.[33] In other words, you could say that Eucharist embodies an
exhaustive curriculum for Christian life. Liturgical scholars are also
assisting the church in recovering the Lord's Supper as more than
memory device ("a reminder ... ") but as eschatological enactment,
one that nourishes the baptized by remembering the past and representing the future. In its recollection of God's saving work from
creation to Passover liberation to the death and life of Jesus Christ,
Eucharist reminds its participants who God is and what God has
done, and, by extension, who they are and what they are called to
do. As a sign-act, Eucharist does not merely symbolize or stand for
these convictions; it in fact becomes an incarnation, an actualization
of these themes.[34] In turn, participants in Eucharist become actors
in this drama of an alternative eschatological reality. They share in
a "foretaste of glory divine." They participate in God's Reign made
present and, in the process, are constituted as a living witness to
the world.

Eucharist as a theological enactment also uniquely reveals the essential *corporate* nature of Christ's Body, an incarnation that counters
the spirituality of Gnostic individualism into which many Christian
youth are presently being formed (" ... for *me*"). Unlike the youth
worship service described above where the focus was on the interior

---

33. Laurence Stookey, *Eucharist: Christ's Feast with the Church* (Nashville:
Abingdon, 1993), 14–24.

34. Couched in this description is an assumption of some form of lively "presence" in the meal. A liturgical reading of the New Testament, including, for example,
the Emmaus story in Luke 24 or Paul's theologizing in Romans 6, convinces me that
New Testament communities believed themselves to be encountering Christ as living
presence in and through their liturgical practices. My reluctance to specify exactly
the parameters of that presence is rooted in my conviction that ritual/symbolic action
by definition resists such specificity.

experience of individuals, the Eucharistic meal requires community in order to become feast. Not only are multiple bodies essential to the mix of Christ's Body, so too are ordinary bodily practices: setting the table, welcoming, saying grace, sharing, eating, drinking, touching. Surely a Gnostic god could only send regrets to such a party. Thus, practicing Eucharist offers youth a grace-filled remediation for individualized, overly spiritualized faith. Through their common bodily practice, it binds them together as Christ's Body offering itself to God and for the world.

The Lutheran liturgical theologian Gordon Lathrop offers another compelling argument for practicing Word and Table worship. He argues that the very pattern of God's self-revelation operates through the juxtaposition of holy things to one another; in this case, the juxtaposition of book to table and of these to the worshiping assembly itself.[35] The earliest Christians, for example, shared with their Jewish contemporaries the *synaxis*, the service of reading from the scriptures in community then interpreting them and otherwise responding to them. (See, for example, Jesus' homecoming at Nazareth in Luke 4:16ff.) What set the infant church apart from the synagogue, however, was that it put the "breaking of the bread" (the Eucharistic meal; see Luke 24) alongside the *synaxis*. According to Lathrop, through this juxtaposition, the Table puts flesh on the Word while the Word opens up the rich significance of the Table. In other words, in the juxtaposition, the ritual symbols (Word and Table) are broken together and "broken open" so that in and through this breaking God may enact a new reality, a new creation, a new Reign. Word and Table "speak" far more in juxtaposition than either could in isolation.

The worshiping assembly also participates in the act of liturgical juxtaposition. Through the breaking together of holy things the assembly finds itself consistently formed and reformed in this crucible of juxtaposition. In other words, the people themselves may also be broken open. I remember my first All Saints' Day after my parents' deaths. Scriptures about the communion of saints and the great cloud of witnesses were broken together with the meal marking Jesus' death

---

35. Lathrop, *Holy Things*. See especially chapter 3.

and life. For the first time, I appreciated and understood the church's historic claims for worship as a joining of the praises of Christ's Body on earth with the eternal praises of the communion of the saints, a communion that now included my parents. In the juxtaposition of Word and Table (and in this case time, as well), *I* was broken open to new appreciation for and deepened gratitude for God's redemption.

Though this brief account of Lathrop only scratches the surface of his extraordinary work,[36] we dare not overlook its implications. Communities that neglect holy things diminish the possibility of the liturgical juxtapositions through which God is made known and acts to redeem the world. Protestants in particular, through their neglect of Eucharist, have often gone hungry when they could be feasting.

I offer one final reason for practicing Eucharistic worship with youth, this time related to the formational ecology of presence, identity, and vocation. While the youth worship described at the beginning of this chapter may have been intended to bring worshipers to a powerful, personal, transforming *experience* of the presence of the living God, without explicit reference to scriptures, without participation in creeds, litanies, or Eucharist, we may rightly wonder how the youth gathered at that worship were able to *identify* the God some were apparently experiencing. The uncritical appropriation of contemporary cultural forms in this worship coupled with the neglect of holy things also fails to provide sufficient attention to how unspoken consumerist agendas — forming youth as consumers of the Christian music industry, for example or, more generally, as consumers of powerfully felt experience — may subvert earnest worshipful intentions. So we might ask, How does the production of experience in youth worship point to anything beyond itself? Eucharist as a means of grace invites experiential encounter with the living God, but it also provides that God with a storied identity as creator, liberator, self-giving servant, and host of the eschatological banquet. In turn it provides its participants with the outlines of Christian vocation.

---

36. Lathrop's *Holy Things: A Liturgical Theology* was followed by *Holy Ground: A Liturgical Cosmology* (Minneapolis: Fortress, 2003) and *Holy People: A Liturgical Ecclesiology* (Minneapolis: Fortress, 2006).

Through the Eucharist, youth learn to welcome outsiders as neighbors and share what they have. They receive and offer hospitality in response to God's presence.

Pedagogical support for formation through Word and Table

For Word and Table to become a central liturgical practice for youthful Christians unaccustomed to sharing in its bounty, we faith communities must be imaginative, intentional, and deliberate in our efforts to form youth into it. This process cannot be left to chance or to osmosis. At the Duke Youth Academy we use a "pedagogy of traction" to assist students in becoming vitally gripped by this life-giving liturgy.[37] The five overlapping components of this pedagogy are these:

1. Robust daily celebration of the Word and Table in a variety of worship styles and contexts;

2. Explicit teaching on the theology of Word and Table;

3. Opportunities for youth to practice planning and leading worship;

4. Deliberate juxtaposition of Eucharist with other spiritual practices, including servant ministry in the community, community agricultural gleaning, and hospitality meals shared with strangers, along with interpretation of these juxtaposed practices in light of one another;

5. Intentional small group reflection between students and adult mentors on the emerging significance of the liturgy to their theological self-understandings and their vision of faithful Christian life.

---

37. This phrase was first suggested to me in a conversation with Charlie Collier, Duke graduate student in theology and ethics and veteran mentor in the youth academy.

Below I describe each component in greater detail. Though my descriptions are set in the context of the youth academy, the content and process I describe have been easily transposed for use in congregations.

Robust celebration of Word and Table

The liturgical theologian Don Saliers, also a principal architect for the reform of liturgical rites in United Methodism, is well known for his advocacy of practicing liturgy "at full stretch."[38] By design, such a metaphor is pregnant with a multitude of hopeful possibilities. I take it to mean an unapologetic robustness in liturgical practice where the central symbols (book, bath, table, patterning of time) are overtly and actively juxtaposed to one another, where artful language and gesture are stirred together with holy symbol in order to conjure revelatory possibilities, and where the entire gathered community understands itself as actively participating in this holy endeavor.

In the case of Eucharist, "at full stretch" means evoking the fundamental phenomenological reality of communal meal-sharing in light of the unity of four basic gestures: taking, blessing, breaking, and sharing. Each day at the youth academy the table is carefully prepared; often it is adorned with art or symbol that evokes something of the thematics or experiences on a given day. Sometimes members of the congregation bring the elements to the table. Through their gestures of careful "table setting" (for example, unwrapping of loaves and pouring of juice into cup), presiders signal to the community that they are in fact preparing for a meal. In addition, hosts presiding at our table "say grace" by offering abundant prayers of thanksgiving. The entire community joins in these prayers, sometimes in song. Such grace-saying invites expressions of gratitude for the stories of God's unwavering faithfulness to God's people, but by it, the community also participates in the re-membering, re-presenting dynamic described above. The communal prayer of Great Thanksgiving invites the triune God (not just any god) into this present gathering to sanctify this holy meal and to make of this gathering a holy people.

---

38. See Saliers, *Soul in Paraphrase*, iv.

The climactic moment in Eucharist is, of course, the breaking of the loaf, a sign-act that expresses sharing in general and the self-giving of Jesus Christ for the world in particular. Finally, bread and cup are shared with the gathered assembly. We receive the meal in a variety of styles over the course of the two weeks, yet every occasion breathes an unhurried expectancy. Servers make eye contact when offering the elements, they speak persons' names, and they never rush. Sometimes the community sings during the distribution, at other times we keep meditative silence.

Teaching on the meaning and significance of worship

On each of its first three days, the two-week academy devotes three seventy-five-minute teaching and learning sessions to the subject of worship. These three worship plenaries focus on: (1) the meaning and purpose of Christian worship; (2) the essential ingredients, patterns, and tensions of worship especially as they relate to Word and Table; and (3) the meanings of Eucharist. Below I offer a brief description of the content and flow of each session.

Session 1: Considering worship theologically

On the first day we begin by posing to the community two related framing questions, "What is Christian worship? and "What is Christian worship *for?*" Participants write down responses and share them with partners as a means to begin the conversation. Then we invite broader sharing. Since the community is so diverse, a rich variety of answers bubbles up.[39] Students describe opportunities to praise God, to reconnect with community, to "fuel up their tanks," to pray, to learn, and more. In response to what worship is for, participants not only talk about meaning and purpose but also of ingredients, patterns, and tensions in worship. For a bit of drama, we invite "characters" into our space, actually youth academy staff members who offer dramatic monologues responding to these framing questions.

---

39. Youth workers cannot normally assume this wide diversity of worship practice and experience for the students in their own congregations. Thus, it may be necessary to visit other communities at worship in order to provide students with sufficient context to enable comparisons with "home."

We hear from "Rev. Dr. Phineus Doddsworth," for example, that the purpose for worship is to train youth to offer praise and gratitude to God, "even if we have to beat it into the little narcissists." On the other hand we also hear the appeal of seventeen-year-old "Blaze Blaisé"' for worship to address her own needs: "Like, who cares about the royal *diaphragm?*" she pleads in an earnest if self-interested way. "Give me something I can *use*." Obviously, these characters are caricatures. But their strong opinions point to important issues like the tension between construing "worship as the glorification of God" and "worship as the sanctification of humanity" or between worship as the means to make persons relevant to God or worship as the means to make God relevant to persons. In a closing move, we listen to another range of voices, this time from the scriptures ("I appeal to you, therefore, brothers and sisters, by the mercies of God, to present your bodies as a living sacrifice, holy and acceptable to God, which is your spiritual worship") (Rom. 12:1); the theological tradition (worship is "the ongoing prayer of Jesus, and the ongoing word and self-giving of Jesus... that brings *us* to expression");[40] and the culture ("I often think of the set pieces of liturgy as certain words which people have successfully addressed to God without their getting killed").[41] As with every step in the process, we invite students to probe what is being claimed for worship in light of what they have named. The purpose in this session is not so much to nail down one definition for Christian worship but for students to think expansively on the subject.

Session 2: The ingredients, patterns, and tensions of worship

On the second day we focus on the ingredients, patterns, and tensions that are essential to worship. Similar to the first session we begin with a framing discussion question, this time, "What are the essential ingredients of worship in your home congregation?" Once again the diversity of the community makes for a varied list. Some

---

40. Saliers, *Worship as Theology*, 27.

41. Annie Dillard, *Holy the Firm* (New York: Harper & Row, 1984), 4; quoted in Saliers, *Worship as Theology*, 21.

students mention preaching, prayer, and music, and others mention confession, Eucharist, the offering, altar calls, and more.

In a second move we look to Luke's Emmaus account (Luke 24) with the suggestion that it provides hints to the earliest church ingredients, patterns, and tensions of worship. This text is a real treasure trove of liturgical theology. Reading between the lines of the narrative, we see, in addition to a compelling story of encounter with the resurrected Jesus, the depiction of a prototypical worship pattern. First, in the form of the dismayed disciples joining with the stranger, the people *gather* in worship to pour out their hearts. Second, as represented stylistically by the shape and content of their interaction with the stranger on the road, the community engages in *proclaiming, interpreting, and responding to the scriptures* in light of their present situations. Third, having prevailed upon this stranger to be their guest for dinner, in an inversion consistent with the Gospel (and with Christian worship), this guest becomes host for their meal by taking, blessing, breaking, and sharing the bread with them. Further, in this *breaking of the bread* (Luke's code for the Eucharistic meal) the church encounters the living presence of the risen Christ. Fourth, the disciples (and the church) are *sent forth* in joy and hope to witness and to serve. To summarize, Luke's Emmaus account suggests a basic pattern for worship in his community:

1. The assembly gathers.
2. The assembly proclaims, interprets, and responds to the scriptures.
3. The assembly participates in the Eucharistic meal.
4. The assembly goes forth in ministry.

Note how we have begun to shift the conversation from worship as a collection of individual ingredients to worship as a *patterning* of holy things. There is an almost natural logic at work here. Communities everywhere build into their assemblies rituals that assist them in coming together and departing. In addition, for the earliest Christians, the proclaiming and responding to the Word was already native to their Jewish heritage. The juxtaposition of that

Word with the Table, however, spoke a new "word": Jesus Christ crucified ... and risen.

Students, though they typically do not know the scriptures, are accustomed to regarding the Bible as authoritative. Reading the scriptures this way is challenging for them, but the logic of the interpretation is also convincing. In reflecting on the text, they are moved to question why, for example, in their home churches, word or table seemed privileged or absent. Thus, they are also challenged to reflect critically upon what previously has simply been a given.

Next, building upon this construal of worship as a patterned relationship of holy things, we introduce the concept of worship as embracing patterns that create crucial *tensions.*

For example, following Gordon Lathrop, we talk about the juxtaposition of word with table. We discuss how when juxtaposed with one another these holy things break open the other to fully reveal the unprecedented and decisive action of God. Thus, not only are book and table essential ingredients to Christian worship, but the pattern of their juxtaposition and the tension that it creates is also essential. Consider Lathrop's example: he suggests that the ancient creed "Jesus Christ crucified" is a case of linguistic juxtaposition. For Israel, "Christ" meant "messiah," the anointed one of God who would deliver Israel from its present oppression. But "Christ" juxtaposed to "crucified" shatters this conventional understanding of "messiah." That the messiah is killed is a nonsensical claim ... unless God is doing a radically new thing. To this linguistic juxtaposition is added a liturgical one: these words are set alongside the table. Therein we discover that Jesus Christ crucified is alive and in our midst. Practically, this juxtaposition suggests that Christians are called to dwell in the tensive space between too-easy triumph and total despair. This tension is what enables God to continue to "speak a new Word" to the church through ancient holy things.

We also note the range of emotions and experiences depicted in Luke's Emmaus account. The disciples come together in fear and despair, but their pathos soon finds itself replaced by the joy of meeting Christ's living presence. Herein lies another tension we judge essential to Christian worship. In order to be authentically Christian, worship must find the means to be honest about naming the world's suffering as it also proclaims resurrection joy and hope. Truthful worship requires expressions of lament, holy fear, and cries for mercy alongside its enactments of doxology and delight. Youth worship that is exclusively perky and upbeat distorts the truth about human life (including the lives of youth) and about God's life. Christian hope and joy are found in the midst of human suffering; they do not replace it. Authentic Christian worship enacts the tension between these realities.

Another of our characters, "Brother Spiritual," shows up to prime the pump about a third named tension: that between freedom and order in worship. Brother Spiritual hails from the Pentecostal tradition. He also raises the issue of social class. Frustrated by the sometimes oppressive "order" that he must endure in his job and family life, he looks forward on Sundays to some "lovin' *dis*-order" in church. He delights in cutting loose with the Spirit. Time stands still as his congregation sings, shouts, and dances for hours on Sundays. He also describes his recent experience of attending the funeral of a friend's parent at an Episcopal Church: "Nobody fell out, but they had a mini-meal." While he misses the accustomed opportunities to "dance with the Spirit" afforded him back home, he notes with some appreciation how the "mini-meal" acted out the story of Jesus' death and resurrection and implied that "all kinds of folks are welcome at Jesus' heavenly banquet."

In the language of this book, Brother Spiritual also demonstrates the importance of worship serving as a context for both the vital experience of God's presence and naming the identity of the God being worshiped. Clearly Brother Spiritual is inclined to tune into God's living presence. Yet he also notices how Eucharist identifies God by telling the story of Jesus and offering a "taste" of God's Reign.

The fourth and final named tension is between received tradition and interpretive innovation. We illustrate this tension by inviting a musical member of the community to demonstrate the extraordinary range of musical innovation possible through a basic chordal pattern. First, our musician strums a bare bones C-F-G-C progression. Next she plays through the likes of Bach, the Beatles, and Bob Marley showing how each brings innovative style and creative freedom to this basic pattern. In other words, the pattern (the chordal progression) and the musicians' creativity require one another for making music. Too little artistic interpretation and all you have are building blocks of music, not music itself. Too much deviation from the pattern and the sounds cease to be intelligible as music.

It's an analogy we use to advocate for Word and Table as the church's basic pattern for worship. We assert that this pattern constitutes the liturgical fugal theme that the church has improvised upon for two millennia. In the next breath, however, we attempt to show how that pattern requires artful and innovative interpretation based on a local worshiping assembly's context and shared experiences. Thus, the pattern requires the community's unique gifts of song, prayer, and gesture along with its unique interpretive responses to the scriptures. To support these claims students view clips of Word and Table worship practiced in a range of congregations from Pentecostal to Roman Catholic and also in contexts beyond North America. Students are able to see for themselves that instead of being synonymous with a formal "high church" traditional *style* of worship, Word and Table in fact form a *pattern* that undergirds an enormous range of innovative cultural and stylistic interpretations.

Session 3: The meaning and significance of Eucharist

On the third day together the subject is Eucharist. The focus on Eucharist in this session is prompted by the fact that this component of worship is often not a regular or well-understood part of worship for students "back home." The session begins with the invitation to conversation partners to describe to one another their experiences of memorable meals. We then pose this question: "What are the key ingredients to these memorable meals?" After more discussion, the community shares aloud responses that are recorded on a board. They include such features as good food, gracious hospitality, gathered company, a special occasion, storytelling, laughter (and tears), thanksgiving, guests, and more. We then suggest that Eucharist itself is best conceived as a meal analogous to our own understandings and best practices of meal sharing. In other words, drawing out the fullness of table hospitality is an excellent means for youth to reimagine the significance of Eucharist.

After this storytelling and imaginative reflection, we pull out what we affectionately have come to call the "list of theological alliterative Cs" (Creation, Crisis, Covenant, Christ, Church, Calling, Coming Reign of God). We use this list repeatedly and in a variety of settings at DYA.[42] In this case, I ask students to look for connections between the meal and these theological categories. Perhaps for the first time, students are invited to imagine the living dynamics of Eucharist as also a feast that constitutes Christ's Body the church alongside of their prior narrow conceptions of it as a "sign that Christ died for me." Such imaginative, expansive interpretation is what we are seeking for all holy things. Finally, we examine 1 Corinthians 11. We pay special attention to the word "remembrance" in verses 24 and 25 — an important theological term, especially for church and youth ministries grounded in the *ordo*. The Greek word for remembrance is *anamnesis*. According to Paul, Jesus says, in effect, "Do my anamnesis." Liturgical and New Testament scholars have noted, however, that *anamnesis* in this context intends more active force than its English rendition "remembrance" conveys. This difference may be illustrated by noticing the distinct shades of meaning implied by "remember" on the one hand and "re-member" on the other. A similar distinction is evident between the terms "represent" and "re-present." In each case, the hyphenated terms possess more active force than their nonhyphenated partners. Each suggests that something is happening in the present. Thus, we are now positioned to better see what Paul sees with respect to the Eucharist. Consistent with Jewish ritual understandings, Paul believes that the Eucharistic meal is not only remembering Jesus' life and death and that the elements are

---

42. DYA is partly indebted to Laurence Stookey, *Eucharist: Christ's Feast with the Church* (Nashville: Abingdon, 1993) and *Baptism: Christ's Act in the Church* (Nashville: Abingdon, 1982) for this list of theological terms. To his list, we have added "Crisis" and "Calling." The alliterative Cs also offer a framework for the theological plenary sessions on baptism (see chapter 4). In addition, I use them to construct a theology of youths' baptismal vocations in chapter 8.

representing his body and blood. In addition, Paul believes the community to be re-membering, and re-presenting them. In other words, when the Corinthians gather to break bread and share the cup, the living Christ is being made present to them. Moreover, through his presence they are being re-membered into his Body. Understood this way, Eucharist functions as far more than a memorial meal to remind youth what Jesus once did for them. It becomes, instead, a feast with Christ and with the church, one that nurtures the "members" of his Body to live as faithful arms, legs, eyes, ears, mouths, and elbows.

The text also invites discussion over the matter of Paul's reprimands directed toward the wealthy of the community who cannot see the connection between sharing in the Eucharist and sharing food with the poor members of their community. I return to this bridge between Eucharist and an ethical way of life in chapter 7.

Students prepare for and lead communal worship

As important as theological education is to understanding Christian worship, the content of the *ordo* is not primarily conceptual: it is embodied in practice. Much depends on whether the scriptures are opened wide or employed only selectively, on whether praise finds its counterpoint in lament, on whether there is a communal meal and who is allowed to preside over it, on who is welcomed to or excluded from the table, on whether the full range of the ritual symbolic gestures is enacted, on the invitation to practice a variety of cultural interpretations and expressions of the *ordo,* on whether whooping can find a place along side of genuflecting, and so on. Students confront these realities directly when, in concert with adult mentors, they join together in small groups to plan and lead services of corporate worship for the community in its second week.

There are certain givens to the planning process. Academy worship employs our lectionary with its preselected scripture passages from the Old and New Testaments already appointed for each day. These passages are chosen in support of a day's theological theme (one of the alliterative Cs). The second given is Eucharist. In short, the Word and Table pattern is required. Worship planning generally takes up five to six hours over several days.

Planning groups begin by studying the scriptures together. They do basic exegesis. They research unfamiliar words or concepts and compare different biblical translations of their assigned passages. They ask and answer questions like these:

- What might this passage have meant to its original hearers?

- What might it mean for us today?

- What do these texts say about our life together here or back home?

- What do these passages have to do with our day's theological theme?

- How do the different passages speak to or interpret one another?

- How do the different passages speak to or interpret Eucharist and vice versa?

Using the answers to these questions, the planning groups next brainstorm with persons appointed to preach for their service. They offer their insights into how the texts may speak to the community and how the community may be "read by" the texts. These insights also provide the means to begin to plan the service itself. Subgroups are appointed to choose music, write prayers or litanies, revise parts of the Eucharistic prayers, plan for decorating the worship space, and consider ways to proclaim the Word (including drama, dramatic reading, biblical storytelling, gesture, dance, and more). The youth academy's artists in residence (see chapter 3) offer their creativity to this part of the process.

The students' budding theological awareness notwithstanding, these planning sessions are taxing. For example, a student may come to the youth academy believing that her sole purpose for existing is to lead the sign-language version of "Shout to the Lord" in worship. Difficulties arise when other members of the planning team question, for example, the propriety of "Shout to the Lord" in a service devoted to the solemn commemoration of Jesus' passion. Mentors repeatedly push students to reflect theologically on these conflicts rather than allowing them to default to personal preference, but that way of thinking goes against the grain of individualistic culture. Moreover, since worship is a bodily activity, it is bodily habits as much as minds that are being challenged. The deeper issues are of bodily proprieties. Are there more adequate or less adequate worshipful postures before a God who is at once transcendent and immanent, suffering servant yet the author of all life? And what to make of the adequacies of one youth's habitual worship gestures with respect to another's? These are questions worship groups seek to resolve in light of normative claims for worship ingredients and tensions. But the process is always inexact and never perfect. That is why we seek to dwell charitably with one another in the midst of these tensions.

One year a group battled over whether blowing bubbles then watching them pop qualified as a ritual gesture properly signifying God's forgiveness of confessed sins. The issues at stake included whether or not sins are utterly extinguished when God forgives them or whether, even when forgiven, human beings must deal with the consequences of sin. A second set of concerns addressed the question of whether or not blowing bubbles conveyed sufficient gravitas with respect to God's forgiveness of sins. Another year the debate was whether or not the Beatles' "All You Need Is Love" belongs in Christian worship. This question goes directly to the tensions between tradition and innovation as well as between identity and experience. Notably, youth's actual engagement with worship wherein something is at stake for them personally is what prompts their theological reflections and makes relevant to them the church's theological traditions of worship. We judge our teaching on worship to be vitally important; without it, youth possess no tools for creative engagement beyond personal taste. Learning about worship is best linked to the task of worship leadership, however, so that it may become more than a matter of abstract interest.

Finally, liturgy planned must be performed. Depending on the actual shape of the service, different members of the planning teams may read scripture, preach, pray, dance, sing or play an instrument, testify, or assist at the table. Many students report that not only the Word and Table pattern but the regular visible presence of themselves and their peers in leadership roles in communal worship is acutely

different from their experiences at home. Perhaps this is an example
of a revelatory, if ironic and unintended juxtaposition — youth set
alongside of holy things? Others note their sense of humility and
empowerment when serving bread or cup to community members,
including adult members. Year in and year out, these student-planned
and -led services manifest careful theological reflection, wide varieties
of styles and cultural interpretations of worshiping practices, and, ultimately, wonderfully varied improvisation built on the *ordo*'s fugal
themes. The students' own investments of themselves, their learnings,
and their gifts in communal worship are crucial for opening them to
its grace-filled logic. Their experience also demystifies worship in constructive ways. They discover that it does not drop out of heaven or
the pastor's head fully formed. They learn how the basic pattern provides a framework for creative interpretation wherein the Spirit may
breathe new possibilities. They find out that you do not need to hail
from some higher order of being in order to offer worship leadership.
They discover why "liturgy" means "work of the people."

Juxtaposition of Eucharist with liturgical and extraliturgical practices

Through these gifts of Word and Table the centrality of Christ's death
and life for the world is made abundantly clear; indeed it is reinforced
daily through our worshiping practice. But worship also enacts a
total way of life for those with eyes to see. Critical to this seeing is
the intentional juxtaposition of Eucharist with other liturgical and
extraliturgical communal practices and themes. For example, in past
sessions of the youth academy we've invited a member of our faculty, Elizabeth LaRocca-Pitts, to teach on the theme of "covenant" in
light of the scriptures and the baptismal covenant. This same professor (also an ordained clergy person) returned that evening to preach
and preside at our community worship. By design, worship had a
Semitic feel to it. The community sat on the floor, sang Psalms and
learned to chant the Shema, Israel's covenantal acclamation to God,
in Hebrew: "Hear O Israel, the Lord our God is one Lord. You shall
love the Lord your God with all your heart, and with all your soul,

and with all your might" (Deut. 6:4–5). The preacher taught in rabbinic fashion from a sitting position, and the scriptures were chosen to chronicle the history of God's covenant making. The Eucharistic Prayer of Great Thanksgiving included passages in Hebrew as well as references to manna in the wilderness and the Passover. Instead of the more typical loaf, unleavened bread was broken. The cup was a piece of earthenware pottery. Like every worship service, the intent of this one was the glorification of God and the sanctification of God's people. In addition, however, through the juxtaposition of Eucharist with a particular theme (covenant), explicitly covenantal biblical texts, and other supportive liturgical symbols and practices, a further crucial theological dimension of Eucharist in particular and Christian conviction more generally was enacted. An organic connection was made between our present-day worshiping community and the great history of God's covenant people. In other words, our students were being invited to see (and taste) their own inheritance. This worship service was participating in God's graceful initiative of providing these young Christians with a sweeping story and, by extension, an interpretive context for making sense of their lives. It not only invited the community into fellowship with God, it identified God (and by extension, God's people) as a community with a specific history.

On another day the theme was "incarnation." In the day's plenary session a member of the theology faculty, John Utz, first recounted some of the historical and theological struggle to construct and then do justice to the formula "fully human, fully divine." In addition, rightly surmising that incarnation is less adequately comprehended than it is encountered through grace, he invited the community into the process of reading and interpreting incarnational poetry.

This session is a rich contemporary example of what the church of antiquity called mystagogy, literally "teaching on the church's mysteries" for those newly initiated into them through baptism. Such teaching functioned only partly for the purpose of explaining Christian theology and practice. Just as significant as explanation for mystagogy was the continued cultivation of capacities to encounter and engage more deeply such grace-filled mystery. Such relational knowing, the kind of knowing that, for example, enables one to be moved by the love of God, is not dependent exclusively on reason or rhetoric. It is a knowing engendered and understood by the body and heart. That is why I describe what I take to be inspired pedagogical strategy on the part of this faculty member. Not only did he invite the students into the theological battles that drove the church to define with precision this crucial piece of dogma, he also sought to nurture their affectively embodied poetic capacities, their abilities to play with symbol and metaphor in light of the incarnation as powerful living reality. I judge this latter strategy, so often ignored, as crucial to equipping persons for more effective participation in liturgy, and ultimately for the formation of a character susceptible to the promptings of a loving yet mysterious God. It is one key to overcoming the gap between "neck-up knowing" and faithful embodiment of the Gospel. The next chapter develops these themes more fully.

That evening an Episcopal priest led communal worship following his tradition's Feast of the Annunciation. Once again the choice of leadership and liturgical style were intentional. In addition to the now familiar liturgical symbols (book, bath, table, assembly, cross, fire, song) our priest friend employed members of our community as acolytes, made ample use of "smells [incense] and bells," and presided carefully at table (at times bowing over the elements and whispering in hushed tones) in such a way as to highlight the mystical incarnational aspects of the service and particularly the meal. It is important to reemphasize that we were not simply trying to be clever in our worship planning and practice, nor were we seeking to tour the liturgical waterfront.[43] Rather, we could imagine no more exemplary way to manifest the grace-filled, if mystical, reality of the incarnation than through the rich aesthetic, symbolic, poetic, ritualized embodiment of such treasure in earthen Eucharistic vessels. If incarnation testifies to God's divinity embodied in earthly form, how better to enact this reality than through iconic liturgical practice where ordinary things may become divinized vessels of grace?

---

43. Though it is true that we hoped members of our community would come to appreciate how the Word and Table pattern could find life in a variety of denominational and cultural worshiping styles.

In addition to the intentional juxtaposition of Eucharist with theological themes and other liturgical practices, Eucharist also finds itself juxtaposed with what I describe as *"ordo-nary"* practices at the youth academy. Chapter 7 develops the meaning of this term in more detail. A small example will suffice at present. Each summer the community participates in agricultural gleaning. Gleaning is a practice described in the Bible wherein the poor are invited to gather produce left behind after fields were reaped or crops were gathered. In the summer of 2002, the youth academy community spent a Saturday gleaning cantaloupe, eventually filling a refrigerated trailer truck with thirty-two tons of the fruit, all destined for regional shelters and food banks. It was a great day, not so infernally hot as previous days, a nice break from the "routine" of academy life and with the added intrinsic pleasure that unlike in the kitchen at home, in this context tossing melons became an officially sanctioned practice of the good life.

At the conclusion of the day, worship leaders turned some packing crates into a makeshift table upon which they placed a few melons plus a loaf and cup, then called us together for worship. The scriptures included the story of Ruth's gleaning, references to the Levitical code around gleaning, and the sheep and goats story from Matthew 25. The preacher-presider for that day was known to our community for her commitments to Christian justice. Her sermon skillfully connected Biblical texts with our day's practice of gleaning and with themes of justice. It also pointed to the Eucharistic meal as the nexus of everything we had experienced. For her, it was obvious that our giving of ourselves to gleaning was prompted by and a grateful response to Christ's self-giving through Eucharist. In other words, the Eucharist of our worshiping issued forth in our living Eucharistically. Such an evocative liturgical setting was full of possibilities for deepening the meaning of Eucharist and, by extension, for deepened comprehension of the nature of Christian life. In their later reflections, students indicated that the power of this juxtaposition was not lost on them.

Multiple opportunities for reflection

Our pedagogy of traction is rooted in a praxis model for Christian formation. Our theories about Eucharist are refined by our practice of Eucharist, and our subsequent reflections on Eucharist then further refine both our teaching and our practice. Reflection is invited in daily covenant group gatherings (seven students, two mentors) and in the worship teams.

Group leaders ask a variety of questions over the course of two weeks. Examples include:

- Where was God in our worship leadership last night?

- How were you surprised by God?

- What have you discovered about yourself in worship?

- What relationship did you sense between the scriptures and preaching and our sharing in Eucharist?

- What was unusual about Fr. Steven's presiding at table this evening?

- What did his gestures signal about incarnation?

- How did our preparing the meal for the AIDS community today then dining with them affect your receiving Eucharist tonight?

- Besides a melon field, in what other unusual places have you worshiped?

- After nearly two weeks of daily Eucharist, how is your appreciation for the meal changing?

Students are also invited to practices of reflection through journaling and meditative prayer.

The five-fold pedagogy of traction with regard to Eucharistic worship represents our best efforts to cultivate in the character of our students' minds, hearts, and bodies receptivity to this unique form of God's gracious self-giving through the church's liturgy. Such receptivity is one key to transformation because it opens students to a crucial source of nourishment for a lifetime of faithful swimming in baptismal waters. It makes clear that God's inestimable love for the world is not ethereal, but is embodied in bread and cup; and it links this offering, this means of grace, to a particular localized faith community and a distinctive way of life. Finally, this form of intentional Eucharistic engagement offers to the young an alternative hermeneutical lens for interpreting the world. It invites them to question whether the frenzied, commodified, individualized life the world seeks to form in them is actually a Christian life. It demonstrates and invites them into the performance of truthful life.

Answers and more questions

So what do the students say about our attempts to recover Word and Table worship and place them in the midst of it? To some extent, it depends on when you ask. My reporting at this point is partly anecdotal, partly the result of interviews with individual students, and partly based on responses to surveys delivered six months after the youth academy. It should be regarded as suggestive more than definitive.

Mentors report that students express a variety of opinions about daily Eucharist in the early days of the academy. Some are enthusiastic. A few intuit or explicitly express that daily Eucharist is one dimension of the "something deeper" they were seeking when they applied to the academy. Others are unimpressed or even hostile. They voice concerns that frequent Eucharist becomes "less special," or that we are "trying to be Catholic" (I am presuming the capital "C") or "traditional" and that "this seems an awful lot like church" as opposed to contemporary youth worship. Students complete a program evaluation at the conclusion of the two weeks. Though it does not ask specifically about daily Eucharist, communal worship (inclusive of Eucharist) consistently receives among the highest ratings of any feature of our community life (approximately 4.8 on a 5-point scale). This would at least suggest that some initial suspicions about or objections to daily Eucharist are overcome in the course of the academy. In the survey six months after students attend the academy, we ask them this leading question: "What parts of worship at home are richer to you as a result of your experience in the youth academy?" Approximately 25 percent of our students name Eucharist. We've also received unsolicited reports from pastors testifying to the possibility of Eucharist gaining traction with some students. One reports a youth academy alumna inquiring why the church did not celebrate weekly Eucharist and expressing the desire to assist with distributing the elements. Several report students seeking training as Eucharistic lay ministers. A pastor of a church adjoining a college campus reports that two freshman and youth academy graduates regularly attend 8:00 a.m. services because that is where Eucharist is offered weekly.

My own participant observer assessment of the transformation that takes place in youth academy worshiping life over the course of two weeks is this: Initially student participation in worship seems inhibited by the fact that community members do not yet know one another, nor are they familiar with the Word and Table pattern. Specifically with regard to Eucharist it seems to take a few nights to work out the anxieties of where to stand, how to receive, and what attitude to bring to the meal. Through this initial period, presiders and staff seek to model serenity, hopeful expectancy, and, above all, hospitality. By the end of the two weeks a marked transformation is palpably present. Students participate in the meal with joy and expectancy. This attitude is evident in their faces, their body language, and their eye contact, as well as the gestures of love and care they offer one another as they move to and from the table. Of course, it is understandable that a group of persons who now have a shared history after two intense weeks together would become more comfortable with one another. At the very center of that shared history, however, is this quirky proclaiming and responding to the scriptures and sharing of bread and cup. And that is the powerful point! What was previously for many teens an unfamiliar and anachronistic practice of "traditional church" became the very occasion for powerfully experienced and affectively embodied encounter with the living God and of deep communion with one another. But this was no teen lovefest sanctioned by some vague deity. Eucharist in concert with its many juxtapositions consistently testified to a God inescapably linked to both cross and empty tomb, who gives God's self through the ordinary goodness of creation, and whose broken body provides nourishment to another broken body, the church, a church that is itself empowered for Eucharistic living for the world.

If Eucharist can be for youth a vital practice and setting for experiencing God and being formed into the identity of God, one wonders why youth worship continues to settle for amplifiers to the exclusion of altar tables. There is no single cause. I would suggest that impoverished congregational liturgical practices, the absence of pedagogies of traction in congregations, and the predominance of lay leadership in youth ministry all prevent youths' deeper engagement with Eucharist. None of these causes suggests a conspiracy. Yet disturbing questions persist. Why do the clergy, most often the caretakers of sacramental practices, steer clear of youth ministry in many denominations? Why are persons discerning calls to youth ministry steered away from ordination tracks that would provide them access to sacramental means of grace?

And in regard to the students in our congregations, how long will we persist in impoverished practices of formation then profess shock and dismay at how un-Christian they turn out? In my tradition, presiders at the table often preface distribution of bread and cup with the saying "The gifts of God for the People of God." Christian youth are part of this People of God. We dare not content ourselves with offering teens an occasional worshipful jolt of empty calories while depriving them of authentic Christian nourishment. They are hungry for so much more.

The pedagogies described above are one step to inviting youth into deeper and more substantive worship of God. I have reserved for the next chapter, however, a further step: the cultivation of students' artistic imaginations. Even a casual observer will easily recognize how much of Christian worship is tied to artistic performance. There is music, symbol, and gesture, and the whole thing is at one level a form of dramatic performance. Cultivating youths' aesthetic capacities, therefore, will only enhance their participation in book, bath, table, and time. Equally important, aesthetic ways of knowing may deepen students' attentiveness to and ability to discern the divine self-communication. Through art they may become attuned to the gifts and callings of the Artist. This is a skill vital not only to youths' worship but to their faithful life beyond the sanctuary.

Three

Being creative and creative being

*Art, incarnation, and youth's embodied communion
with God and neighbor*

Frisbees fly each summer evening at the youth academy in the forty-
five minutes between dinner and communal worship. The quad in
front of the Duke University Chapel is the perfect "court" for a
hybridized version of Frisbee-tennis, a game where two teams of
twenty or so stake out two large grassy rectangles bounded by
flagstone walkways and hurl disks toward each other. Contrary to
conventional Frisbee practice, the object is to land your disc on the
opponents' green space (for them *not* to catch it, in other words), and
strategies range from deft targeting of unguarded corners to knocking
a front line player silly with a laser beam to the forehead. Admittedly,
a game involving competition and sweat, glory and shame, victor and
vanquished may be construed by some as theologically problematic,
especially for a community claiming to share all things in common
through deep baptismal unity. But Frisbee-tennis rocks, and, besides,
the game itself is not the point at the moment.

As it happens, the two weeks of the Duke Youth Academy overlap with the highly prestigious American Dance Festival (ADF), an
internationally renowned celebration of modern dance that makes its
home in the theater directly across the chapel quad (aka Frisbee tennis
court) from the Divinity School. ADF also runs an intensive academy
for high-school-aged modern dancers. The two buildings even sport
dueling banners: the green and blue DYA banner draped from the
Divinity School's arched entryway facing off against the flaming red
ADF banner hung from the corresponding archway on the building
across the quad.

Over the years this juxtaposition has made for some interesting alchemy between the young Christians and the young Artists gathered for their respective academies.[44] One particularly memorable year featured a series of close encounters between both camps. At the outset each community practiced its early evening rituals separately. While the Christians dominated the quad space with their Frisbee warfare, the Artists congregated closer to their theater awaiting that evening's performance. Each group made the pretense of studiously ignoring while actually intensely scrutinizing the other. Differences in appearance were striking. Unlike the Christians oppressed by a burdensome dress code, the Artists were brightly and lightly clad, revealing all manner of interesting tattoos and piercings. They were also brash and flirty. The Christians, on the other hand, also labored under an oppressive PDA restriction.

This studied noninteraction reached its zenith a few days into the academies. When the Christians came out to play after dinner one night, they discovered the Artists in outrageous foil and paint costumes — bodies entirely draped and painted in shiny metallic shades of green or orange or blue or yellow like so many Ozian Tin Men — already occupying the quad. The Artists weren't just standing around; they were engaged in a form of extremely slow-motion choreographed movement. Like grandfather clocks whose moving hands are perceptible to those who stop and pay attention for a few moments, the Artists danced at a snail's pace in the direction of their theater doors. The Christians were flummoxed and a little indignant. Beyond the sheer oddity of it all, the Artists had invaded the Christians' court! A few brave Christians inquired of these slow-paced pilgrims their artful purpose, but they received neither answers nor even eye contact, only stony-faced silence. The slight and barely discernable dance continued.

At which point the Christians decided to play Frisbee-tennis anyway. As the Artists slow-danced toward the theater, the Christians hurled their discs across the very same space seemingly oblivious to

---

44. As this essay will suggest, it is possible, indeed it is even desirable, to be Christian and Artist in the same body.

it all — the only difference being the occasional heroic horizontal leap to prevent the loss of the green Tin Man's teeth to a Frisbee strike. Was this evidence of Christian charity?

On the Monday following this Friday evening encounter, however, one of the Christians made a breakthrough. Gesturing to the Artists (once again appearing "normal"), he said, "Would y'all like to play?" At first his invitation was met with awkward silence. But then the artists conferred, and many did play. And continued to do so nightly.

If you're hoping for the happiest of endings here you'll be disappointed. Though the Artists continued to play Frisbee-tennis, the fullness of the Reign of God did not come. The Artists never followed the Christians from the Frisbee tennis court to join them at the evening's Eucharistic table, nor did everyone then dance the night away in the ecstasies of newfound bodily, aesthetic, and spiritual communion. The two camps did sense something of their shared humanity while playing: they came to enjoy conversation, the raucous team camaraderie, and the peculiar charge and sexual energy of differently formed bodies mingling in close proximity. But this coming together was way more détente than divine. At 7:15 every night, the groups retreated to their opposite sides of the quad, one to worship, the other to dance.

In the spirit of a chapter about the arts, I offer this anecdote as an extended parable. At a variety of levels it captures the complex and tensive relationship between Christian theology and the arts and, more pointedly, between ministry practices related to the Christian formation of teens and to artistic practice, sensibility, and aesthetic in the world. Historically, the relationships between theology and art and between church practices and artistic endeavors have possessed the very same oil and water qualities that characterized those evening gatherings on the chapel quad. Though it is a safe bet that neither group of students realized it, their dissonant interactions were shaped by that history.

At times, art and theology have opposed one another. The Christian iconoclastic impulse, for example, remains an active one to this day, while much of the impetus toward modern art is driven by artists' desire to escape the perceived imperialism of a theological world view. Art and theology, therefore, often have attempted either to ignore or marginalize one another, to accuse each other of epistemological cheating, to notice with distaste each other's differences, and, effectively, to play their own games and then go their own ways.

This occasional enmity has implications closer to home. Ask a group of high school students to name the different groups at their school, and, in addition to goths, jocks, and preps, they'll likely name Christians and artists separately. Even closer to our own doorstep, I once overheard a zealous youth worker offer this description of his youth group to a wide-eyed entering seventh grader: "We don't do that artsy fartsy VBS crap here," he enthused, as if to insist that the substance of Christian faith resides in a realm far deeper and more significant than the facile materiality of matchstick crosses.

Fortunately, in other eras, theology and the arts, when shaken together briskly, have powerfully seasoned one another and the world. One need only consider the names Mozart and Michelangelo to recognize the truthfulness of this assertion. Yet, unlike equations in chemistry class, the comingling of these ingredients has never begotten some cozy new compound. Even in the best of times in the history of the relationship between theology and aesthetics, or faith and artistic practice, the partners have maintained their distinctiveness and at least a little bit of mutual suspicion. We might read the present scholarly theological interest in the relationship of theology to art as a hopeful sign of renewed and deepened relationship, but we ought not be surprised if the artists are wary.

Nevertheless, cultivating artistic literacy and aesthetic sensibility in the young is critically important to forming them for faithful Christian life. The Christian doctrines of creation and incarnation as mode and content of God's self-revelation are essentially artistic. How that connection between creation, incarnation, and art is absolutely critical to youths' right apprehension and practice of the *ordo*'s holy things is the task of this chapter.

Like great art, holy things are performed, imagined, encountered, pondered, and engaged. Practicing holy things is not the equivalent of studying the AP calculus textbook. Thus, my account also requires a fuller epistemological description of how human beings best apprehend and live truth — including *revealed* truth. I have hinted elsewhere at my affinity for bodily, heartfelt, symbol-laden, and extrarational human knowing capacities as channels for receiving and acting upon God's grace. Here I explain why forming youth into these ways of knowing matters essentially, and how we in the church may cultivate artistic literacy and aesthetic sensibility in our youth for the sake of Christian formation and by way of the *ordo*. I describe the DYA's Arts Village and its practices, showing how academy poets, potters, musicians, dancers, and storytellers not only teach *about* theological themes of creation and incarnation in light of the *ordo* but through their particular media assist students in *encountering* these doctrines as living, graced realities. In a final move and by way of offering some examples of student creations and comments, I'll suggest how the practices in the Arts Village both deepen and depend upon other academy practices of Christian life. To reiterate, engagement with art is not an extra-curricular activity for Christians. It is essential to the health of the formational ecology and therefore to faithful formation of the young.

The arts in relation to theologies of creation, incarnation, and revelation

Creation

Genesis 2 two portrays God as artful potter, fashioning a clay person, then animating that person with God's own breath. Later church tradition describes God the potter as re-forming, through the waters of baptism, human "vessels" or pots that have become misshapen or spoiled through sin.[45] God's creativity is portrayed as artful work. God is neither project manager, nor technician, nor gene-splicing scientist, nor paper-pushing bureaucrat, but artist par excellence.

Portraying God's creativity as artistic endeavor seems to sanction human artistic creativity as well. Indeed, some would argue that since

---

45. Thomas M. Finn, *Early Christian Baptism and the Catechumenate: West and East Syria* (Collegeville, MN: Liturgical Press, 1992), 89.

God is known as creator, human capacities for imagination and creativity are near the heart of what it means to be formed in God's image. Yet we should exercise caution over making too easy an analogy between God's creativity and our own. First, because according to the tradition, whereas God creates ex nihilo (from nothing), human beings create using materials provided for them by God. In other words, human creativity is a second-order, derived creativity, always dependent upon God's loving provision of creative "raw materials." Second, whereas God's creativity is always and everywhere a good thing (as the scriptures testify, "And God saw that it was good"), the human creative impulse may become distorted by misplaced pride or hubris, and the results can be disastrous. The story of the Tower of Babel teaches that sometimes human beings are too creative for their own good, and, in the process, they are prone to mistaking themselves for God. Later in his life, Robert Oppenheimer, chief architect of the atomic bomb, offered this Babel-evoking confession: "The physicists have known sin," he lamented.[46] Given this sometimes distorted impetus to creativity, we need further justification before we too easily find provision for human artistic expression in a theology of creation.

Incarnation and eikon

Fortunately for Christians, the doctrine of creation is always tied to that of incarnation. Incarnation (containing the Latin carnus, flesh) is the central Christian conviction that Jesus is at once fully human and fully divine. Incarnation provides a means to link the creative activity of God with the same Jesus who came to live in the world, and in the process, to redeem creativity for Christians. Closer to the ground, theological consideration of incarnation may better explain how and why practicing the arts is vital to Christian formation.

For assistance in this task let us consider icons, or images, those ancient and enigmatic two-dimensional paintings of the principal figures in Christian tradition. Iconographers, artists most often associated with Orthodox Christianity, portray Biblical characters in

---

46. Quoted in Parker J. Palmer, *To Know as We Are Known* (San Francisco: HarperCollins, 1993), 2.

simple two-dimensional style but with inviting gestures and evocative eyes that seem to draw observers into the very lives being portrayed. Icon expert Jim Forest suggests that the impetus to this kind of art is none other than the incarnation itself.[47] He notes that Paul describes Jesus to the Colossians as "the image [eikon] of the invisible God, the firstborn of all creation" (Col. 1:15). Being "of... creation" means, according to Paul, that Jesus is indeed carnus (flesh). He shares human birth, blood, joy, tears, and also death. Jesus is in every way "of creation" like us. Yet Jesus is also eikon, "the image of the invisible God." Jesus who is flesh is no less than the embodiment of the loving transcendent mystery of the universe.

Clumping the human and divine natures into one person creates an extraordinarily difficult intellectual problem. It would appear that, by definition, divinity must trump humanity, so, not unexpectedly, the church has sometimes erred in the direction of overemphasizing Jesus' divinity at the expense of his humanity. One solution to this recurring problem was to emphasize the distinction between Jesus' humanity and his divinity (the "two-ness" of the two natures) as if these natures drew a line down the middle of the poor guy and agreed never to cross it so that each could retain its own integrity. But Paul's description of Jesus as eikon or image refutes such oversimplification. It is through (not in spite of, or across the line from) his very humanity that Jesus' followers detect in him the eikon of God. Further, as eikon or incarnation, he does not merely point to God, he participates in God; he is God. Thus, as the Orthodox say, Jesus as incarnation not only reveals divinity, he also redeems, transforms, even divinizes creation.

Given this conviction of creation transformed through incarnation, we can see how iconography found a place in Orthodox spirituality. The fact that the figures portrayed as icons gesture to us invitingly or gaze at us evocatively illustrates this incarnational sensibility. On the surface icons are simple oil-painted figures on wood, yet the artists who create them fashion them with the intention that they "invite

---

47. Jim Forest, "Through Icons: Word and Image Together," in *Beholding the Glory: Incarnation Through the Arts*, ed. Jeremy Begbie (Grand Rapids: Baker, 2001), 83–84.

us in" to some deeper mystery. That is why the Orthodox claim to venerate icons as "windows into heaven." They do not worship the paint on wood, but because of their incarnational convictions they are attuned to the ways that their art evokes and participates in transcendence toward which it points. In other words, by attending to the art, the Orthodox may also commune with the Artist. Icons do more than represent God for the Orthodox, they re-present God.

Of course, Orthodoxy is using a broadly recognized characteristic of art for theological purposes. Artists everywhere (and of all religious persuasions) work within the parameters of the apparent ordinariness of the stuff of creation — water, clay, oil, fiber, pigment, wood — along with the pulsing bone and sinew of their own bodies — to create and reveal far more than the sum of these raw materials. Art is art precisely because it creates something new out of ordinary stuff and, in the process, transforms our ways of seeing or being. This "more than face value" dynamic in which artistic creativity participates is what the Orthodox justifiably tap into. These incarnational sensibilities are not the exclusive property of the Orthodox, however. They belong to the whole Body of Christ precisely because of the incarnation.

For example, the church's worshiping life is pregnant with iconic potential — and I don't mean merely that some congregations hang pictures in their sanctuaries. The church's holy things, its principal worshiping symbols (book, bath, table, time), all participate in the "more than" dynamic of incarnation. The water bath, for example, was readily perceived by the churches of antiquity as gathering around itself an evocatively thick association of meanings: birth, life, cleansing, and pleasure on the one hand; awe, terror, judgment, and death on the other. This associative power of the water bath is what made it iconic and theologically rich for the ancient church.

However, unlike the Orthodox, Western churches have historically adopted two different but equally unhelpful and unartistic approaches to these holy things. Roman Catholics have often stamped out the "more than" character of these symbols by attempting to rope and brand them in the name of theological precision. Thus the drive to specify exactly how Christ is present in the Eucharist. The result is a flattened symbol, one deprived of its power to participate in the dynamic of "more than." Protestants, on the other hand, responded to this flattening by denying the possibility of the church's holy things for bearing iconic, incarnational power. Both groups have forgotten what the church once knew.

Augustine, one of the church's early and great theologians, once said of the Eucharist, "it is your own mystery that you receive."[48] The qualifiers "your own" in Augustine's phrase points to the manner in which human beings are invited to be stewards of God's creation. In love God the creator provides to human beings the wheat and the grapes, but through artful stewardship and God-endowed human creativity these basic ingredients are transformed into the bread and wine offered to God at the table. But Augustine insists that the deeper "mystery" is that through incarnation, bread and wine are transformed once again into Eucharist — Christ's own life, death, and resurrection for the world — and returned again to his followers in love. We, in turn, through our receiving, find ourselves transformed. Fully appreciating this incarnational mystery which Augustine describes requires an artist's incarnational sensibility. Thus, the Christian practice of the arts is to be commended as a central means for young Christians to become attuned to the central reality and manner of God's grace-filled presence and activity in the world.

Incarnation helps underwrite artistic expression in other ways, as well. It refutes an age-old religious tendency to create hierarchical distinctions between spirit (good) and matter (bad). Beginning with Plato and echoed by a chorus of Western thinkers ever since, earthy materiality gets blamed for a whole host of down-and-dirty problems while the spiritual realm floats above it all like an angel on a cloud. According to this way of picturing the world, thinking elevated thoughts in ivory towers receives high marks, while birthing babies, planting crops, and painting pictures are regarded as necessary evils or sinful wastes of time.

One need not travel too far along either trajectory of this spirit/matter split in order to stumble over supposed justification for the

---

48. Augustine of Hippo, *Sermon* 272.

oppression of whole peoples. Women, for example, have suffered historically because they have been deemed too earthy to be of spiritual worth. This unfortunate split was also responsible, in part, for the iconoclastic controversies in the church which resulted in the destruction of vast quantities of Christian art in different periods of the church's history. Such a split makes possible the construal of art as idolatrous instead of iconic. Yet the doctrine of incarnation claims that none other than God takes on the earthy materiality of creation in and through Jesus, and therefore endorses and redeems the material world. It means that God gives God's self to us through flesh and blood; that spirit and matter are organically intertwined; and that therefore the everyday ordinary materiality of our lives including our book, bath, table, and time, are infused with this mystery of grace.

Incarnation and Logos

The theological use of the Greek word *Logos* ("Word") in John's Gospel strengthens the relationship between God's artful creation, the doctrine of the incarnation, and the necessity for cultivating the human artistic impulse as a means to forming faithful life. The Old Testament testifies to God's creation through the spoken word. As Genesis tells it, "And God said, 'Let there be....' " Playfully, we say that God's creative power is tied to God's way with words. Later the writer of the Gospel of John was inspired to associate this creative power of God present from the beginning with Jesus: "And the Word [*Logos*] became flesh and lived among us" (John 1:14). Here we see clearly the integral connection of creation to incarnation.

According to Malcolm Guite, the oldest English word for "human being" is best rendered "word-bearer."[49] The complexity of our languages distinguish humans from the rest of creation. And language also empowers human beings to create worlds of thought and imagination in which to dwell. This is literally true in the J. R. R. Tolkien trilogy, for example, in which we find ourselves so wrapped up in the story that we feel Frodo's fears and shed tears of joy at the reunion

---

49. Malcolm Guite, "Through Literature: Christ and the Redemption of Language," in *Beholding the Glory*, ed. Jeremy Begbie (Grand Rapids: Baker, 2001), 33.

of the company of the ring. But this creative power of language to create a world may also be subverted, for example, by naming a nuclear missile "peace-keeper." In response, Guite observes that in the incarnation, the Word himself became a word-bearer. Though born "without a word" Jesus grows in his own facility with language, and through his adult ministry demonstrates how words may be employed redemptively. The Gospels witness to his amazing power for storytelling through parables, for rhetorical brinksmanship with the Pharisees, and to his highly developed insights into poetry and metaphor in describing himself as "Bread of Life" and "Living Water." Guite suggests that by virtue of the Word being incarnated as word-bearer, Jesus also "redeems language."[50] He employs language to reveal the truth about himself and the world. And he does so artfully. "*I* am the Truth," says Jesus. Only a poet could render truth by fashioning himself as living metaphor!

As was the case with the scripture's describing Jesus as *eikon*, rendering Jesus as *Logos* also allows the possibility of language that is artfully fashioned pointing to and participating in incarnation. By extension, such rendering also places upon Christians the responsibility for appreciating and using such language. To put it bluntly, Christians must become poets!

Dominant epistemologies and the abandonment of artistic knowing

Unfortunately, most of our youth are not taught to use language poetically or to value such use. They are mainly taught to use language technically and scientifically, to quantify, verify, specify, and objectify, as if epistemology, the study of what constitutes credible human knowing and how that knowledge is acquired, is best done through such means.

In my classes, I often illustrate the problem of competing languages and the competing epistemological systems they represent using a full-color cartoon with the character Ziggy and his dog, Fuzz, standing atop a mountain glorying in a magnificent sunrise. As light beams

---

50. Ibid., 34.

streak across the panel from the rising sun to Ziggy's mountain, he lifts his hands in applause and exclaims in the talk bubble, "Go God!" When I ask students to interpret the comic theologically, they rightfully point out that Ziggy proclaims faith in a loving creator God, that one feature of God's loving creativity is to divide daily activity from nightly rest, that Ziggy is moved by such a heavenly display, and that he rightly expresses affectively-laden gratitude and bodily praise for God's good work.

In a second, step, however, I ask them to convert Ziggy from believer to modern day rational empiricist and to replace the "Go God" in Ziggy's talk bubble with language appropriate to his new epistemological frame. After some initial head scratching students soon come up with all the right jargon. In contrast to the simple "Go God" of believer Ziggy, science Ziggy observes that the phenomenon of sun-rise is actually an optical illusion (the earth, of course, orbits the sun), that the brilliant colors are the result of particulate matter in the atmosphere — made all the more spectacular these days by humanly manufactured atmospheric pollutants — and that for reasons of natural selection human beings have evolved to pay attention to powerful visual phenomena and to experience emotion in response to them. (For example, it makes good survival sense to notice, be afraid, and run away when a volcano blows up.) Nowhere does Ziggy the empiricist credit divine creativity, because empiricism can find no evidence for it. In fact, Ziggy the empiricist's explanation of this phenomenon actively excludes the possibility of beautiful sunrise as gratuitous gift from a loving creator God for Ziggy's enjoyment and response of praise. Based on the empirical evidence, such a response would be irrational.

In class, we move on to discuss which epistemological stance is true. This discussion often leads to further reflection on the characteristics of the knowing in the contrasting descriptions. As Parker Palmer notes, scientific knowing lays claim to "facts" that it can prove by way of the scientific method.[51] No doubt, this kind of knowing has transformed our world and our lives, sometimes even for

---

51. Palmer, *To Know as We are Known*, 22. See also chapter 4, "What Is Truth?"

the better. But scientific knowing has turned out to be less than the panacea we may have once hoped, and it can indeed have destructive consequences. For example, scientific inquiry proceeds with the expectation that the knower will maintain distance from what she seeks to know. Distance ensures objectivity. But such separation is actually illusory. Biology students peering through microscopes at pond water may imagine they are looking down on an alien world, but, in reality, students and paramecia all swim in the same biological soup. Still, the method requires that persons proceed *as if* separation between knower and known is real, and, in fact, its procedures actually support this illusion.

A further consequence of this false premise is that this assumed separation may be construed as grounds for hierarchical distinction. As knower I come to understand myself as sole *subject;* all else becomes the *object* of my inquiry. I am lord and master of the paramecia! In quasi-theological terms, it is as if the world becomes my apple for the picking. Separating myself from all the possible objects of my knowledge sets up a dangerous, if implicit, moral stance: I am superior to everything else.

A third characteristic of this way of knowing is that it proceeds by cognition and excludes emotion. Cool reason sifts the evidence to get at the facts. Allowing emotion into the equation can only mean that autonomous subjects risk getting too close to the objects of their inquiry. When objectivity is lost, so is the reliability of that knowledge.

The contrast with Christian knowing is stark. First, the goal of Christian knowing is not separation of knower from known but loving relationship between knower and known. The biblical stories of God's salvation testify that God invites human beings to be subject to one another and, in an even more dramatic reversal, that God becomes subject to *them* through the incarnation. Instead of a rigid distinction between knower and known, between subject and object, Christians are invited into relationships of mutual subjectivity with one another, their world, and with God. The truth of creaturely existence for Christians is, ultimately, one of relationship, not separation. Palmer uses the language of Jewish theologian Martin Buber to strengthen this point. The difference between these epistemological frames, he says, is between an "I-It" separation (hierarchical distinction between subject and object) and an "I-Thou" relationship (mutual subjectivity).[52] This distinction may appear as little more than semantics, but language matters. I am, for example, far less likely to exploit another if I regard that other as "thou" rather than "it." I am far less likely to drive a Hummer if the planet's ecology and my yet unborn grandchildren are to me revered "thous" not disposable "its." I am far more likely to refer to my patient as "Mr. Roberts" than "the gallbladder in 3A" if my epistemological frame is Christian and not merely scientific. Thus, there are deep moral implications to these contrasting epistemological perspectives. The one has difficulty finding room for loving relationship; the other requires it.

Second, the focus of Christian knowing is not merely individual objectified pieces of the puzzle but the big picture, the search for Truth with a capital "T." Why is there something instead of nothing? Why are we here? Where are we headed? What are we supposed to do in the meantime?

Finally, as Ziggy's praise exemplifies, Christian knowing is often transacted by way of the body and the heart. Christians claim to intuit or feel God's presence, to love God and neighbor, to joyfully praise God or to lament the world's sufferings. None of this makes rational sense to science, yet Christians trust this affective way of knowing to be authentic. Emotional knowing is distinctive in another way, as well. Emotional knowing is a participative "knowing in the midst of." It requires and engenders bodily interaction with other bodies in the Body of Christ. It is a relational knowing that unites knower with known. Ziggy's praiseful adoration of God is a perfect case in point.

I hope this epistemological excursus helps those who care for and work with youth to better understand their environments of formation. Our youth's schooling is also oriented primarily to scientific knowing in the name of economic competitiveness. Science and math dominate the curriculum. Students are taught reading and writing not to be embraced by the beauty of literature but because our economy

---

52. Ibid., 50.

requires persons who can communicate in the idioms of technical rationalism. Cognition, not emotion, is king, though as Elliot Eisner notes, even cognition has lost its "scope and richness," reduced to meaning only "thinking with words or numbers by using logical procedures for their organization and manipulation and not thinking in its broadest sense."[53] Everywhere the language is truncated — witness instant messaging in which whole conversations are reduced to combinations of letters (LOL!) and smiley faces. In addition, given America's current fascination with testing and our national perception that our students' academic performance lags behind that of students in other nations, arts curricula in the schools are repeatedly reduced or cut out altogether. The result is fewer and fewer occasions for students to wonder, to be moved, to create, to reflect.

In addition to the explicit curriculum, the separation of knower from known also shapes implicitly the values the school teaches. Such separation means that students do not imagine themselves as engaged in a communal journey with fellow learners toward a common goal of mutually constructed knowledge. Instead, they are formed to be isolated individuals competing with other isolated individuals for high grades and the economic rewards that go with them. Further, since students are taught to objectify their subject matter, they seek "mastery" over it rather than a lifelong relationship with it. Learning and thinking become instrumental means to some usually economic end.

Reclaiming artistic knowing for Christian formation

After this critical consideration of dominant ways of knowing at present, we make our way back to Christianity, to incarnational theology in relation to *Logos*, and to forms of artistic expression that involve words — words that participate in Christian epistemology by virtue of their being artfully crafted into poetry and story. Our task is to form youth more highly sensitized to the power of words to bear

---

53. Elliot W. Eisner, *The Educational Imagination: On the Design and Evaluation of School Programs* (New York: Macmillan, 1979), 98. The author's heuristic proposal for "explicit, implicit and null curricula" provides an extremely helpful lens for critically reading contexts for education and formation.

the spark of the divine. And this means attending to the skillfully expressive forms of language.

It is no accident that the Bible is not written in the style of a Microsoft user's manual. Instead the Bible is composed of stories and poems and heightened speech rich with metaphor. Yes, there is also a good bit of legalese, but when the child in Deuteronomy asks the parent the meaning of those rules and statutes the parent explains the law by telling a story that appeals to the imagination: "We were Pharaoh's slaves in Egypt; and the Lord brought us out of Egypt with a mighty hand" (Deut. 6:21).

And that is the point. The use of artful language is, for Christians, anything but quaint or cute or frivolous; it is an essential means to communicate incarnational truth. Youth who learn to speak and listen to this language are formed to encounter the living Word. Without this formation they are doomed to the equally empty certainties of fundamentalism or empiricism.

Entire libraries are devoted to the knowing engendered by the artistic crafting of language. I will content myself with three possibilities: (1) the relationship between story and personal and communal identity; (2) the capacity of metaphoric language to link diverse realities and claims to truth; (3) the power of poetry to awaken and transform perspective.

The art of story

We are indebted to the past generation of theologians for their work in recovering the importance of story to Christian identity. For a generation accustomed to imagining story in terms of Mother Goose or Dr. Seuss, stories might be considered simply as child's play. Yet even a cursory glance at the scriptures reveals the importance of story to Israel and to the church. At every pivotal moment in its history — escape from slavery, wilderness wandering, crossing into the Promised Land, surviving exile — Israel told and retold the stories of its journey with God. Clearly, the intent was for Israel to remind itself of who and what it had been in light of God's saving actions in the past in order to lean faithfully into God's promised future. As a case in point, Joshua retells those stories on the banks of the Jordan, then affirms, "as for me and my household, we will serve the Lord" (Josh. 24:15). Later, the story of Jesus' life, death, and resurrection becomes so important to the church that it includes four versions in its scriptures and patterns its time to enact this story.

How do stories exert formative impacts on communities? Novelists and movie scriptwriters appreciate how certain plot lines shape and require certain kinds of characters, and the same dynamic is at work in cultural or communal stories. In the story of Manifest Destiny, for example, there's no place for whiney dependent types who are afraid of their own shadows. What was needed were so many rugged Paul Bunyans capable of carrying wagons, families, and oxen across the vast prairie on their broad shoulders. By contrast, the Gospel stories seem to require communal interdependence and to eschew a "pull yourself up by your own bootstraps" individualism. These examples of contrasting stories and the identity of the characters they require reveals the reality of competing stories in our world today. Will our students be formed by the stories of the life, death, and resurrection of Jesus Christ or by what Stanley Hauerwas describes as the contemporary "story that they have no story except the story they choose when they have no story."[54] The answer is not a simple one, but requires at root that youth learn to see themselves as story-formed, story-telling, story-living people. Then, of course, they must learn the details of their own storied identity as followers of Jesus. Whatever else may be said, this much is certain: Imagining one's self as storied, as participating in God's unfolding story, and as leaning faithfully into the future based on the trajectory of that story requires a very different way of reading and imagining the world than technical rationalism or scientific empiricism. Since students are actively formed in a competing epistemological frame at school (and its implicit competing story), the church cannot assume that they will automatically grasp or appreciate either the mode or content of artfully storied epistemology. Youth need frequent opportunities to hear stories, tell stories, wonder at stories, and see themselves as actors or

---

54. Stanley Hauerwas, "Preaching as though We Had Enemies," *First Things* (May 1995): 53.

participants in stories. The next chapter will consider these practices in more detail.

The art of metaphor

Streams of living water. The Living Word. The Bread of Life. Cast your bread on the waters . . . I love metaphor. I love its allusive, illusive character. I love the way it reveals truth to those with eyes to see while confounding those who think they've already got truth all sewn up. And I love how it can bind into relationship so many different ideas and realities.

Metaphor is also the principal linguistic tool human beings possess for describing transcendent experience. For Christians, metaphor is words that evoke Word. Christians could not talk about or make sense of their faith without metaphor. Consider the names for God: Father, King, Lord, Wisdom, Mother Hen. Consider names for Jesus: Lamb of God, Prince of Peace, Alpha and Omega, Son of Man, Living Water, Bread of Life, as well as the aforementioned Word. Consider names for the Church: Body of Christ, Pilgrim People, Ark of the New Covenant. You get the idea. Faith and theology proceed by way of metaphor. One cannot be a thoughtful person of faith without dabbling in metaphor. Therefore churches' endeavors to expand youths' capacities for playing with and appreciating metaphor assist them in better knowing and encountering God.

Take bread, for example.[55] In an *ordo*-grounded approach to youth ministry, bread appears everywhere: as part of liturgical recitations of the salvation story (manna in the wilderness, loaves and fishes, wedding banquets) or the Lord's Prayer ("Give us this day our daily bread. . . . "); as the gift of hospitality at community meals (often in culturally specific forms — tortillas, rice cakes, corn bread); as a sign of justice in relation to preparing and sharing food with the poor and homeless; in the biblical practice of agricultural gleaning; as a

---

55. Bread is not merely a linguistic metaphor; it is also an iconic symbol, one often engaged ritually in the church. Yet a symbol bears its symbolism by virtue of its metaphoric quality, so in this case I choose to focus on the linguistic meanings of bread.

key ingredient of sabbath feasting; and, of course, at the Eucharistic table. These many contexts for bread are what enable students to comprehend its multivalent theological meanings. Bread as metaphor evokes and participates in creation, self-giving, justice, hospitality, community, stewardship, feasting, the Body of Christ, and the in-breaking Reign of God. Youth who begin to "get" this resonant and evocative power of the linguistics of bread are not only youth whose metaphoric capacities have been enlivened, but youth who are being formed to appreciate and participate in God's graceful gifts of treasures in earthen vessels. They are word-bearers and word-crafters better formed for imaginative attentiveness to and relationship with the Word. Their faith is shielded from gnostic-leaning, etherealized spiritualities or wooden literalizing that effectively deny the incarnation and that turn so many Christians into practical atheists. Bread as metaphor may manifest Jesus Christ, but it ever remains one of the material realities of earthly life, including the Christian practices of hospitality and justice.

The art of poetry

We move now to a consideration of poetry which, of course, is not only laced with metaphor itself but also extends the power of metaphor in imaginative directions. Among the many distinctive features of poetry is its capacity to transform our perspective in relation to something we thought we fully understood. Poetry invites us to see or imagine in new ways — fog creeping in on "little cat feet," for example. All good poetry provides us with new and richer insight into our lives in the world. That, according to Walter Brueggemann, is exactly why the Old Testament prophets were also poets.[56] Their language confounded ruling managerial types who had domesticated Israel's high calling with their measured speech. Through poetry prophets awakened a new way of seeing in a people perishing for lack of vision.

---

56. Walter Brueggemann, *The Creative Word: Canon as a Model for Biblical Education* (Philadelphia: Fortress, 1982). See chapter 3.

John Utz's DYA class session on incarnation, in addition to constructing a bridge between theology and worship through holy things as described in the previous chapter, also displays how poetry may awaken prophetic vision. John spends the first half of the teaching session dutifully tracking the historical controversies and heresies that led to conciliar claims for Jesus as fully human, fully divine. He devotes the second half of his session to poems on the incarnation by Denise Levertov.[57] Several years ago, after listening to students read the poems out loud, and not very clear on the meanings of them myself, I joined a small group of five or six students working on interpreting them with an adult mentor. They were discussing the author's use of the imagery of the newly born lamb as defenseless and dependent. Very quickly I noticed that one of the students demonstrated incredible skill in unpacking the dense imagery. At one point in reference to a particular line she said, "It's as if Levertov is trying to convey just how vulnerable God became in the incarnation, how much of a risk he took. I've never thought about God that way before, as vulnerable, or dependent even." Admittedly an extraordinary case, it is nevertheless true that this student's cultivated skill with poetic language became key to her deepened theological awareness. In an extended conversation several days later with the same student, she related how she had run all the way back to the dorm after Dr. Utz's session to call her mom and describe her extraordinary encounter with this poetry. It turned out that she loved poetry and literature (no surprise there), but that her high school English teacher and classmates seemed bent on using literature to debunk faith. This was the first time she'd ever witnessed it employed so powerfully in the service of faith. Wiping away tears, she described the pain of previous English class encounters with literature and the joy of this most recent one.

At the risk of overanalyzing her experience, I suggest that this student acquired more than new intellectual insight into the use of metaphoric imagery to depict the incarnation on that day. She also

57. For example, "Agnus Dei," by Denise Levertov, in *The Stream and the Sapphire: Selected Poems on Religious Themes* (New York: W. W. Norton, 1997).

experienced or *encountered* something of the loving mystery of incarnation born, in this case, by way of the fragile yet enormous power of poetic speech. Through those words she was made present to Word. Through the poetry she experienced what it is like to know in love as we are known by the preeminent Lover. Her epiphany was not simply *about* the incarnation, it was a participation *in* the incarnation, prompted by metaphoric language that moved her to the core of her being.

Art, the life of the heart,
worshipful receptivity, and response to God

We began this chapter by observing how the scriptures by way of *eikon* and *Logos* provided the grounds for the more developed theologies of incarnation. We saw that the fact that these terms bear artistic implication is no accident. Incarnation and art share in many of the same dynamics. Both value the material as offering its own beauty yet also use the material to point to truths beyond themselves. In addition, as with incarnation, encounters with art may transform for the better the ways human beings interpret or live their lives. By way of illustrating these claims we explored inconography and poetic language, one an example of visual art, the other of the literary arts.

We turn now to considering Christian worship by way of the *ordo* as a form of performing art. The purpose of this exploration to this point is to affirm how appropriate and natural it is for Christians to use art in relation to their faith given the incarnational nature of God. Indeed, the nature of incarnation *requires* that Christians be attuned to artistic sensibilities and artistic ways of knowing if they are to be in full relation with the God who creates them.

Though I've not used the language of revelation to this point, inevitably, that is what incarnation is about — God making God's self known in the world through Jesus Christ. Thus, all of the prior discussion on incarnation has significance for revelation. Here, we focus on revelation but from a particular angle. I am interested in describing human capacities for *receiving* God's revelation. Thus, I will focus not primarily on the incarnational *content* of God's revelation (Jesus Christ, fully human and fully divine) nor the *mode* of God's revelation (transcendence disclosed artfully in and through material, including the material of holy things). Instead, I will pay more attention to human *experience* of God, how human beings perceive and receive the grace God reveals. This focus is in keeping with lifting up vital experience of God's presence as a key dynamic in the faithful formation of youth. Making this move requires that I pick up again the subject of epistemology, what human beings know and how they know it, especially the epistemological importance of bodily and affectively-laden knowing for Christian faith and life. By way of a preview, in this section I note how human experiences of and encounters with art overlap with their experiences of and encounters with God, especially in and through their practices of corporate worship.

I'll never forget my one and only personal meeting with Michelangelo's David. Never before had I encountered anything so beautiful, so powerful, so awe-inspiring. I was speechless. Tears welled up in my eyes as David and I stood gazing at each other. That experience is stamped in my memory as singular, holy even. Since that time, I've had similar experiences with other art forms — everything from performing a Bach mass, to attending a daughter's modern dance recitals, to singing Charles Wesley's "Christ the Lord Is Risen Today" on Easter Sundays. Reflecting on these encounters, I note that part of the power of art and the pleasure I take in its many forms is that it affects me *affectively*. Art stirs my emotions. It can carry me to ecstasy, fill me with rage, offer me peace, make me weep.

I am not alone, either. At the time of this writing, for example, New Yorkers were publicly engaged in two very different artistic/aesthetic conversations. In one case, they struggled over the most fitting replacement for the destroyed twin towers of the World Trade Center. Should that site be remade as a solemn memorial, as a defiant restoration of capitalism, or some combination of both? The conversations are not merely architectural. They are more about what sort of design sets the appropriate emotional tone for a site now so emotionally freighted. In a second case, consider the delight with which New Yorkers received the exhibition of bright banners flying above the walkways of their Central Park. The architectural artists Christo and Jeanne-Claude constructed thousands of tall gates draped with orange fabric over the park's paths in the winter of 2005. Citizens who had not visited the park in years came out in droves to stroll under these gates and to enjoy the new perspective this art brought to this familiar landmark. Many spoke of the ways the experience lightened their hearts.[58] Art does that to us. It moves us at an intuitive, visceral level. Certainly participating in art is not unintellectual, but it is never only or even primarily cognitively so.

By comparison, notice how Christians also employ the language of the heart to describe their experiences in worship. They say, "Your words really touched me, Pastor," or "My, we danced with the Spirit today!" or "God, it was dead in there this morning." Or "Wow, that choir anthem sent chills down my spine." Christians often describe their religious experiences, their encounters with the presence or absence of God, as being mediated emotionally — which is also to say, bodily.

What to make of the overlap between religious and artistic experience? At minimum we can say that artistic experience and religious experience often seem to be mediated for human beings by and through the same embodied, heartfelt ways of knowing. A bit bolder claim might suggest that Christians' religious experience, their ability to receive God's loving revelation in worship, is prompted by and mediated through their participation in artful media. Throwing caution to the wind we might even suggest that given what we know about the nature of incarnation, art's ability to move human beings makes it a primary channel for God's self-revelation precisely because of its capacity to speak to the human heart. Thus, it is no accident that Christian worship drinks deeply at the well of artistic expression. Art is a medium uniquely capable of participating in God's own revelatory means of self-communication. And art speaks to the deepest regions of the human spirit. All the more reason for us to provide

---

58. For Internet links to all of the *New York Times* stories on the "Gates," see *www.nytimes.com/ref/arts/design/gates-ref.html?excamp=gggnchristo*.

youth "eyes to see," and "hearts to experience," and bodily postures to receive this graceful self-giving.

The significance of the heart resides not only in its capacity to open persons to grace-filled revelation but to form their lives in faithful response to God's love. The church of antiquity sought to form in persons "affections" (enduring positive emotional dispositions including love, peaceableness, compassion) and to root out their passions (sinful emotional dispositions including hatred, lust, violence, pride, etc.), because it believed that displaying the right emotions in the right situations was key to holy living in right communion with God and neighbor. By contrast, a millennium later, Descartes' dictum "I think therefore I am" declared the Enlightenment's preference for thinking above feeling as the key variable in the equation of moral life. In the process, morality in general came to be described less in terms of virtuous emotional dispositions housed in persons and more along the lines of vexing ethical dilemmas to be worked through intellectually. For the ancients the moral concern was, "What kind of persons should we Christians be?" Enlightenment moderns asked instead, "What's the best way to solve this moral problem?" Interestingly, at the turn of the new millennium scientists struggling to uncover the biological workings of the human brain have begun to reemphasize the crucial role of emotion in human knowing, being, and acting, particularly with regard to social and moral life.[59] According to science, the place where the rubber hits the road in daily human moral living is far more likely to be linked to an emotional disposition to care — a bodily-affective habit of compassion for homeless people, for example — than it is to intellectual consideration of vexing ethical problems such as "What are the moral implications of homelessness?" In straightforward scientific terms this is true because the

---

59. Antonio Damasio's *Descartes' Error: Emotion, Reason, and the Human Brain* (New York: Bard Avon Books, 1998) provides an excellent entrée into this conversation. See also Frans DeWaal, *Good Natured: The Origins of Right and Wrong in Humans and Other Animals* (Cambridge, MA: Harvard University Press, 1996); Joseph LeDoux, *The Emotional Brain: The Mysterious Underpinnings of Emotional Life* (New York: Touchstone, 1996); and Daniel Goleman, *Emotional Intelligence* (New York: Bantam Books, 1995).

networks of our brains privilege feeling our way into action rather than thinking our way into action.

How does all this tie together? The implications for the formational significance of embodied emotion are wide-reaching and profound. The science implies that the same emotional capacities in human beings that mediate transcendence, the experience of and communion with God's grace-filled presence, and regard for the sublime incarnational character of art, may also be crucial to loving neighbor as self. The body is the context through which we become present to God and learn to receive or avoid the neighbor. In short, a rightly formed body and heart are key to connecting with God *and* to the good life.

Thus, worship becomes a school for the body and the emotions. By practicing ritualized bodily gestures and playing with evocative holy things, Christian liturgy awakens in its participants joy, delight, and gratitude but also lamentation for failures and compassion for suffering. Forming persons in these distinctly Christian dispositions of the heart may then shape their daily lives beyond the sanctuary. But such a worshiping "curriculum" for the formation of the heart proceeds by way of a thoroughly artistic "pedagogy." Worship is full-blown performance art complete with director, actors, and audience. God, clergy, and people often fill those roles interchangeably. Worship includes song, dance, poetic speech, passionate dialogue, and visual beauty. It includes all the other trappings of theater as well: holy things as props, suspenseful buildup, climax, and audience response.

Once again, though the focus this time is on human receptivity and response to divine revelation, we see the critical role of the arts and the cultivation of artistic sensibilities for Christian formation. Christian life, including Christian worship, is an artistic endeavor mediated through body and heart. Cultivating in young Christians the artistic capacities that take their emotions to school will promote both their authentic communion with the God who is known to the human heart and more authentic life in a community of people seeking to be known to one another in love. We turn now to the task of undertaking this formation in the lives of youth.

DYA's Arts Village

Each summer the youth academy invites five or six theologically trained "artists in residence" to join the community. Typically this group is representative of one or more species of the literary, visual, and performing arts. Artists generally participate in all aspects of community life in addition to their specific leadership responsibilities. Thus they are intimately aware of daily themes, moods, worshiping activities, and other practices.

The village itself is housed in a church near Duke's campus. The decision to locate the village in a congregational setting was partly logistical (it boasts a stage and ample classrooms) and partly theological (the arts are at home in the church). During a typical academy, students spend approximately two hours working with each of the artists in residence and sometimes spend additional time with the artist and artistic medium they enjoy the most. Students are also treated to a well-conceived theological introduction to practicing the arts offered in the form of performance art by the artists in residence.

Though there is no typical studio session, most artists attempt to provide basic introductions to their media and as much time as possible for working within each medium. What makes the Arts Village a theological endeavor, however, is its subject matter and the type of creativity and reflection artists in residence invite from their students. Artists who work with materials (painters, potters, photographers, jewelers, and more) often make use of Christian symbols related to holy things (basins, lamps, crosses, chalices, patens) as subjects for student creation. Likewise, literary artists tend to draw from primary *ordo*-inspired metaphors (bread, water) in teaching students how to create poetry, keep a journal, or write literature. Dancers often work on the significance of embodied liturgical gesture for creating and transmitting religious story and meaning. Musicians call attention to the theological aesthetics of tone, rhythm, chordal progression, and lyrics.

Rather than attempting to describe what goes on in every studio, let me take you through a typical session as musician in residence. First, I teach students to sing samplings of different forms of Christian music from chant to classical to hymnody to gospel to contemporary, then invite them to discuss which forms they prefer. Sometimes I even conduct an informal poll and post the results. Students often surprise one another by the diversity of their preferences. Then I push a bit deeper by asking, "What is your favorite form of Christian music from the examples we encountered? What makes it so?" Inviting students to reflect on their musical tastes raises the issue of aesthetics. As the theologian and church musician Frank Burch Brown suggests, this question makes them consider how they perceive music as artistic expression in the first place, what factors or dynamics are involved in their enjoyment of certain forms of music, and what standards they use in exercising preference for some musical forms over others.[60] Youth tend to voice strong opinions about music while neglecting any substantive argument to back up their assertions. Asking questions of aesthetics such as: "What makes music music?" "What makes you enjoy music?" and "How do you judge music to be good, bad, or elevator?" is an invitation for students to construct thoughtful arguments for their preferences.

In a second move, after playing or performing the diverse musical selections again, I typically ask questions of context: Does this music belong to a certain time or certain people? Is it appropriate only to those times and those communities? How do Christians negotiate differing musical preferences in congregations? Are there some musical forms that are inherently more or less appropriate for Christians? This constellation of questions continues to push on the issues of musical diversity, inclusivity, and taste.

By way of a third move, I repeat the musical selections but this time focus on emotions and mood as bearing the potential for encountering God, asking, How does this musical piece make you feel? Why? How are Christians supposed to feel in worship? And finally, Is there a fittingness between the musical melody, rhythm and tone, and the sung lyrics? This third round of questions seeks to get at the relation between theological conviction and musical aesthetics.

60. The critical reflective questions in this section are inspired by Frank Burch Brown, *Good Taste, Bad Taste, and Christian Taste: Aesthetics in Religious Life* (Oxford: Oxford, 2000), 195 and also chapter 8.

Youth often complain that worship in their congregations is not lively enough, and I would be the first to admit that they are often justified in their complaints. This discussion, however, prods them to consider whether perky emotional energy — the kind of music that has a good beat you can dance to, for example — should be the sole criterion by which to judge music in worship. Should congregations, for example, be singing "Pharaoh, Pharaoh" to the tune of "Louie, Louie" on Holy Thursday, or is there music that captures the Passover overtones of the day equally well but that better expresses its pathos? Like Brown, I am convinced that the capacity to become more appreciative of a wider variety of artistic expression is linked to growing in theological awareness and Christian character.

The session as I conceive it invites students to consider the historical and ever-increasing diversity of musical tastes in the church. Such broadened exposure prepares them for participation in myriad Christian musical forms at the youth academy and perhaps for their lives after the academy. As Brown says in reference to encounters with musical diversity, "To enjoy another's enjoyment is already an act of love."[61] The goal is more than loving tolerance of unfamiliar musical genres, however; it is growth in appreciation of what God may communicate along with the full aesthetic range of the Gospel being communicated. Encounters with musical difference are critical to this goal. The session challenges students to become aware of how diverse musical expressions may bear or support diverse theological meanings by way of lyrical and tonal phrasing and their corresponding emotional resonance. If God speaks to human despair as well as to human hope, to secret sin as well as to public righteousness, and if the purpose of worship is more than feeling good about ourselves, then students who learn to be open to a range of music acquire a powerful means to grow in their faithfulness. Of course these proximate goals are undergirded by the foundational hope that through the Arts Village students will be opened to the incarnational nature of Christian faith and the manner in which it is revealed.

---

61. Ibid., 24.

Every artist's studio time is shaped differently. There is at least one shared dynamic, however. All of the artists participate in a *praxis* pedagogical model that includes preparation, participation, and reflection. Artists describe their medium and teach students about the tools of the medium, then invite students to participate actively in that medium, then also devote time to facilitating student reflection on the significance of the medium and its resonance with Christian life. Not every artist orders a session exactly this way, but these three ingredients are essential to each session.

Implications of artistic practice for youth ministry

Practicing the arts in youth ministry affects multiple dimensions of community life. First, if DYA is an accurate indication, ministry through the arts generates a unique vibe and a different kind of energy for the community. In contrast to theological plenaries which sometimes go off with headbanging intensity, the afternoon Arts Village breathes relaxation, enjoyment, and peace. It is as if time spent practicing the arts is not only creative but also re-creative of bodies, minds, and spirits. Second, practicing the arts in light of the *ordo* provides students opportunities to grapple with holy things on their own terms and by way of their imaginations. Third, for some students, practicing the arts is critical for vocational discernment. As was the case with the youthful poet described above, when students are blessed by opportunities to practice artistic forms they love together with other artistic Christians, they may discern a sense of calling for their lives. Finally, less utilitarian than these impacts (but perhaps the biggest blessing of all) is the addition of beauty to the life of a community. Everywhere at DYA there are examples of literary, performing, and visual arts celebrating and revealing God's grace.

The most likely area of impact of the arts will probably be corporate worship. One year DYA students fashioned pottery oil lamps that illumined the crypt beneath Duke Chapel for Eucharistic worship. Another year students took black-and-white photographs of bleak urban landscapes in which also discernible were outlines of the cross. These were offered in a worship service focused on Jesus' passion as a means to show his solidarity with the world's suffering. On still another occasion, brilliant aqua-blue pop art banners with baptismal themes adorned the chapel at a service of baptismal renewal. Students have also shared poems and litanies in worship created in the village. Others have danced or choreographed movements for choir anthems. Still others have offered dramatic presentations of biblical texts or in response to these texts. Others have adorned the worshiping space with fabric and symbols. Others have sung or played instruments. The community also chants, praises, and sings hymnody with ever-increasing gusto over a period of two weeks.

Congregations sometimes practice what I describe as the vacation bible school (VBS) approach to the arts. Each day children convene with the expectation that they "learn" a Bible story (the story of Jesus' passion, for example) then "have fun" doing art, or singing songs about Jesus' death and life, or acting out a dramatic version of the story. Seldom do VBS teachers and leaders stop to consider that the real "learning" from that day may actually occur in the shaping and handling of a wooden cross, in the singing of "As I Survey the Wondrous Cross," or in shouting, "Crucify him!" as part of a class reenactment of the story. As we have seen, however, the incarnational character of God's revelation in Jesus Christ and the incarnational character of the arts engender a relational "knowing in the midst of" that makes participation in them critical for those seeking to be formed into deeper relationship with this God. Thus the Christians really do need the Artists. Indeed they need to become artists (or at least to imagine and think and feel with an artist's touch) for the sake of their lives with God and their lives for the world.

So where does all this leave us? In the first chapter, I suggested that any ministry, but especially a liturgical youth ministry grounded in book, bath, table, and time, necessarily begins in worship. I also asserted that liturgy grounded in the *ordo* provides a generative context for youths' formation into the presence and identity of God along with practicing their proper vocations before God and for the world. In chapter 2, I examined more closely actual practices of youth worship suggesting how attention to holy things, especially, in this instance, to reclaiming a place for youth at the table, may renew and deepen youth worship while at the same time holding out the potential for more effective formation of youth. The present chapter's appeal to the arts further supports the critical importance of attending to the body in the formation of Christian youth and to the need to cultivate in them aesthetic, affectively embodied ways of knowing for the sake of deepened communion with God and neighbor in the liturgy and beyond.

I turn now to another of the holy things: the *ordo*'s book. Readers may be relieved to retreat from artsy aesthetics to the more familiar terrain of the dependable Bible. Youth ministry has long championed the Bible's central place in its practices of formation, so this conversation should be a familiar one, right? Exploring the book through the lens of the *ordo*, however, may confound some of our conventional wisdom about its proper use for the formation of youth.

Four

The Book becomes script

Youth practice storied performances
of the Bible

The Bible is the church's book. To be Christian is to be immersed in its pages. That youth need to read and learn the scriptures would seem to be one thing Christians of all stripes could agree upon. Judging by the millions of youth-friendly Bibles sold annually and by the bookstores full of resources intended to fortify youth's reading of the Bible, everybody already gets this. No-brainer. Next chapter, please.

But a funny thing has happened on the way to the best-seller's list. The Bible holds the distinction of the most purchased yet least read book in North America. Most youth, following their parents' lead, do not read the Bible. Biblical illiteracy is a major contributor to what Christian Smith describes as teens' "incredible inarticulacy" with respect to their faith.[62]

Conventional wisdom places the blame for the decline of literacy on the broader culture. As Neil Postman argues, the advent of television hastened the transition from oral or written communication to communication through visual media with commensurate dumbing down of the thought process as one result.[63] Nowadays children and youth are as likely to learn scripture from an animated tomato as from pages of the Bible. For Postman, as for many of us, watching a vegetable act out a Bible story is a less adequate form of trans-

---

62. Smith, *Soul Searching*, 131.
63. Neil Postman, *Amusing Ourselves to Death: Public Discourse in the Age of Show Business* (New York: Penguin, 1986).

mitting biblical knowledge than actually connecting with the text or connecting with human "texts" telling or living the story.[64]

No doubt declining verbal literacy is a partial cause of teen's biblical illiteracy, but lodged against youth this critique seems a little unfair. Why blame them for their cultural inheritance? Besides, there's more blame to pass around, especially to the churches. First, in their zeal to render the scriptures youth-friendly, denominations and their allied publishing houses have increasingly turned to the market. *Revolve*, a New Testament with the look and feel of a fashion magazine targeted for teenage girls, is a perfect case in point.[65] *Revolve* is the most highly publicized Christian youth resource of this decade, garnering national press exposure and strong sales. It represents a strategic effort to make the Gospel available to teenagers through a culturally accessible medium — the look, language, and practices of women's fashion. Unfortunately, as we shall see, *Revolve* also uncritically promulgates consumerist, individualist, therapeutic, and patriarchal readings of scripture. In the process it also obscures the identity of God.

But *Revolve* is merely symptomatic of a deeper malaise: the tearing of the pages of the book from the fertile soil of the *ordo*'s ecology that constitutes the church's distinctive life. *Revolve* could only evolve in a church culture that has come to regard reading the Bible alone in one's bedroom as the normative practice. In other words, many congregations have forgotten that the book tells a story that most fully comes alive in the context of liturgical engagement with bath, table, and time as performed in the Spirit-filled community. Here we find one more example of holy things bearing much fruit together or withering on the vine in unnatural isolation. Moreover, the church's failure to perceive the book's organic interdependence with holy things is in part responsible for enabling distorted interpretations of it to fill the

---

64. I'm referring here to the popular Christian video series "Veggie Tales," in which talking cartoon vegetables recount Bible-based stories with neat morals and snappy tunes.

65. *Revolve* is published by Thomas Nelson publishers, with new "updated versions" appearing ever year or so. It is also now available in both New Testament and "complete Bible" (without Apocrypha) versions.

vacuum. *Revolve* is a case in point here with its dumbing down of the communal biblical story to a buffet of self-help snippets.

This chapter explores in some depth how the unreflective presumptions of *Revolve*'s editors and publisher actually prevent faithful reading and performance of the scriptures. It also proposes a more adequate vision for reading and performing the church's book through the *ordo*. The means to this end include examining the Bible's own self-understanding as storied and its use of typology to create a plotline. Finally, I point to practices that will assist in teaching youth how to read and perform the Bible as story. These practices include using narrative pedagogies for reading scripture, restoring scripture to the ecology of the *ordo*, and performing scripture's stories beyond the assembly.

Revolve: *Good intentions paving that road*

The *Vogue*-like cover grabs you. Three sophisticated teen girls with perfect white teeth, made-up eyes, and flowing hair smile in close-up, beckoning your attention. Their look is tan and fit, the strappy top and bare shoulders of two of them signal summer sexy. Perhaps their glossy-lipped smiles reveal a spiritual joie de vivre, or maybe they're just laughing because it's fun to be so beautiful. The masthead reads: *Revolve: The Complete New Testament.* But the breathless blurbs below — "Are You Dating a Godly Guy?" "Beauty Secrets," and "Guys Speak Out" — tell a different story. So what is it, girls? A Bible? A fashion and lifestyle mag?

Both! A quick glance inside reveals the entire New Century Version of the New Testament. But it won't take two seconds more to figure out that this isn't your Aunt Ada's illustrated King James. Young women smile glowingly (and knowingly) from nearly every page — except when some beefy guy speaks for his gender about his preferences in women. Of the hundreds of beautiful faces almost none are blemished by braces . . . or *blemishes* for that matter. Permanent physical disfigurements or handicapping conditions? Girl, no way! You won't even see glasses unless they're of the sun-shielding variety.

Adding to the fun are recurring "special features" that enhance *Revolve*'s fashion mag look and feel. In addition to the aforementioned "Are You Dating a Godly Guy?" and other quizzes, and along with "Beauty Secrets" and "Guys Speak Out," *Revolve* offers features like "Radical Faith" (invitations to trust God's providential care more deeply), "Blabs" (an advice column), plus a full-page calendar for each month of the year with daily suggestions for practicing Christian life. Also featured are "Bible Basics," "Top Ten Lists," "Bible Bios" (of female biblical characters), and "Check It Out," short descriptions of a variety of charities and service organizations with web addresses listed to encourage further investigation. Each feature is enhanced with its own distinctive font, graphic layout, color theme, and, usually, a photo of an attractive teen. Calendars look like calendars, lists like lists, "Blabs" like an advice column, and so on. These highly visual features are interspersed between the biblical text on each page and contrast with it. The proportion of biblical to extrabiblical materials in *Revolve* is approximately even.

I devote extra attention to *Revolve*'s glossy layout and style for several reasons. First, to the publisher's credit, this is no amateurish knockoff. *Revolve* is professional in voice and polished in look. The editors obviously have studied piles of *Seventeen*, *In Style*, *Cosmo*, and *Vogue* for content ideas and prose style. The publisher also invested heavily in *Revolve*'s graphically pleasing layout. That they went to such expense testifies to the first of many ironies involving *Revolve*: while adolescent girls may be biblically illiterate they are fluent in fashion. They know without thinking its idioms, its gestures, its looks, and its bodily proprieties. They are experts because they have been formed from birth in a culture that values fashion and celebrity more than most anything else. Thus, as the producers of *Revolve* no doubt understood, anything less than a first-rate effort at the fashion genre would have been doomed (by definition after all) to failure. What could be more unfashionable than an out-of-fashion fashion Bible?[66]

---

66. For further insight into the production of popular cultural artifacts, see Michael Warren, *Seeing Through the Media: A Religious View of Communications and Cultural Analysis* (Harrisburg: Trinity, 1997).

I also devote attention to *Revolve*'s layout as a preliminary means to raise critical questions about its premises. For example, do the editors presume the life of fashion to be commensurate with life in Christ? Or do they imagine the fashion mag genre to be morally neutral, simply an attractive gimmick to introduce girls to the scriptures? Does this make *Revolve* into a subtle bait-and-switch scheme? If so, why would the editors presume that Christ's abundant life requires bait? Or perhaps they imagine themselves to be redeeming the culture of fashion by juxtaposing it to the New Testament?

Closer scrutiny of the content of *Revolve*'s features provides some answers to these questions . . . but also raises further questions. Clearly, *Revolve*'s editorial content is way tamer than a typical fashion mag. For example, it comes out strongly against all forms of sexual promiscuity. In contrast with a *Cosmo*-esque "Top Ten Positions Guaranteed to Drive Your Man Wild," readers find "Top Ten Random Ways to Have Fun with Your Friends." The magazine also speaks directly from its Christian perspective to teen girl crises like anorexia, abuse, and rape. It counsels girls to reach out for help or to offer help but says little about the cultural forces (the culture of fashion, for example) that objectify girls and their bodies.

Therapy, individualism, consumption, and the evolution of Revolve

Philip Rieff, in his classic text *The Triumph of the Therapeutic*, chronicles the shift in Western culture from one primarily influenced by the theology of the church to one more expressive of the therapeutic thinking and values of Sigmund Freud and his twentieth-century intellectual descendents.[67] Therapy, as Rieff frames it, is not so much the name given to the practice of psychological counseling as it is a metaphor for contemporary Western culture. It signals that human beings and their personal needs have taken precedence over human

---

67. Philip Rieff, *The Triumph of the Therapeutic: Uses of Faith after Freud* (Chicago: University of Chicago Press, 1966).

obedience to God.[68] As Rieff says, "For the culturally conservative image of the ascetic, enemy of his own needs, there has been substituted the image of the needy person, permanently engaged in the task of achieving a gorgeous variety of satisfactions."[69] Further, with respect to the turning of religion into therapy, "Any religious exercise is justified only by being something men do for themselves, that is, for the enrichment of their own experience."[70] Hence, instead of loving God and praising God forever, in a therapeutic culture the chief end of the human being becomes acquiring a personal sense of well-being and self-satisfaction.

A further consequence of therapeutic culture's focus on the self is the loosening of communal obligations. It invites the "revolt of the private man [against] all doctrinal traditions urging the salvation of self through identification with the purposes of community."[71] In fact, that pursuit of personal well-being has become "the end, rather than a by-product of striving after some superior communal end. . . . "[72] Rieff would agree that at present the self-determining autonomous individual reigns supreme over any claims to the necessity of interdependence of persons in community.

Therapeutic culture also provides a fertile seedbed for consumerism. If fulfilling personal needs is the purpose of life, then shopping for goods and fulfilling experiences becomes the chief means to that end. Consistent with Rieff's insights, one commentator suggests that the intent of contemporary business, political, and cultural interests is to construct human selves who perceive themselves to be "empty" and, therefore, in need of filling up by way of consumption.[73]

Judging from the title *The Triumph of the Therapeutic*, readers might understandably conclude that Rieff believes the culture of

---

68. My sympathetic reading of Rieff's analysis of therapeutic culture should not be interpreted as an argument for the complete dismissal of counseling. Girls wounded by abuse or rape, for example, will most likely require precisely that.

69. Rieff, *Triumph of the Therapeutic*, 241.

70. Ibid., 251.

71. Ibid., 242.

72. Ibid., 261.

73. Philip Cushman, *Constructing the Self, Constructing America: A Cultural History of Psychotherapy* (Cambridge, MA: Da Capo, 1995), 216.

therapy to have routed Christian culture and sent it off to Siberia. Though he does, in fact, believe the conquest to be complete, he contends that therapy's ascendance was achieved through years of subtle infiltration rather than overt battle followed by exile. In contemporary terms, the cultural transition could be likened to the workings of a computer virus. Imperceptible at first, the virus works its devilry in the background until it eventually controls the whole machine. Similarly, Rieff argues that therapy, not theology, gradually came to infiltrate and presently to dominate the church. The church edifice may still be around, but what goes on inside is more self-help than salvation. Put differently, the turning of Christianity into therapy has meant a subtle transition from focus on God and neighbor to a focus on fulfilling the desires of needy individuals.

With respect to youth, the sociologist Christian Smith largely confirms Rieff's claims for the therapeutic character of contemporary religious convictions. "What we heard from most teens," comments Smith on his team's research findings, "is essentially that religion makes them feel good, that it helps them make good choices, that it helps them resolve problems or troubles, that it serves their felt needs."[74] Calling this an "instrumental approach" to religion, Smith goes on to say religion becomes a " . . . tool for people to use to get what they want, as determined not by their religion but by their individual feelings and desires."[75] He is describing a decidedly therapeutic instrumentalism.

Also confirmed by Smith is the individualistic character of teens' faith. Again summarizing his research findings, he says, "American youth, like American adults, are nearly without exception profoundly individualistic, instinctively presuming autonomous, individual self-direction to be a universal human norm and life goal. Thoroughgoing individualism is not a contested orthodoxy for teenagers. It is an individual and pervasive doxa, that is, unrecognized, unquestioned, invisible premise or presupposition."[76]

---

74. Smith, *Soul Searching*, 148.
75. Ibid., 149.
76. Ibid., 143.

This deeply rooted unselfconscious individualism is the result of powerful cultural formation. Like their therapeutic values, teens' individualism is powerful, in part, because it operates beneath their radar. And because cultural transmission so often operates subconsciously, persons frequently have great difficulty grasping the forces that shape their engagement with the world. Smith plays with the youthful vernacular to drive home this point: "[N]obody *has* to do anything in life," he says summarizing youth's attitudes, "including anything to do with religion. 'Whatever' is just fine, if that's what a person wants."[77]

The problem with therapeutic, individualistic, and also consumerist faith is that it is not Christian. A God identified exclusively as therapist is not the God of the Bible. Absent are God's capacities as creator and transformer of the cosmos, judge of human sinful proclivities, and prophet for communal justice. Neither do the scriptures locate individual persons alone in the cosmos (see Psalm 8). The Bible's approach to faith is relentlessly communal. And, although they are often over-burdened by bags full of purchases, shoppers are not blessed by name along with the poor and the peacemakers.

If the present content of "faithfulness" bears less resemblance to Christianity than it might, the further problem is that most teens and their leaders are so thoroughly formed as therapeutic, individualistic consumers that they are prevented from seeing how these cultural forces hold them captive, or worse, how they are effectively morphing the practices of youth ministry and the faith of teens into so much sentimentality. As Smith notes of his team's thousands of interviews, "Hardly any teens spoke directly about more difficult religious subjects like repentance, love of neighbor, social justice, unmerited grace, self-discipline, humility, the costs of discipleship, dying to self, the sovereignty of God, personal holiness, the struggles of sanctification, glorifying God in suffering, [or] hungering for righteousness...."[78]

---

77. Ibid., 143–44.
78. Ibid., 149.

Consuming Revolve

Here to save the day is *Revolve*. The editors of *Revolve* claim to know how tough it is for girls in contemporary North American culture. They jump into the breech by counseling prayer — and *shopping*. One of the "Top Ten Random Ways to Have Fun with your Friends" recommends the following: "Go shopping and see who can get the coolest item for less than $10.00."[79] Thank goodness *Revolve* girls know that cool doesn't have to cost an arm and a leg. Elsewhere the editors recommend to readers, "Take your sister to the mall and buy her a gift, just 'cause."[80] This suggestion is reinforced by the full-color graphic of a credit card imprinted with the words "charge it." Savvy *Revolve* girls know that giving gifts to sisters satisfies best when costs are deferred.

Consumption is more than a special treat, however: it is an essential daily practice for *Revolve* girls. The first "Beauty Secret" features a smiling model with creamy white skin who urges the reader, "[a]s you apply your sunscreen, use that time to talk to God. Tell him how grateful you are for how he made you. Soon, you'll be so used to talking to him, it might become as regular and familiar as shrinking your pores."[81] On the surface only a cynic could grumble against offering gratitude to God while preventing premature wrinkling and erasing oily buildup. Among the many intriguing implications of this earnestly intended piece of advice, however, is the editors' assumption that Christian girls practice a daily beauty regimen requiring the consumption of beauty products. Apparently *Revolve* girls possess both the leisure to spend time in the sun (or they hold down farm jobs) and the resources to buy products that screen their faces and shrink their pores. In other words, being Christian apparently coincides with being a middle-class consumer. The irony only grows with the suggestion that prayer may one day become as natural and normal as buying products to beautify one's face.

---

79. *Revolve*, 5.
80. Ibid., 325.
81. Ibid., 5.

In addition, here and throughout the editorial content of *Revolve*, God is designated with masculine pronouns. Are girls to conclude that God is a silent male admirer, a mystery date for whom girls must scrub their faces to sparkling? Fortunately, if God is a guy, at least he's enlightened about teen girl life. Like their favorite hairstylist or the clerk at the makeup counter, *Revolve* girls can thank God for helping them look good and for understanding how hard they have to work at it. God's in touch with his feminine side.

The editors' stated intent for "Beauty Secrets" is to "show ways you can beautify your inner self."[82] Besides facial care and prayer, they offer advice on exercise, nutrition, hydration, clothes buying, lipstick application, and so on. These fashion practices are intended to be linked with or made analogous to spiritual practices. For example, advice on lipstick application offers an occasion to caution girls against negative speech. And more than once, these "Secrets" remind girls that God "looks at the heart not at the outward appearance,"[83] as, for example, with the claim that "Exercising to the Glory of God" through service to others is a sign of "true beauty."[84] Yet it all seems a bit disingenuous. "Beauty Secrets" never offers photos of ordinary or plain-looking girls, and never questions the premises of the cultures of fashion and consumption. If beauty is not about appearance for *Revolve*'s editors, then why does *Revolve* devote so much space to helping girls find the right products and services to work on it?

Therapeutic Revolve

Posted on the office door of the New Testament scholar Richard Hays two doors down from my own office is a cartoon depicting this scene: A book shop customer asks the clerk where to find a Bible. "That would be under 'self-help,' " the clerk responds.[85] It's supposed to be a joke, but therapy is very much at the heart of *Revolve*. As noted

---

82. Ibid., "Introduction."
83. Ibid., 22.
84. Ibid., 217.
85. Cartoon by Peter Steinen in *The New Yorker,* July 6, 1998, 33.

above, in a therapeutic culture individuals seek to maximize the fulfillment of their perceived needs. Persons are no longer oriented to ends beyond themselves. Living the good life means simply that I am happy.

Above all else, *Revolve*'s editors want girls to be happy. In the recurring advice column "Blabs," girls ask and editors answer questions like the following: "I'm nearly fourteen and I have never even had a boyfriend. Am I the only one?"[86] Or, "How can I quit doing bad stuff?"[87] Or, "I know you're not supposed to have 'it' before you're married, but is it okay to think about 'it'?"[88] Admittedly, the responses of "Blabs" are not sugarcoated. Repeatedly, "Blabs" condemns premarital sex and lustful fantasy as sinful. This line in the sand seems hardly to be settling for the moral relativism, the "anything goes, I'm OK and you're OK" attitude often attributed to therapeutic culture. But form trumps content in this case. An advice column operates from the premise that girls have unmet needs that must be fulfilled. Situating it in the pages of scripture proposes to readers that scripture itself is a book of therapy.

Revolve reinforces therapeutic culture in additional interesting ways. One quiz deals with the all-important teen girl dilemma, "Are you an introvert or an extrovert?"[89] Again, the focus of this quiz is the reader and not God, and in this case the language is explicitly therapeutic rather than theological. Even more revealing is the quiz: "Are You Crushing Too Hard?" This quiz checks up on whether girls' levels of boy craziness fall within acceptable limits. After answering five multiple-choice questions girls are instructed to tally their scores and refer to a key. According to the key, "if you scored between 0 and 9, you are level headed! Right on. You're not carried away about guys. Sounds like you've got your priorities in order." Of course, you could also be a lesbian. Scores between 10 and 16 mean you are "a little boy-crazy, but not abnormal. Still you might want to get in the scripture and refocus on God. Remember, all your fulfillment is in

---

86. *Revolve*, 6.
87. Ibid., 13.
88. Ibid., 27.
89. Ibid., 10.

him." "Yes," a slightly boy crazy but not abnormal girl might reply, "but when I try to get into the scriptures, at least in *Revolve,* I keep running into all these gorgeous hunks of man flesh when I turn the pages." Finally, scores between 17 and 24 mean that "you are totally crushed out. Chill out, girl. God's gonna provide you a man when the time is right. No need to become a stalker. Check your priorities."[90] At the risk of completely spoiling the fun, here is my take on all this: "Be patient and God will fulfill all your desires. And in your case, girls, that fulfillment comes through a man."

Admittedly, I am mixing together my critique of therapeutic Christianity as seen in *Revolve* with specific critiques of *Revolve*'s theology as, in this case, its unreflective patriarchy. To be fair, I agree with some of its theological assertions and disagree with others. For example, the feature "Radical Faith" consistently exhorts girls to extend themselves beyond their personal comfort zones for the sake of the Gospel — though it says little about how to do this. The more fundamental critique remains, however. *Revolve*'s earnest desire to be a help to young female Christians is completely overwhelmed and undone by its unquestioned therapeutic premises as evidenced by its uncritical appropriation of the fashion mag genre and fashion culture more generally. As with "Are You Crushing Too Hard?" *Revolve* expects that girls' experiences, including their hopes for romantic love, provide the normative context into which scripture must fit rather than the other way around. *Revolve* assumes that all teenage girls are supposed to have crushes (on boys), purchase beauty products to care for their faces, pursue romantic relationships, then hang in there for God to bring them the man of their dreams. In other words, *Revolve* implicitly urges upon girls a scripted North American middle-class life trajectory leading to personal happiness. Only secondarily and in light of this already determined therapeutic vision of a self-fulfilled life — and applied to that life trajectory like so much spiritual mascara — do the scriptures appear to pretty up the picture.

Interestingly, and to this point, "Blabs" features a discussion on mascara and other fashion practices:

---

90. Ibid., 222.

Q: What does the Bible teach about women wearing pants, and make-up and cutting their hair?

A: What you have to know about the Scripture is that some passages are what we call "prescriptive" (they tell us what to do today) and some are "descriptive" (they talk about Bible times). Today it is generally not a scandal for women to wear pants, wear make-up, or cut their hair.[91]

Honestly now, how could the editors of *Revolve* have possibly responded in any other way? An answer that rejects fashion as nonsense or even sinful does not boost sales of a fashion Bible. Neither should we be surprised that they do not use this question as an opportunity to critique the fashion industry's premises: women as incomplete without beauty products or styling — or men; fashion as proffering therapeutic self-fulfillment; and women's bodies as shaped by fashion to be objects of male desire. Nor are we shocked that they offer no theological response to the fashion industry, such as: Christians resist cultural practices that objectify or otherwise dehumanize persons; Christians resist self-creation and self-fulfillment through consumption as forms of idolatry; Christians live simply, sharing all things in common. Finally, we note how in their response, *Revolve*'s editors assume the Bible functions as a rule book. It's a complicated one — "you need to let us adults tell you which rules still apply" — but a rule book nonetheless.

We are not shocked or surprised by any of this because therapy is the controlling interpretive metaphor for *Revolve*. And therapeutic culture requires that some scriptures be read "descriptively" rather than "prescriptively" in order that the personal happiness of individual girls be assured through the scriptures. Interestingly, *Revolve* says little about the Christian vocation of girls. We are left to our own conclusions as to whether Paul's admonitions to women in 1 Corinthians 14 are prescriptive or descriptive. We do know there's at least a sports exemption: the assignment on *Revolve*'s September 27 calendar reads, "Go to a football game tonight and worship God through

---

91. Ibid., 27.

your cheering and joy!"[92] You go girls! — even if it is just to cheer for the guys.

Revolve-*ing around whom?*

Clearly, teenage girls are the main characters of *Revolve*. It is a book for and about them. Remarkably, this targeting is accomplished between the words of scripture which, ostensibly, is a book about God. Achieving such a stunning reversal is possible only through the prism of unquestioned and unfettered individualism. Note this "Blabs" exchange:

Q: Why is religion — the set of rules, traditions, rituals — necessary if you have individual faith in God that you feel content with?

A: Religion is not necessary. That's like saying, Why are the rules, traditions, and rituals necessary to play basketball? They're not. But they help the game move smoother and faster and give you a guide. That is like the whole religion thing. It helps give you some direction on how to create a deep relationship with God the Father without getting majorly side-tracked.[93]

Leaving aside the issue of the near total incoherence of this response — how *do* you play the game of basketball without following the rules? — let us explore the therapeutic individualism undergirding it. The questioner assumes — and "Blabs" does not challenge this assumption — that "individual faith in God" is, in fact, possible, normative even. But from whence does such faith derive? Does it fall out of heaven and hit girls on the head? Is it transmitted through the spiritual ether? No, it is a gift of the Spirit mediated through Christ's Body the church. "Oh," the questioner might reply, "but I don't go to church. I read my Bible and pray." To which we would ask in return, "Where did you learn those practices?" Without the church there would be no witness of prayer, no story of God collected in the scriptures, and no resurrection body to witness to God's redemption. Apparently, none of that matters so long as I am spiritually fulfilled.

---

92. Ibid., 267.
93. Ibid., 304.

North Americans' presumptions of individual self-construction are so deeply ingrained, however, they often cannot see how false they are. Thus, "Blabs" has no problem imagining the "religion thing" as a nonessential and only potentially helpful means to cement girls' personal relationships with God. Showing no more insight than their adolescent questioner, *Revolve* editors fail to acknowledge how personal identity is inescapably communally constructed — like through the fashion thing. Apparently, neither can they see that there would be no personal faith without the church and its odd collection of "rules, traditions, rituals" — aka, the liturgy's *ordo*. The result is a tacit endorsement for individualistic, anticommunal, and spiritualized faith.

Notice also the telling phrase in the teen's question: "...that you feel content with." Clearly, in the imagination of this teen, the purpose of Christian faith is to fulfill her personal needs. It is a faith that orbits around her and her predetermined agenda. No doubt, mixing it up in a congregation where people are prone to whine and complain or disapprove of her fashion tastes will only detract from her personal relationship with God. Again, the questioner is not to blame here, but the grown-ups aren't helping.

Resolving not to Revolve

Revolve and resources like it are not the answer to fostering teen biblical literacy or deepening their Christian lives. These resources suffer from a failure to understand how using some forms of contemporary culture may actually be destructive to the efforts to promote faithful life in teens. In *Revolve*'s case, the culture of fashion is not a neutral medium. Operating from a presumption of scarcity, fashion contradicts the Gospel's claims for abundance. Repeatedly, the fashion culture trumpets to girls and to women their own inadequacies while also exhorting them to purchase fashion's remedies. Thus, fashion also forms young women as consumers of products and experiences to enhance their individual identities and personal satisfaction. Unfortunately, promises of fashion fulfillment are at once tantalizingly close and ever illusive. Fashion may promise redemption, but the business of fashion survives by keeping women (and surely men as well) feeling unsaved.

It is truly astounding, therefore, that the most visible biblical resource for teenage girls at present is a fashion magazine. Fashion's underlying premises — consumption, a therapy lifestyle, individualism — are antithetical to Christian faith and life. For youth ministry retailers to perpetrate this kind of deformation upon unsuspecting youth is unconscionable. And to do it between the words of scripture . . . are you serious?

Conceiving the Bible as storied

Fortunately, the book itself — especially as it is employed through the *ordo* — offers some clues not only to how it should be read but also how persons can be better formed to know and act upon its contents. The interpretive key that the *ordo* provides is appreciation for the storied nature of the Bible.

Once upon a time, describing scripture as story could only mean relegating it to the world of child's play. Wanting to be grown up like the scientists, theologians and biblical scholars spent most of the twentieth century searching for the truth *behind* the Bible's stories.[94] Mostly they succeeded in explaining what the Bible was not — not a history book, not a science book, not distinctive from other ancient literature. Presently, however, we have rediscovered how stories play an essential role in shaping communal vision and identity. To be more precise, stories like those contained in the Bible do not answer questions merely by getting at the facts — a way of knowing pursued by science; rather, they create for tellers and hearers an interpretive field that disposes them to make sense of and live their lives in light of those stories. But stories that shape cultures are not always consciously interpreted or even understood.[95] As is often observed by

---

94. See Stanley Hauerwas, *The Peaceable Kingdom: A Primer in Christian Ethics* (Notre Dame, IN: University of Notre Dame Press, 1983), 25.

95. Stephen Crites, "The Narrative Quality of Experience," in *Why Narrative? Readings in Narrative Theology*, ed. Stanley Hauerwas and L. Gregory Jones (Eugene, OR: Wipf and Stock, 1997), 69.

scholars, persons do not so much tell stories as they find themselves told by them. Stories become embedded in cultural practices including often in unconscious, habitual human dispositions to think, feel, and act in story-determined ways. Following this line of thought we can say that consumerist therapeutic individualism is itself a dominant cultural "story" in North America at present. This situation makes even more crucial the recovery of the Bible itself as a compelling story, one that offers a consciously authentic alternative to our current unreflective narcissism. By recovering the Bible as storied we may also hope to form the practices of Christian youth with dispositions to think, feel, and act in ways consistent with the stories of Jesus Christ.

There are several corollaries to conceiving the Bible as storied. First, unlike the approach of *Revolve* — fitting snippets of scripture into an already determined North American middle-class female teen therapeutic life path — engaging the scriptures narratively creates a *world* for *hearers* to enter. For the stories of scripture are principally about God, not about beauty-challenged adolescents. This assertion is sufficiently important to bear repeating: The Bible is about God — God's character, God's identity, God's creating, saving, and sustaining activity, about who God is and what God does — and only secondarily about us. The Bible holds the key to identifying God. Our identity is derivative. The Bible's stories about God include accounts of creation, of God's repeated self-offering through a succession of covenants, of God's freeing Israel from slavery and guiding them into the Promised Land, of the apparent loss of favor and hope resulting in exile, of Jesus' answer to that crisis through his ministry, death, and resurrection, of the Spirit's establishment of the church that grafts Gentiles into God's covenant promises, and of the inauguration of God's Reign and its promised fulfillment.

Many scholars suggest that these varied stories of God actually constitute "chapters" in the one unified "story" of God's salvation. Others refer to this one grand biblical story as "salvation history." Whatever we decide to call it, God remains the central character and primary actor in these stories and in this story.

There is a second corollary to reclaiming the Bible as storied and the biblical sory. As Walter Brueggemann suggests, there is a "givenness" or giftedness to the biblical stories.[96] We do not create the biblical story: we receive it as a gift from God and from the church. And, as members of the church, we are blessed to pass it on to others. In other words, receiving and giving this story is essentially communal. Unlike *Revolve*, which seems to regard scripture as an enrichment tool for self-creation, regarding scripture as storied means that the community precedes the individual. For Stanley Hauerwas, one essential truth of the storied Bible's story is that it reminds Christians they are not self-made.[97]

One further value to encountering Bible as storied also deserves mention. When children ask their parents to tell them a story, they expect through the telling to experience wonder and delight. This is part of a story's gift to its tellers and hearers, and the Bible is no exception. When we learn to engage the scriptures in narrative terms instead of regarding the Bible as a terribly disorganized concordance, our imaginations are freed to help us reclaim the giftedness of the biblical story. So, too, may our hearts be stirred by the witness of Israel, of the church, and of the saints to go and live as they did. Scripture as story invites persons into authentic encounters with the living God.

Holy things aid in reading the scriptures as story

Liturgical practices of bath, table, and time support narrative participation in scripture. Indeed, through these ritualized performances the church demonstrates its understanding that communal identity and continued formation derive from worshipers' participation in a

---

96. Walter Brueggemann, *The Creative Word: Canon as a Model for Biblical Education* (Philadelphia: Fortress, 1982), chapter 2.
97. Hauerwas, *Peaceable Kingdom*, 27. See also Stanley Hauerwas, "Character, Narrative, and Growth in the Christian Life," in *A Community of Character: Toward a Constructive Christian Social Ethic* (Notre Dame, IN: University of Notre Dame Press, 1981), 129–52.

shared narrative. Below, I briefly describe the relationship of time, table, and bath to the storied book.

Patterning time

The church's decision to worship on the first day in light of Israel's seven-day week is one example of its distinctive patterning of time consistent with its faith in the newly unfolding chapters of God's story of salvation through the resurrection of Jesus Christ on the first day. Subsequent creation of Christian festival days and seasons juxtaposed to their Jewish predecessors represents the further transformation of time into a witness to Jesus' birth, ministry, death, and resurrection. This yearly cycle, culminating annually with Holy Week and Easter, serves to tell and retell the church's distinctive story. Indeed, this ritualized patterning of time was key to the church's proclamation of its story long before the widespread availability of Bibles in pews. For that matter, pews themselves are a relatively recent addition to sanctuaries since in a previous era they would have gotten in the way of congregational enactment of the Bible's stories. Pews are an indirect witness to the loss of congregational participation in God's story.

In fact, the lectionary evolved to support storied temporal patterning. Keyed primarily to the Gospels, the lectionary assists the church in telling the story of Jesus in light of its patterning of time. During Advent, for example, at once the beginning and ending of the Christian year, the lectionary includes biblical accounts of hope for a savior as well as accounts of the church's longing for the return of Christ as cosmic king. At Epiphany, which means "manifestation," the lectionary chronicles Gospel accounts pointing to the mystery of God at work in the ministry of Jesus of Nazareth. We hear of Jesus "setting his face to Jerusalem" at the beginning of Lent and of the climactic consequence of his journey to the cross through one of the Gospels' passion narratives read and enacted during Holy Week. From Easter dawn and on through the Great Fifty days from Easter to Pentecost, the lectionary shares the stories of Jesus' resurrection and of resurrection life in the Spirit-born church. Thus the Bible's Gospel story is placed in synchrony with the church's patterning of time and amplified by this patterned resonance.

Some pastors find the lectionary a rigid or repetitive imposition on the freedom the Spirit promises. Instead of preaching from texts proscribed by the lectionary they opt for catchy sermon series with titles like "Seven Roads in the New Testament" in support of which they cherry-pick supportive biblical texts. By ignoring the lectionary, however, they fail to tap into the formative potential consistent with the church's patterning of time — the coincidence of events in Jesus' life as testified to in the Gospels and marked by seasons and days. Instead of marking Pentecost and with it the gift of the Spirit and the birth of the church, they tackle series sermon number 4: "On the Road to Perdition." Mistakenly opting for "creativity" over "repetition" — a false dichotomy if there ever was one — they actually create the conditions for congregational biblical illiteracy by chopping up or simply ignoring the church's story and substituting bits and pieces of the Bible to proof-text their own agendas. They steer the church "On the Road to Oblivion." Subversive youth workers interested in forming young Christians would do well to dust off the lectionary. What could be more powerful, engraced, and radical than inviting youth to journey with Jesus from cradle to grave and beyond through the Christian year? The story in its fullness is transformative. It doesn't require thematic improvement.

Bath and table

In addition to the patterning of time, the *ordo*'s other holy things, bath and table, richly enact the stories (and story) of the book. As we have seen, the church once understood its ritual meal as the multivalent enactment of multiple biblical stories including, centrally, Jesus' sacrificial self-giving and resurrection presence. Not only does table enact the book's central story, however; it is essential for lived understanding of it. Richard Hays suggests that "we come to understand the death and resurrection of Jesus as we participate in the shared life of the community, enacted in meals shared at table."[98] Stanley Hauerwas adds, " . . . scripture can be rightly interpreted only within

---

98. Richard B. Hays, "Reading Scripture in Light of the Resurrection," in *The Art of Reading Scripture*, ed. Ellen F. Davis and Richard B. Hays (Grand Rapids: Eerdmans, 2003), 231.

the practices of a body of people constituted by the unity found in the Eucharist."[99] Here we find echoes of Gordon Lathrop's insistence on the juxtaposition of book and table to display the fullness of God's revelation in Jesus Christ. Each of these scholars is pointing out the mutually interpretive power of the *ordo*'s holy things, in this case, especially, of word and table. Similarly, as I will show in greater detail in the next chapter, the church also once understood its baptismal rites as the incorporation of persons into the story of God's covenantal promise to Israel and into the story of Jesus' life, death, and resurrection. Such ritual enactment of these stories and the overall story is accomplished through the expansive and associative qualities of the symbols of bread, wine, and water. Reclaiming the rich practices and interpretations of bath and table will assist in restoring a narrative appreciation for scripture.

Biblical sanction for reading the Bible as storied

That the Bible is to be read as the unfolding story of God's redemption is itself a biblical claim. Brian Daley explains: "[T]he driving impulse behind the Christian Gospels, as well as the letters of Paul, seems to have been...that [Jesus] must be recognized by the community as *Messiah*, as the one promised by Israel's scriptures and pointed to as 'coming' by the Law and the Prophets."[100] Thus, the biblical writers themselves witness to their own faithful reception of the scriptures as Israel's story as well as to their imaginative reinterpretation of these stories as they testify to God's continuing unfolding Story of redemption in Jesus.

Typology as the interpretive key to scripture and the ordo

Critical to reading the Bible as story is grasping typological or figural interpretations of the scriptures. Typology is a method of

---

99. Stanley Hauerwas, *Unleashing the Scripture: Freeing the Bible from Captivity to America* (Nashville: Abingdon, 1993), 23.

100. Brian E. Daley, S.J., "Is Patristic Exegesis Still Usable?" in *The Art of Reading Scripture*, ed. Ellen F. Davis and Richard B. Hays (Grand Rapids: Eerdmans, 2003), 74–75.

interpretation as old as the Bible itself. It proceeds by way of imaginative "reception and reinterpretation; of seeing new meaning in old texts."[101] Distinct from the Old Testament writers and editors, the New Testament writers worked from the assumption that Jesus as messiah was the central antitype pointed to by many other Old Testament persons and events, which therefore were considered "types" or "prefigurements" of Jesus. Richard Hays frames the interpretive predisposition of Christian typology slightly differently but with a similar intent by calling it a "hermeneutics of resurrection,"[102] by which he means that for the church, this image of Jesus as the risen Lord is the very heart of the Bible's witness. He argues, therefore, that the New Testament writers were justified in interpreting the Old Testament as pointing to and anticipating God's revelation in Jesus.

The propriety of this sort of interpretation is a point of some controversy in current biblical scholarship. But the fact that the early church, including the writers of the New Testament, engaged in typological interpretation is indisputable. The apostle Paul, for example, portrays Jesus as succeeding through sinless obedience where sinful Adam had failed (Rom. 5:14–15; 1 Cor. 15:45). In the language of typology, Paul makes Adam to play the type to Jesus' antitype. Similarly, Matthew creates a Gospel portrait of Jesus in which Moses' story functions as its prefiguration. Like Moses, Jesus comes to deliver Israel from slavery, this time a slavery to sin and death. Succeeding where Moses falls short, however, Jesus, through his resurrection, crosses over the Jordan to the Promised Land of life beyond death. In each case the New Testament writers search Israel's scriptures to discover in Jesus both the recapitulation of God's past saving activity and present fulfillment of it in this chosen one. In the process, these typological interpreters succeed in weaving individual biblical stories into one grand story.

Readers may be inclined to think that if Jesus is the antitype and all the Old Testament is type, then the Old Testament is rendered unnecessary. Precisely the opposite is true. Far from dismissing the

---

101. Ibid., 75.
102. Hays, "Reading Scripture in Light of the Resurrection," 231.

Old Testament as irrelevant, each of the previous examples highlights how the typological interpretations of New Testament writers make the Old Testament "indispensable . . . in bearing witness to the Gospel."[103] That is finally why I advocate retrieving and teaching skills for typological interpretation of the Bible. Typology provides the means to read the scriptures as unfolding story and therefore supports the formation of communal identity around this story.

Implications of typological readings of scripture

There are four implications of narrative and typological interpretations for the church's encounter with the Bible. In turn, these affect my suggestions for fostering biblical literacy in youth.

First, to reiterate, typology supports narrative readings of the Bible and narrative readings of the Bible encourage typological interpretation. Typological interpretations, particularly of the Old Testament by writers of the New, assist in connecting the dots between what may otherwise appear to be a chaotic jumble of unrelated biblical episodes. Typology enables biblical stories to become "chapters" in a grand unfolding biblical story. Even those sections of the Bible that are patently nonnarrative — the Psalms, the Levitical codes, the Wisdom writings, the Epistles — are best understood as responses to the biblical story of God's unfolding redemption or attempts to form communities that embody that story. Thus, the Bible itself testifies to the validity and importance of reading the Bible as storied. Practically speaking, any approach to learning scripture or any purported scripture resource that diminishes its intelligibility as story — ignoring or editing out entirely the Old Testament as in the case of *Revolve* or reducing the Bible to a rule book or advice column or turning the Bible into preacher-chosen proof texts — is unbiblical.

Second, typology asserts that we come to know and understand adequately the story of Jesus as we know and understand the stories of the patriarchs and matriarchs, of Noah, of Moses, of Miriam, of Ruth, of David and the events of their lives. We make sense of Jesus as the embodiment of new creation or new covenant only to the

---

103. Hays, "Reading Scripture in Light of the Resurrection," 233.

extent that we grasp his prefigurations in Moses or Noah. The New Testament writers understood this intuitively and already have done for us much of this work of tying type and antitype together. Typology continued in the theological traditions of the church of antiquity as with Origen, for example, who never met an Old Testament text that he couldn't turn into an type for Christ.

Third, in contrast to overly rigid and reductive approaches to engaging scripture, including moralizing, snippet-clipping, rule-booking, and proof-texting ones, typology offers a rich and expansive interpretive method. As the biblical writers and scholars of antiquity demonstrate, ever wider and deeper typological readings of the Old Testament made for ever richer theological sense of Jesus. Their profound knowledge of Israel's scriptures made possible their rich figurations of Jesus as "paschal lamb," "living water," "bread of life," and "good shepherd" along with the ideas of the new Adam and new Moses. Each of these metaphors evokes a different dimension of God's salvation story, and each contributes more nuanced awareness of the significance of the saving activity of Jesus Christ. Thus, according to Daley, instead of "flat doctrine," typological readings of the Bible as unified story offered the ancients (and potentially us as well) "a kind of unquenchable fountain whose scattered drops all reflect the one mystery of Christ."[104]

Fourth, associative and expansive readings of the book that typology affords are equally critical to tapping into the richness of bath, table, and time. Conversely, rich practices of bath, table, and time can contribute insight into storied and typological readings of scripture. As noted, these holy things enact persons into dimensions of Jesus' story. Moreover, to the extent that Jesus is regarded as the antitype for all of God's previous saving work in Israel's scriptures, holy things also recapitulate these older stories and enact persons into them as well. This was the understanding of the writer of the book of 1 Peter. He asserts that God's deliverance of Noah through the flood and establishment of covenant with him prefigures Christian baptism into

104. Daley, "Is Patristic Exegesis Still Usable?" 77.

Jesus Christ (1 Pet. 3:18–22). Simply put, from a typological perspective the waters of the flood anticipate the waters of the font. In this way baptized persons are also immersed in the stories of Noah as they are being incorporated into the life, death, and resurrection of Jesus Christ. Viewed from the other direction, baptism into Christ recapitulates and fulfills God's covenantal promise to Noah and his heirs. Jesus is the new and lasting covenant bringing all other covenants to fruition. With respect to the table, Paul's framing of Jesus as "paschal lamb" is likewise indebted to typological sensibility (1 Cor. 5:7–8). Paul's choice of this image and the story it represents signals that in fulfillment of the deliverance begun at Passover, Christ framed as paschal lamb now offers his own body and pours out his own blood for the sake of the world. As with the liberation of Israel from slavery in Egypt, Christ, through his self-giving, now offers liberation from all forms of slavery to sin along with his companionship on the journey to the new Promised Land — God's everlasting Reign.

As we observed with bread and cup in previous chapters and shall explore with respect to water in the next, every incidence of these symbols and the stories they are attached to in Israel's scriptures provided the opportunity for typological interpretation in light of the church's bath, table, and time. Encouraged by the multivalent resonances of symbols, early church interpreters readily used typological interpretation to show how, for example, the waters of creation in Genesis prefigured new creation available through the baptismal waters, how the manna in the wilderness of Exodus prefigured the Eucharistic bread that sustains Christians on their own wilderness journeys, and how Israel's Pentecost celebration of harvest and gift of Torah prefigured the church's own Pentecost holiday of Holy Spirit sustenance. And this is just a sampling!

Requirements for instilling storied biblical literacy in youth

By this point readers will probably not be overly surprised to learn that I advocate recovering for youth an appreciation for scripture as stories composing God's salvation story. In the paragraphs that follow I suggest three strategies: (1) Employing narrative biblical pedagogies with youth; (2) Telling and ritualizing the story in worship; (3) Inviting youth to "perform" the biblical story through ministry. I also describe how these strategies work best when practiced in concert with one another.

Employing biblical narrative pedagogies

From an educational standpoint, reclaiming a narrative appreciation for scripture means teaching youth to read the Bible in storied chunks rather than as a collection of single verse snippets designed to answer their developmental questions. Youth ministers seeking to teach this form of biblical literacy will regularly engage the book by way of biblical storytelling, dramatic reenactments and skits, or, simpler still, through communal readers' theater where different students read aloud the lines of different biblical characters with a narrator filling in the conversational gaps. Reading the scriptures in this way demonstrates the storied nature of the text. It also reinforces the communal nature of the storytelling. Repetition is key. Stories themselves cry out for it. The stories we love most are the ones we know best.

But the many stories constituting the biblical story are also so numerous and varied that they will require years of repetition in order to become familiar. Perhaps that is one reason why the church lectionary journeys through the story of the life of Jesus each year.

Narrative appreciation for scripture may be further underlined by following up on storied scripture tellings with questions like these: What is this story about? What is God doing in the story? How do the story's characters advance the plot? How are they involved with what God is doing? Leaders may also attend to deepening youth's skills for typological interpretation through a different line of questioning: Of what other stories, characters, or symbols in the Bible does this story remind you? What might these connections mean? Where do you find differences in these related stories? Finally, this form of narrative pedagogy also invites questions of youth's identity: Where do you see our church, youth group, or yourself in this story? What story from your life or out of our common life does this story make you want to tell in response?

Even as the knowledge of individual stories comes slowly, youth are easily capable of grasping the storied Bible's basic plotline. DYA's list of theological alliterative Cs (Creation, Crisis, Covenant, Christ, Church, Calling, Coming Reign of God) offers an excellent short-hand outline for linking the different stories that together constitute the grand biblical story. This list also lays out a basic chronology that can supply students with important points of historical context. It is vitally important, for example, to understand that God's series of ever-more-beneficent covenants with Israel precedes in the narrative the covenant offered through Jesus Christ. Church curricula some-times recommend the creation of an actual timeline (on a classroom wall or by way of a length of string with pictures or event names at-tached) where, in this case, stories related to creation, then crisis, then covenant, and so on may be named and grouped in such a way as to demonstrate visually the Bible's narrative trajectory. These sugges-tions may seem too basic or too remedial for teens — or at least the teens in *your* congregation. If so I apologize, but keep in mind that the research suggests that the large majority of teens do not know the biblical story — or even that the Bible tells stories.

Telling and ritualizing the story in worship

Perhaps the most important aid in fostering this storied biblical lit-eracy in youth will be the restoration of the Bible to its liturgical context. For it is in this venue that the Bible becomes automatically public, aural, communal, performative, and participative. Each of these characteristics is consistent with and supportive of the practice of reading the Scripture as storied. The lectionary also remains the best way to tell the *whole* story in its fullness. Each week it prescribes readings from the Old Testament, Psalms, Epistles, and Gospels. And more than just a verse or two: these readings constitute narrative or thematic units. Often the Old Testament readings prefigure the New Testament texts. As noted, over the course of a year the lectionary takes a congregation through the life of Jesus. In its three years it covers much of the Bible.

The youth academy employs its own lectionary with all the features described above. With only fourteen occasions to worship instead of fifty-two, however, it is a leaner one than those available to the churches. Nevertheless it represents our best effort to tell the whole story of salvation from Creation to Christ to Coming Reign with the other alliterative Cs in between. We also make frequent use of Psalms that actually reprise this unfolding story. Psalm 136, with its hopeful refrain, "[God's] steadfast love endures for ever," is a good example of the power of rehearsing and repeating the story. Typological organization of the scriptures is evident with Old Testament prefigurations linked thematically or episodically to the Gospel texts. Robust ritual practice around table and font supports the telling of this story, just as the telling deepens worshipers' practices of these holy things. In addition, preaching always gestures toward the table, while in the meal we feast on the Word.

DYA's practices of teaching the Bible as storied, and enacting the story in worship, are blessed by the good work of a professional biblical storyteller. A student quickly recognizes when she shares her gifts in communal worship that while the words she speaks are drawn verbatim from the scriptures, her tone of voice and inflection, plus her bodily gestures, transform those paper words into living drama. In worship and at the Arts Village students learn further from her how to hear scripture as story and how to tell it that way as well. Admittedly, she is unusually gifted as an artist, and not every congregation boasts someone like her, but she does not hold a monopoly on teaching youth to read and hear the scriptures as if they were participating in living drama. These skills are, after all, learned by doing.

Encountering so much scripture in worship is a novel experience for many DYA participants, but more surprising still is finding themselves on the telling end instead of exclusively on the hearing end of the equation. Because of our commitment to liturgy as the peoples' work, youth regularly serve as lectors in communal worship. Tentatively at first but with increasing confidence and skill, students proclaim the biblical texts aloud then quickly branch out to dramatic enactment and choral readings. Some are so adventuresome as to apprentice themselves to our biblical storyteller. As a participant observer, here is what I notice: Youth become better tellers *and hearers* of the biblical story in worship when they assume responsibility for the telling. Though that is only a theory, my sense is that the students at first are startled into attention to the scriptures by the shift in the dynamics of power. At home the scriptures belong to the clergy, in public anyway, and seldom do they hear the Bible proclaimed in their own voices. This role reversal also signals a shift in agency. When youth are invited to share in the work of liturgy they become proclaimers as well as hearers. In turn, their agency prompts further concern for responsible proclamation of the Bible. "What does this word mean?" "How do you pronounce 'Yahweh?'" "Am I speaking too fast?" These are questions prompted by youths' concerns to exercise their liturgical agency responsibly. Further, responsibility for proclaiming requires a level of understanding, or, in the case of dramatic enactment, bodily engagement with the story in order to proclaim adequately. Could it be that vesting youth with responsibility for leadership in public worship deepens their participation in public worship . . . and their biblical literacy as well?

Performing the biblical story

A third strategy toward forming narrative biblical literacy in youth is faithful performance of the scriptures in community. Performance of the Word includes but also extends beyond the sanctuary. As Richard Hays and Ellen Davis note, "Scripture is like a musical score that must be played or sung in order to be understood; therefore, the church interprets scripture by forming communities of prayer, service, and faithful witness."[105] I can best describe what I mean by performing the biblical story by telling a story.

In a past youth ministry I was privileged to know a young woman I'll call Kate. She was unusual in appearance: she dressed like a hippy when being a hippy was not even remotely hip, but she was also exceptionally bright. Kate attended youth group by parental mandate and regularly pointed out to me the illogic of Christian faith, including the many inconsistencies of the Bible. She knew all too well the

---

105. Davis and Hays, *The Art of Reading Scripture*, 3.

Bible's many "failings" as a science book or a history book. Through the blessings of providence, however, she also regularly signed up for church mission trips even while professing disbelief. On these trips she served with people who were often very sick or very poor yet also very faithful. Like others on the trip she lived simply and worked hard. Kate also participated in worship where she encountered the scriptures daily, scriptures that included this prophetic word:

> The Spirit of the Lord is upon me, because he has anointed me to bring good news to the poor. He has sent me to proclaim release to the captives and recovery of sight to the blind, to let the oppressed go free, to proclaim the year of the Lord's favor. (Luke 4:18–19)

A funny thing happened to Kate through her participation in mission. Instead of merely considering the stories of the Bible in the abstract as was often the case back home, in mission she encountered the biblical story in a context where she and her peers also *performed* the Bible's story in light of Jesus' announcement of God's Reign. Kate gave daily care to the poor and sick. In return she was blessed with a recovering of her own sight. Kate received the gift of getting involved with God's establishment of a new Reign, which in turn made possible her reception of the Bible's truth, illogical as it may have seemed in settings where faithful performances were absent. No doubt, my frequent Sunday night moralizing to Kate and others "not to pass by persons in need" failed to persuade her. Instead, her participation in a community that was actually performing the Word opened her eyes to the truth of the story. Sarah Coakley suggests that the resurrection transforms our understanding and imagination.[106] For Kate it was practicing resurrection life, that is, exemplary performance of the story, that worked transformation in her life through grace.

Athanasius, a fourth-century bishop of Alexandria, explains as well as anyone this vital connection between learning the biblical

---

106. Sarah Coakley, *Powers and Submissions: Spirituality, Philosophy, and Gender* (Oxford: Blackwell, 2002), 130–52; quoted in Richard B. Hays, "Reading Scripture in Light of the Resurrection," 235.

story and performing it: "For searching and right understanding of the scriptures there is need of a good life and pure soul, and for Christian Virtue to guide the mind to grasp, so far as human nature can, the truth concerning the Word. One cannot possibly understand the teaching of the saints unless one has a pure mind and is trying to imitate their life."[107]

One especially critical performance of the story is offering hospitality to strangers. I will address hospitality in depth in chapter 7, but it bears mentioning here as well. The Bible itself repeatedly witnesses to this practice. Abraham and Sarah welcome strangers to eat and rest, and, according to the story, in doing so actually welcome God (Gen. 18:1–15). In the Eucharist's interesting inversion, the invited guest becomes the host who therefore opens the table to any and all. Clearly, offering hospitality is an important dimension of performing the biblical story. Welcoming outsiders, serving them, and listening to their stories may also serve an important critical function, however, by assisting Christians toward more faithful reading, interpreting, and performance of their scriptures. Strangers, by definition, confront us with difference. Their differences from us may challenge our unquestioned assumptions about ourselves, including our assumptions that we have a monopoly on understanding God's Word or that we alone are God's chosen. In other words, persons different from us — those who speak a different language, inhabit a different culture, or who do not share our social location — these are persons we need to listen to so that our own readings of the biblical story do not become too comfortable or self-serving. Different faith communities will define "the stranger" differently. For some it may be poor immigrants or gays or pacifists. For others it may be fundamentalists, rich corporate types, or warriors. By welcoming strangers into our midst I do not mean to suggest that we will automatically amend our readings or performances of the biblical story or our convictions about what the Bible means. I am suggesting, however, that if the Bible itself testifies to strangers bearing God, then we need to

---

107. Athanasius, *Incarnation of the Word of God;* quoted in Stanley Hauerwas, *Unleashing the Scripture,* 37.

seek friendships with them for the good of our own souls as well as for theirs.[108]

Joining narrative pedagogies with liturgical enactment and faithful performances

The best strategy for cultivating storied biblical literacy in youth is to join together the three strategies described above. Youth will require repeated opportunities to narratively engage and reflect upon, ritually enact, and otherwise perform this story. As a community, they may offer hospitality to strangers, share bread with hungry persons, provide comfort to the sick or the old, reconcile with and forgive their enemies and each other both in and beyond the liturgical assembly — but always in explicit and intentional relationship with the biblical stories these practices enact. This intentionally structured pedagogical reciprocity between telling stories, ritually enacting stories, performing stories, and reflecting on stories creates the conditions for forming in youth a biblical story-formed imagination and identity.

Critical to the intended reciprocity will be the ecological vision and imagination of youth leaders. Skillful youth leaders will, first, create environments of formation where Bible, worship, and faithful biblical performance take place in recognizable proximity to one another. They will also facilitate reflection that invites youth to note the organic connections and overlaps as well as the tensions between these dimensions of biblical engagement.

Biblical literacy for youth cannot be achieved by applying a little rouge to the Bible's cover or making it the must-have fashion item of the current cultural season. Instead, I propose to foster biblical literacy by creating the conditions and employing the pedagogies for the Bible to be properly encountered as narrative, one that tells the story of God's redemption of the world. That way youth may hope to discover who God is and who God intends them to be and not

---

108. See Stephen E. Fowel and L. Gregory Jones, *Reading in Communion: Scripture and Ethics in Christian Life* (Grand Rapids: Eerdmans, 1991), especially chapter 5.

merely justification for our culture's consumerist, individualist, and therapeutic agendas. As we have seen, storied readings of the Bible are communal rather than individual and are oriented to ends beyond mere self-satisfaction. Reading the Bible as story also enables the full rendering of the character and identity of God. In turn, that portrait may become a mirror in which youth begin to see their own reflections — however dimly at first. Imagining their own lives in light of God's story and God as a participant in their growing stories is equally a manifestation of God's redemptive presence and God's call to youth to take up a distinctive way of life. Storied biblical engagement with youth is, in other words, a means to participate in God's identity, God's presence, and youths' own vocations before God and for the world.

Lest the congregational transformation required for fostering storied biblical literacy in youth seem too daunting for mere adults, I hold out the hope of discovering surprising allies from unexpected quarters. One DYA alumnus reported that upon return to his home congregation he noticed the absence of Old Testament readings in his community's worship. Innocently as a lamb, no doubt, he observed to his pastor, "It seems like we're missing half of our story." Soon weekly Old Testament readings appeared in that community's liturgy.

Recovering biblical literacy is an essential piece in the ecology of formation. It is rightly pursued in concert with the practice of reflection upon book, bath, table, and time. In the next chapter I consider how a community organized around the *ordo* both creates the context for and engenders youths' meaning-making activity with respect to God, themselves, and the world they live in. In other words, I am interested in how the *ordo* may assist youth in becoming theologians.

Five

Contemplating the bath

Doing baptismal theology with youth
through the ordo

In the mid-1980s, the theologian Edward Farley issued the classic challenge to the field of Christian religious education. Noting the virtual army of Christian educators serving denominational and congregational staffs, the proliferation of professionally produced full-color curricular resources, the school-like appendages attached to nearly all church sanctuaries across the continent, and the array of educational choices tailored to every age level, he wondered, "In light of all that, how can it be that the majority of Christian believers remain theologically uneducated?"[109] Fast-forward twenty-five years to the sociologist of religion Christian Smith's conclusion of his recently published study: most youth know little or nothing about the distinctive theological content of Christianity, and, therefore, they are equally ignorant of the implications of Christian faith for their lives.[110] In the case of Christian youth at least (though Smith believes that youth are simply mirroring the ignorance of their elders), it appears that Farley's challenge to Christian educators to foster theological literacy is still unmet a quarter of a century later.

Learning to think theologically in light of the biblical story is a critical practice for Christian youth. With the continuing help of Edward Farley and others, I suggest why theology matters profoundly to youth and, indeed, to all Christians. Then, consistent with other chapters, I describe how we go about teaching youth this practice at

109. Edward Farley, "Can Church Education Be Theological Education?" *Theology Today* 42 (July 1985): 165.
110. Smith, *Soul Searching.*

the Duke youth academy and therefore, by extension, how you might do something similar in your own contexts. I include an explanation of our theological curriculum as taught by members of the Divinity School faculty as well as illustrations of their creative pedagogies or the means they employ to engage students in learning. Our approach to teaching theology to youth depends upon the fact that our community life, fashioned around the *ordo,* provides a rich context and the basic building blocks to support theological reflection. I show how teaching theology at DYA seems to be affecting the lives of student participants and their faith communities. Not that DYA is the only possible solution to the problem of cultivating theologically savvy youth, but it is the context I know best and it shows: (1) that it matters; (2) that it is possible; and (3) that it can be done in a way that values and reclaims the practices of the congregation as generative resources for theological discernment.

Like the rest of this book, this chapter includes a few additional subtexts. First, in light of the *ordo*'s embrace of book, bath, table, and time, I attempt to show how and why the practice of these holy things is an essential component of theological reflection. In addition, I offer a short dialogue with educators, Christian and otherwise, on the role of critical reflection in teaching theology.

Where, oh, where did theology go?

Edward Farley offers several possible explanations for the absence of theology from youth's consciousness. Arguing from a critical sociological perspective, he suggests that the gap between theologically educated clergy and theologically illiterate laity actually serves the power interests of clergy in the same way that other specific bodies of knowledge with their own indecipherable jargon serve doctors and lawyers and tax professionals. Laity, says Farley, may listen to theologically thoughtful sermons delivered by theologically trained clergy but never are they invited to do the work of theological reflection themselves. They remain dependent on somebody else's theological skills or theological opinions. This ensures their passivity and the continuing asymmetry in relations of power between laity and clergy (along with clerical job security).[111]

Speaking from a historical perspective, Farley points to a gradual narrowing of the meaning of theology. Once, claims Farley, theology was a *habitus*, a thoughtfully reflective Christian practice and way of being. Now theology is an academic subject. Instead of learning to think theologically as an essential dimension of Christian life, seminary students thus take courses in Bible, Ethics, Congregational Studies, Worship, Pastoral Care, Christian Education, Youth Ministry, and, yes, Theology.[112] Put slightly differently, instead of thinking for the purpose of living in relationship *with* God, theology has become a collection of mind-numbing technical questions and answers *about* God. This compartmentalization has made theology seem irrelevant to ordinary Christian believers trying their best to follow Jesus.

Indeed, such a suspicion of theology persists to this day. I was raised in the Deep South, and when it came time for me to consider seminary, more than a few parishioners expressed concern for what "those people" would do to my soul. Indirectly, their suspicions also pointed to a perceived separation between thinking about God and loving God. For some at least, thinking theologically has become the antithesis of loving God and loving neighbor. Consistent with the vision of theology as faithful *habitus*, the youth academy attempts to assist youth in recovering theology as a discipline of thoughtful reflection in the service of loving God and loving neighbor.

A possible third reason for the absence of theologically literate youth might be that learning to think theologically is difficult. I was a student of Edward Farley's at Vanderbilt Divinity School at the time of his challenge to Christian educators. He was a principal architect of a curricular revision at Vanderbilt which came to be known by the catchphrase "minister as theologian." Like any other self-important graduate student, I used this phrase often, though I

---

111. Farley, "Can Church Education Be Theological Education?" 167–68.
112. A full account of this shift may be found in Edward Farley, *Theologia: The Fragmentation and Unity of Theological Education* (Philadelphia: Fortress, 1983).

confessed privately that I didn't understand it. I took a course in systematic theology from Farley, wrote tortuous weekly essays on topics like the difference between sin and neurosis, aced the final exam and the course, yet still could not explain what it meant to reflect theologically on life. Troubled by the fact that I wasn't getting it, I ventured across the street to the now defunct Scarrett Graduate School for Christian Education where I took a class from Charles Foster called "Minister as Theological Educator," a course I now recognize was constructed, in part, as a response to Farley's challenge. The course troubled me further and moved me greatly, but evidently it did not teach me to think theologically either. My senior thesis, read by both Farley and Foster, was titled "Youth Ministry: A Theological Approach." In it I included thirty-five pages of sociological, anthropological, and psychological analysis of teenagers but *no* theological reflection on youth or ministry with youth. On the title page Farley fittingly wrote, "This is a start, but only a start..." and went on to explain that I had not drawn upon the theological resources or theologic itself in a paper with "theology" in the title. Perhaps my story is partial testimony to the difficulty of fostering theologically trained persons in the church even when the efforts to that end are credible. It took years of ministry in the parish and additional study for me to begin to articulate what it meant for me to think theologically and to recognize when I was doing it.

In an era in which churches are terrified to make any demands on their youth for fear of losing them, challenging students to take on a sometimes complex intellectual discipline with no immediate payoff might seem like lousy church growth strategy. Learning to think theologically does not carry the same immediate appeal as, say, going on a ski trip.

Why theology for youth?

So it is a fair question to ask why we should teach theology to youth, especially in light of theology's unfortunate caricature as a mind game for religious eggheads. Farley suggests that the very nature of faith is to be a truth-seeking, reality-grounded enterprise.[113] At the same time, however, he notes that the human sinful predicament means that most philosophical constructions of the world (by this he means the way philosophers describe how and why the world is) are likely to be distorted in self-serving ways. For example, it served the interests of the educated European male elite of the Enlightenment to construct political philosophies that defined themselves as exemplary humans while women and persons of color were portrayed as less than human. For Farley, theology as a servant of faith's truth-seeking is essential for exposing such tendencies to sinful distortion of the world. Thus, theology is a critical watchdog essential to Christian life. A church that fails to think theologically will inevitably distort the truth it seeks to proclaim. That is why, according to Farley, all church members must be taught to think theologically.

Flying closer to the ground than Farley, I contend that teaching youth fundamental Christian theological beliefs *and* providing them the theo-logic to employ those beliefs for reflection on their lives in the world is crucial to forming in them a distinctive Christian identity, as is their becoming fluent in the biblical story. Theological awareness enables youth to understand the implications that flow from their identity "in Christ." Absent theological understanding of their story, youth, like the Israelites in the land of Caanan, may go after other gods — therapy, consumption, and power, to name a few. As Christian Smith suggests, this wandering is not necessarily the result of active rebellion; remember, most church teens claim to like their churches. Instead, it is the result of their inability to distinguish between what Christians believe and what the culture espouses.

At DYA, we see our own evidence of this ignorance in the admissions essays of academy applicants. As you might expect, many students who wish to attend DYA are eager-beaver overachiever types. Perhaps not surprisingly, their statements of faith and their efforts at theological reflection are often tied to their strong work ethic. In effect, many claim, "God blesses me and loves me because I work so hard to become good at what I do." Grace seems absent

---

113. Farley, "Can Church Education Be Theological Education?" 159–64.

from their vocabularies. This claim may be a bit strong, but neither are these youth the last laborers into the vineyard! Remember, many have a track record of excellence. Understandably, they want to get their Christian faith right in the same way that they overachieve at their schools and in their extracurricular pursuits. In theological terms, however, they often get it completely wrong. Because they do not understand grace, they do not know what it means to be Christian. I contend that their failure is the result both of the absence of theological education for youth in congregations *and* of the formative impact of living in a culture of merit by way of their families and their schools. This "culture of merit" is one of those other gods attractive to Israelites and overachieving adolescents who do not know their own God well enough. Youth cannot be or do what they do not know. Plainly put, the answer to "Why theology?" is that theological literacy and reflection is key to youth's pursuit of faithful, truthful, well-lived lives in Christ.

Baptism: DYA's primary theological curriculum

Plenary Sessions

Given these answers to the "Why Theology?" question, readers will not be surprised to learn that we devote several hours nearly every day over the Academy's two weeks to teaching theology and helping students learn how to reflect theologically on issues of concern to them and their world. To be sure, theological teaching and reflection occur all across the landscape of community life — in worship teaching and planning sessions and in worship itself, at the Arts Village, at opportune moments in the midst of practicing servant ministry, in small reflection groups, informally at meals — but the primary and most explicit setting for this work is the daily two-hour morning plenary session led by members of Divinity School faculty. This setting is where the Academy most closely resembles a school — students and mentors sit at desks in a large classroom. They open Bibles and other reading materials before them. Many take notes. Professors wear portable mikes to span the large space as they teach.

We have several goals for these sessions. First, we want to introduce students to the discipline of theology. This includes explaining
that there exists a vocabulary, a tradition, and a process for reflecting
on who God is, how God is known, and what this knowing means
for God's people. In addition to the general theme of baptism, every
session introduces a specific theological theme from the list of alliterative Cs (Creation, for example) and uses as sources both the
scriptures and voices ancient and contemporary from the theological
tradition.

Second, we attempt to show how theology may be critical as well
as constructive, that it may call into question practices, beliefs, and
habits that students previously did not consider problematic. As an
example, I highlight below Stanley Hauerwas's theological advocacy
for Christian pacifism as it contrasts with the church in the United
States generally supporting its own country's use of military force.

Third, in addition to learning theological content and methods, we
hope for students to be moved by our faculty's passion for theology.
We purposely choose a very diverse flock of faculty to plant seeds in
students' vocational imaginations. Key to displaying passion is not
merely turning red in the face and raising one's voice. It consists of a
teacher's skillful arrangement of learning methods (pedagogies) that
effectively engage students.

Baptism as theological curriculum

The youth academy's theological curriculum proceeds from deep and
wide theological appreciation for the practice and meaning of Christian baptism in the church. Baptism is the ever-flowing river of living
water upon which the other holy things of the *ordo* float, so it is fitting from a theological standpoint that our curriculum is based upon
it. Nevertheless, the fact that baptism, though more or less completely
off youths' radar screens of importance, is actually a power-packed
theological heavyweight is not immediately self-evident to students
and therefore requires more than a little explaining. That is why the
first two DYA theological plenary sessions are devoted to it. Below
I describe the content of these two sessions in some detail. Their
content is critical to demonstrating how the *ordo* may function as a

generative source for theology. In addition, the pedagogical processes could readily be used in congregations.

Session 1: "Water-born imagining"

I lead the first session, titled "Water-Born Imaginings." This session includes three movements:

1. Considering the human significance of water;
2. Considering the significance of water in the biblical story;
3. Doing theology in light of numbers 1 and 2.

The following paragraphs describe these movements in more detail.

Considering H_2O. First, in a move that is purposefully similar to considering the phenomenology of meal sharing described in the chapter on table, I invite students to brainstorm on the human significance of water. They quickly generate a list that fills the chalkboard. They name many variations on the themes of life, death, power, terror, peace, transport, scarcity, abundance, baptism (clever), formation, mixing, recreation, and transformation.

Based on this list we move to a discussion of water as a naturally occurring human symbol, one that accumulates around itself multiple and sometimes even contradictory meanings, emotional valences, and moral freight. Look back at the list, and notice that this is indeed the case.

I then suggest that the church of antiquity appropriated water's rich symbolic range for its theological reflections on the significance of baptism for Christians. Thus, baptism for the early church came to mean death of the old self, new birth into the life, death, and resurrection of Jesus Christ, the terror of judgment, the joy of redemption, and power for formation, re-creation, transformation, and so on.

The point of this exercise is twofold. The first is to invite students into the practice of cultivating their aesthetic ritual symbolic imaginations consistent with the alternative epistemological stance we seek to form in them. In this case students are invited to claim and perhaps also experience the metaphorically rich symbolic range of the baptismal waters for Christians. The second point is to encourage students for whom baptism may mean only one thing ("a sign that Jesus washed away my sins") or nothing ("Gimmee a break, I was three weeks old!") to reimagine its significance based on the multiple possible meanings of the symbol.

Considering H$_2$O in the book.   In a second move, we return to the great board of brainstorming, this time to recollect water-related stories in the Old and New Testaments. Again the board fills quickly, this time with references to creation, Noah, the Moses miniseries (Baby M floats in basket until plucked by Pharaoh's daughter, uses water-involving plagues, leads people through Red Sea, smacks rock with rod to turn on the spigot, and more), Israel's crossing of the Jordan to the Promised Land, the Elijah/Elisha tandem and their water-related miracles, Jonah's big fish story, and so on. Jesus, of course, is at the center of the New Testament responses. He is born out of the water of his mother's womb; he heals with, walks on, and sends demon-possessed pigs into water. He also calms seas, generates his own big whopping fishing tales, and implies that he is a liquid metaphor — "Living Water." In the tragedy of his passion, Jesus thirsts, and his death is evidenced by the flow of life-sustaining water from his body. Later the church is born as Paul ventures across the waters of the sometimes tempestuous Mediterranean, and others follow Paul to baptize in Jesus' name. The book of Revelation concludes with a vision of the fullness of the Reign of God where the waters of the river of life flow to the heavenly city.

Gathering all these stories on one chalkboard assists students in contemplating how the waters of baptism may symbolize the great sweep of salvation history from God's mighty acts of creation through covenant making with Israel, redemption in and through Jesus Christ, the gift of the Spirit and birth of the church, to Christ's promised return and the fulfillment of God's Reign. These water stories linked to baptism are the same stories that compose the grand story of God's salvation discussed in the previous chapter. Their relation to baptism is made more clear when students read actual ancient prayers offered over the baptismal font that include these stories in abbreviated form.

I also try to explain something of the ancient church's sensibilities regarding this ritual action. Similar to the church's *anamnetic* understandings of Eucharist, baptism was understood not only to *represent* Jesus' death and resurrection (among other salvation stories) but to *re-present* it (and them). The church believed that all of God's past saving activity was recapitulated, made powerfully present, at the occasion of baptism. Similarly, baptism not only assisted candidates and congregations in *remembering* God's saving history, it *re-membered* them *into* that history, joining them through that ritual action with all who ever have been or one day would be blessed by God's salvation. Baptism also made the future present. The baptizing church believed itself to be a sign of God's unfolding Reign. Thus, to be baptized was to be grafted into the continuing story of God's redeeming past, present, and future.

In summary, this second move is designed to assist students in recognizing the intimate connection between bath and book, that is, between the sweeping water-born stories of God's salvation as recorded in the Bible and the ritual/symbolic actions practiced in baptism. I also work to retrieve baptism from the backwaters of students' spiritual imaginations and to free it from reductionist attitudes like "it's *just* a symbol" or "it's just an *empty* ritual" without actual significance. This kind of reimagining in relation to the holy things of the *ordo* is critical to youth's theological education.

Doing baptismal theology. In a third move, I bring out the explicit theology. First, I offer a quotation from the liturgical scholar Thomas Finn. Faith in the early church, says Finn, "was the result of symbols deeply lived."[114] Next I trot out a principle of liturgical theology for interpreting the scriptures, but only after dressing it up with a fancy name: the Aquatic Hermeneutic. I facetiously call it "Aquatic" to signal that we are investigating water. "Hermeneutic" is a term from literary theory meaning roughly "the science or art of interpretation." Thus the Aquatic Hermeneutic is the science or art of interpreting the New Testament in light of the practice of baptism in New Testament

---

114. Thomas M. Finn, *Early Christian Baptism and the Catechumenate: West and East Syria* (Collegeville, MN: Liturgical Press, 1992), 5.

faith communities. This way of interpretation is partly inspired by the typological readings of the Bible I described previously.

I begin by reminding students that, contrary to conventional wisdom, Christian communities were baptizing, sharing Eucharist, and patterning time long before they had ready access to scriptures. Protestants, especially, fancy the early church as a community not yet "corrupted" by ritual and where everyone communed with Jesus through the spiritual ether. The few ideas along this line that are not completely wrong are backwards. Long before there were Bibles in every pew, indeed long before there was anything resembling a New Testament (or a pew for that matter), Christians were honoring the Lord's Day, baptizing converts, and sharing Eucharist. They did not have any conception of spiritual ether, either. As Finn suggests, faith was transmitted through bodily participation in living symbols — holy things. Thus, in regard to the Aquatic Hermeneutic, it is appropriate to read the New Testament while keeping in mind that the writers of the Gospels as well as Paul and others were members of — or at least frequent participants in — worshiping communities that were already practicing baptism. They frequently witnessed baptisms. They watched as persons descended into rivers or pools naked as the day they were born. They saw them bob back up sputtering with joy and with water streaming off their bodies. They paid attention to the anointings, the gifts of new clothes and lighted candles. They witnessed lives transformed. Not only were they witnesses, but they had also experienced baptism themselves because they, too, were deeply living their symbols. Thus, the Aquatic Hermeneutic means reading the scriptures with this fact in mind and assuming that these biblical writers are often reflecting on the practice and meaning of these "deeply lived symbols" in their theological writings.

In the case of Matthew, for example, the account of Jesus' baptism by John is not merely a newspaper report of where Jesus got wet, when Jesus got wet, who got Jesus wet, and how wet Jesus got (though it does include all those details; Matt. 3). It also contains hints and reflections about what Matthew thinks baptism means not only for Jesus but also for persons presently being baptized into Matthew's church in the name of Jesus. The fact that a dove descends upon Jesus hearkens back to Noah's dove — the one that returned to the ark with an olive branch: evidence of creation renewed. By implicitly linking the Noah story to this story of Jesus' baptism, Matthew is doing baptismal theology for those with eyes to see by way of the Aquatic Hermeneutic. He is signaling that baptism has something to do with new or renewed creation. He is also suggesting that just as the flood became an occasion for new covenant relations with Noah and his descendents baptism is a sign of entry into a covenant community and a communal way of life. This is the all-important source for the theological claim that is at the very heart of the academy. Construing baptism as covenant is what enables us to proclaim to students that baptism is not simply an isolated ritual moment in their pasts or futures; it is an enduring communal way of life through time. Youth rightly live out their baptisms over a lifetime in local faith communities.

Paul, himself a witness to multiple baptisms and blessed with the richest sort of ritual symbolic imagination we seek to cultivate in students, ponders the theological significance of baptismal practice in his letter to the Romans. No doubt, witnessing firsthand the descent of candidates into the baptismal waters and their splashy reemergence is what moves him to imagine that baptism is into *Christ's* passion and into the hope of *Christ's* resurrection (Rom. 6). Later theologians, inspired by Paul, described the font as both "grave" and "mother."[115] As with Matthew, we see for Paul how baptismal practice in the churches functions as a generative theological source. The deeply lived symbol is what prompts Paul's theological reflection on it.

Readers will note that I have been alluding to the list of theological alliterative Cs. So far I've commented on Creation, Covenant, and Christ with respect to baptism. Listing the remaining Cs on the board (Crisis, Church, Calling, Coming Reign of God) I make this claim to the group: "Baptism has implications for every significant theological theme of the Christian faith."

---

115. Cyril of Jerusalem, *Catecheses*; quoted in Finn, *Early Christian Baptism and the Catechumenate*, 48.

For the remainder of the session I invite students to test the veracity of this claim. They work in small groups to cast the Aquatic Hermeneutic's net broadly by finding and reading baptismal texts and searching first for clues to the texts' baptismal nature, and second for how each text may be related to the list of theological alliterative Cs.[116] I invite groups to share their findings, and then conclude by noting that this same list of baptismal alliterative Cs outlines the curriculum for the plenary sessions for the next two weeks.

Session 2: "Learning to swim in baptismal waters"

"Learning to Swim in Baptismal Waters" is the title of the second day's plenary session. It is the second of the academy's foundational sessions and is often led by the Roman Catholic theologian Teresa Berger. It contains two primary moves. First, by using a case study (either an excerpt from the film *This is the Night* or the dramatic account of baptism in third-century Rome in Will Willimon's *Remember Who You Are*),[117] she invites students to name points of commonality and contrast between the case study and the practices of baptism in their own faith communities. Because the practices of baptism and those related to preparing for baptism and its aftermath are so richly elaborated in these case studies, students tend to respond first with contrasts. They note the dramatic ritual/symbolic activity as well as the rigor and discipline expected from candidates for baptism. Other students, perhaps formed by Protestant suspicions of too much ritual and of works righteousness, are more critical. In

---

116. I assign texts including but not limited to Matt. 3 and 4; Mark 10:32–44; Acts 2; Rom. 6:3–11; 1 Cor. 12; 2 Cor. 5:17–20; Gal. 3:26–28; Col. 2:20–3:17; 1 Pet. 2:1–10, 3:18–22; Rev. 21–22. A text is identified as baptismal if it references water or baptism, if it implies a baptismal practice ("putting on Christ" suggests the gift of new clothes in association with baptism, or "illumination" suggests the gift of lighted candles), if it contains language that functions as baptismal code (Paul's "*en Christo*" — to be "in Christ" — is to be baptized), or if scholarship suggests a baptismal link (1 Pet. is frequently described as a collection of sermons and teachings for the newly baptized).

117. *This is the Night* (Chicago: Liturgy Training Publications, 1992). William H. Willimon, *Remember Who You Are: Baptism, a Model for Christian Life* (Nashville: Upper Room, 1980), 15–21. See the appendix for Willimon's baptismal story.

her second move, Berger chronicles the decline of this ecology and the consequences of this decline.

Unearthing a baptismal ecology in the church of antiquity. By displaying the ancient baptismal pattern in its entirety through a case study, Professor Berger invites students to notice the basic ingredients of baptismal life in antiquity:

1. A period of formation in preparation for baptism called the "catechumenate," lasting as long as three years. Candidates were invited to "practice" Christian living prior to their admission as members. Practices of the catechumenate included prayer, fasting, keeping vigil, tending to the needs of widows and other poor persons, learning the creeds, studying scripture, receiving exorcisms and laying on of hands, and attending worship (except for Eucharist, which was for members only).

2. Participation in baptismal rites of initiation into the church. Baptisms were scheduled for Easter dawn. They were often done by immersion, with candidates naked. Baptisms sometimes were accompanied by full-body anointings to seal out the devil or to seal in the Spirit. Sometimes the newly baptized were given white robes (what Paul calls as "putting on Christ") and lighted candles as signs of their illumination.

3. Receiving Eucharist as the food for the baptized. For the first time, new members were welcomed for the entire service of worship and were invited to feast at Christ's banquet table.

4. Mystagogy, living in community and learning how to respond faithfully to the gift of baptismal identity in Christ. The newly baptized were invited to learn more about their calling to ministry as new brothers and sisters of Jesus.

Berger draws several implications from this pattern. First, outlining the pieces of this pattern strengthens the claim made in the previous day's session that baptism is more than a single moment in time; it is an enduring communal way of life shaped through participation in the *ordo*. With the exception of feasting at the table, candidates were invited to practice that way of life in preparation for baptism. Members of the congregation served as mentors and sponsors nurturing catechumens toward that way of life. Indeed, all the energy of the congregation was directed toward manifesting baptismal life for the world. The congregation possessed a clarity of purpose not always evident in faith communities in the present day. Berger's descriptions help students to understand the shape of DYA life and our desire for them to learn to swim in baptismal waters. DYA functions similarly to the formation through teaching and practice that once accompanied baptism. It is catechetical and mystagogical through and through.

Decline of the baptismal ecology and its consequences.

Second, Berger shows that when one or more pieces of the pattern were lost to lapses of memory or discipline, baptismal life became impoverished, as did the understanding that baptism did in fact provide the church a way of life. For example, as time passed, some churches came to baptize persons in a perfunctory and undisciplined fashion. They expected nothing from candidates by way of preparation for baptism (catechesis) or reflection on the vocational significance of baptism (mystagogy). At the same time, these and other churches minimized their baptismal rites. Instead of using tubs or rivers full of water (fullness of bath) at Easter dawn (fullness of time), in association with proclaiming at length the central stories of the scriptures (fullness of book) and leading to the Eucharistic feast with Christ (fullness of table) — and all of this framed theologically by the alliterative Cs — they opted for thimbles full of water at no particular time. Still other traditions have retained many of the pieces of the puzzle of baptismal life, but have forgotten how they fit together to form a unified ecology. Persons are baptized as infants, receive First Communion at age eight or so, are confirmed several years later, and may or may not ever consider the vocational significance of their baptisms. Berger's aim is to help students connect puzzle pieces or assist students in the recognition that the pieces do in fact constitute the ecology of baptismal life — what we elsewhere describe as the *ordo*.

Baptism and confirmation

Readers will note that I have said little about confirmation to this point. In many but not all Christian denominations, confirmation is a rite of passage undergone by younger adolescents. Nowadays, confirmation has morphed into its own independent rite, whereas it was once an ingredient of the ecology of baptismal initiation.[118] In Catholicism it has attained the status of sacrament; in varieties of Protestantism it holds the rank of "important thing we do but we know not why." Its roots are in the laying of hands and the confirming prayer of the bishop, all accomplished immediately following baptism and just prior to Eucharist in the church of antiquity.

At present, confirmation typically is oriented to teens, and responsibility for preparing teens to be confirmed often falls to youth workers. My own recollection is that my senior pastors were always deeply committed to *my being deeply committed* to confirmation. On the plus side of the ledger, confirmation was also one of the few events in the life of the church where youth ministry overlapped with other ministries, in this case, adult-centered worship and the spiritual lives of families. Because of its twisted history, its present orientation to youth and its potential implications for the wider faith community, confirmation offers a wonderful illustration of what went wrong and what may again go right in relation to forming youth into baptismal life.

Hippolytus, presbyter at Rome in the early third century, tells us that immediately after baptism, the new members were led to the bishop, who laid hands upon them and prayed for God to confirm all that they had just undergone at the font. Clearly, confirmation in that context was one component of complexly interwoven rites of

---

118. I speak of both "baptismal life" and "baptismal rites" at times, and this may be confusing. When I speak of baptismal *life* I have in mind that way of life the church offered to converts that included preparation for baptism by way of the cate-chumenate, the actual baptismal rites, Eucharist, and reflection on the gift of baptism for the purpose of taking up baptismal vocation (sometimes called "mystagogy"). Baptismal *rites* are the dramatic moments of initiation and new birth within this way of life that included water baptism and also anointings, recitation of the Creed, new robes, and laying on of hands by the bishop (later called confirmation).

baptismal initiation all jammed into one dawn drama and each designed to support the other. A funny thing happened on the way to
church growth, however. Bishops got busy! As the church grew and
more parishes emerged, bishops could not make it to every Easter
vigil service to confirm the new Christians. Sometimes there was a
delay of weeks or even months before the baptized received their
laying on of hands. Consequently, over time the church forgot the
organic relationship that once existed between baptism and confirmation, and in the process began to invent new meanings for these
now separated rites.

What are the consequences of this unintended separation? I often
encountered them in pastoral conversations with parents of con-
firmands. Sometimes parents believed that confirmation was about
"joining the church but not about becoming Christian." No one in
third-century Rome could have contemplated a split of this kind.
The ecology of baptismal life, punctuated by those dramatic initiating rites, made it clear that one was being baptized into a covenantal
communal way of life (joining the church) *and* into the life, death,
and resurrection of Jesus Christ (becoming Christian). In antiquity,
baptism made manifest the Body of Christ as both mystical relationship and sociological reality. Yet in my day, other parents claimed
that baptism was about washing away sin while confirmation was
for receiving the Holy Spirit. In other words, confirmation completed
what baptism had only started. Here they implied, contrary to church
fathers, that the font may be a tomb (death to the old self) but it cannot be a womb (a source of spiritual rebirth). Once again, we see that
assigning specific and exclusive meanings either to baptism or confirmation is possible only when awareness of their original ecological
interdependence is lost. The powerful range of meanings of the unified rites disappears when everything falls to pieces. In the case of
confirmation, meanings are attributed that were never intended.

Since confirmation now carries eons of institutional freight in many
congregations, it is not likely to go away even if, as we have seen, its
foundations as a solitary rite are dubious. How much more com-
mendable, therefore, if confirmation and the events leading up to it
are reimagined as a grace-filled season for learning to swim more

deeply in baptismal waters. Such a construal is a way to partly re-member the baptismal theological ecology long lost to history and to assist the young in understanding that at their baptisms they embarked upon a lifelong journey with God. Understood this way, confirmation may become a season and a rite for teens to remember their baptisms (in terms of significance if not actual experience), to reexamine the gifts of grace received through baptism and the claims baptism made upon them, and to chart a course for their future navigations upon baptismal waters. (See chapter 8 for a detailed consideration of baptismal vocation for youth.) Confirmation may also become a season where the covenantal, communal theology of baptism is practiced across the congregation. Through the appointment of adult mentors to support youth's confirmation journeys and through public ritualizing involving the entire congregation, the faith community makes manifest its essential role in forming faith in the young.

Baptism as theological curriculum

These two foundational plenary sessions at DYA attempt to equip students to consider baptism as both theological wellspring and all-encompassing practical way of life via the *ordo*. They portray baptism as God's way of making faith in the world — including in students' churches back home. DYA's aim, therefore, is not finally to trump or deprecate life in those congregations, but to assist students in reclaiming the centrality and underlying motivations of their local faith communities' practices of holy things. Many DYA graduates do in fact testify that they have come to appreciate better what their churches do and why. These sessions also attempt to demonstrate how theology is born out of the these distinctive practices (baptism in this case) and is undertaken for the sake of the church's faithful life and witness for the world — and not simply to scratch some silly intellectual itch. These foundational sessions also set the table for the plenaries that follow. Proceeding by way of the alliterative Cs resident within baptismal theology (Creation, Crisis, Covenant, Christ, Church, Calling, Coming Reign of God), Divinity School professors invite students into theological conversation. They proceed by way of the Aquatic Hermeneutic, by continued cultivation of enlivened ritual symbolic imagination in light of table and time, by attention to the book and other theological sources, and by referencing the myriad formative practices of the catechumenate and of mystagogy as the basis for Christian baptismal life.

Pedagogies for teaching theology with youth

Senior faculty at the Divinity School brave enough to teach in the youth academy sometimes come to me with fear in their eyes as the day of their teaching draws near. They feel out of touch with the current teen generation. They have heard that teens demand to be entertained and that they have the attention spans of chipmunks. "How can I make it *interesting?*" they ask me. This is a question of pedagogy, that impressively jargony term concerned with how curricular content is learned. It is a little ironic that master educators worry about pedagogical practices only when faced with the prospect of teaching high school students; one would think that they would wish for their teaching to be *interesting* to all audiences and that they would have already figured out that lecturing for two hours is equally excruciating for adults — it's just that we adults have learned to endure it politely. When a fish lands in my boat, however, I'm not one to throw it back. I'm all for excellent educational practice even if it is motivated by fear. "Yes," I agree, "if you bomb, they're likely to tie you down and pierce one of your body parts. You *do* need to make it interesting." And so the pedagogical imagination is born.

In this section I highlight some of our faculty's excellent pedagogical practices (whether inspired by fear or grace) in these theological plenaries. In plain English, I show how they assist students in learning to do theology. This is more than a matter of technique. Concern for pedagogy is not reducible to picking the right *Readers' Digest* jokes to highlight the "substantive" parts of one's class. Rather, there is an art to joining the right content with the right pedagogies.

Certain pedagogical practices are imposed on our teaching faculty. Actually, we *strongly encourage* faculty to continue to cultivate students' imaginations with respect to the ritual and symbolic holy things of the *ordo*. In addition, we request that they engage the scriptures in relation to their topic narratively and theologically. We do this because it is our experience that students are unfamiliar with either the narrative progression of scriptures (what I previously called the story of God's salvation) or the theological interpretation of that story. Far more common for students is the "Open the Book and Read the First Verse that Appears and Apply It as a Word from God" method. Third, we encourage faculty to speak about the lived implications of their theological themes in relation to the many practices of baptismal life. Finally, we encourage faculty to create space in their sessions for dialogue. This is often accomplished by way of small discussion groups or Q and A with the professor.

In addition to these broad pedagogical "suggestions," faculty bring their own pedagogical practices into the classroom. I describe some of them in the paragraphs that follow. Readers may wish to borrow many of these teaching techniques, and that's just fine. My deeper intent in sharing them, however, is to point out how the adroit fit between curricular content and pedagogical practice may engender student learning.

By way of a fun place to begin, one Old Testament faculty member, Stephen Chapman, once taught on covenant, including signs of the covenant. He asked for student volunteers to step forward, walked them through the ritual steps for circumcision, then asked for another volunteer to be circumcised. There were no takers, but there was plenty of amused anticipation.

I've mentioned John Utz's teaching at several different points in this writing. His subject is Christ's incarnation. Utz suggests that poetry's use of metaphor approaches the truth of incarnation in a more mystical, experiential manner than intellectual discussion. It is a brilliant example of pedagogical and curricular match.

Amy Laura Hall, a theological ethicist, teaches every year, most recently on the theology of creation. Inevitably, however, Hall's session turns into a conversation with the young women in the community about their formation as objects of male desire (a sinful distortion of creation) rather than subjects of their own lives. With charisma matched only by Oprah, Hall leads them in a kind of town meeting dialogue about issues of fashion, romantic love, sex, double standards for child-rearing and career (once while holding her own new baby in her arms), all in relation to a theological appreciation for the doctrine of creation. Men in the community are not excluded from the conversation, but they are not at its center. It is as if they are allowed to overhear some very frank girl-talk. This pedagogical dynamic actually heightens interest for the entire community, men and women alike. At a recent DYA reunion, a thoughtful young woman, now a college senior, described the impact of re-imagining her body through Hall's session. She said that when she returned home, her father surprised her with tickets to see a popular hip-hop artist. She told him that after all she'd learned, she couldn't support entertainers who objectified their own and other women's bodies. He responded with frustration over sending her to "that religious camp."

Other sessions are notable for the ways they link concrete Christian practices with theological issues. In a session on unity and diversity in the church inspired by the baptismal text in Galatians — "There is no longer Jew or Greek, there is no longer slave or free, there is no longer male and female ... " (Gal. 3:28) — the congregational studies professor Daphne Wiggins leads students in addressing issues of difference and inclusivity in congregations. In particular, she challenges students to create then practice on one another the means to talk honestly about differences like race, class, and sexual orientation in order to affect Christian reconciliation. In a related session, Greg Jones, dean of the Divinity School, and his wife, Susan Pendleton Jones, teach on discerning the activity of the Holy Spirit in the church. Among other practices, they advocate for the cultivation of "holy friendships": lovingly accountable relationships wherein friends agree to believe in and cultivate the best in one another in part by refusing to allow the worst to go unchallenged. Very often, student graduates comment to us that one of the lasting impacts of the youth academy is in the way they conceptualize and practice friendship when they return home. Some describe the sometimes difficult and lonely search for new friends capable of telling and hearing the truth in love.

Of all the DYA professors, Stanley Hauerwas has a pedagogical approach that springs most uniquely from his character. Hauerwas is at once cantankerous, curmudgeonly, and an avowed Christian pacifist. His work clothes, closely cropped beard, angular face, and piercing eyes give him the appearance of a Mennonite farmer looking to rumble. Especially at the turn of the twenty-first century, with America flexing its military muscle across the planet, Hauerwas's advocacy for Christian pacifism locates him in the distinct minority, even among American Christians. Appropriately, therefore, Hauerwas's teaching methods are rooted in the traditions and practices of the Old Testament prophets — those who understood themselves as speaking sometimes harsh words of God's truth to communities that would prefer not to listen.

Though I will describe more of the content of his teaching session below, I paraphrase his opening statements here: "If you worship in a church where the American flag is visibly present, your salvation is in jeopardy. If you worship in a church that celebrates 'God and Country Day,' your salvation is in jeopardy. If you worship in a church that honors mothers on Mother's Day, your salvation is in jeopardy...." And the litany continues. As the cumulative weight of these words delivered in Texas twang begins to wash over the students, their bodily responses are palpable: some shrink, some stiffen, some laugh, some glare. None are left unmoved. Now this is typical Hauerwas. I once watched him speak with similar effect to a gathering of five hundred pastors. He began with searing irony by suggesting that pastors invite their parishioners to bring their guns from home and place them on the altar so that pastors could bless them alongside the Eucharist. Some pastors chuckled while others raged.

While this content may be uniquely Hauerwas, the pedagogy comes straight out of the prophetic tradition. The Old Testament scholar and Christian educator Walter Brueggemann describes the intent of the prophets as "disruption for justice."[119] He claims that it is the prophet's job to "break or challenge or criticize the consensus for the sake of a new word from the Lord."[120] He understands the prophets as

---

119. Brueggemann, *Creative Word*. See especially chapter 3.
120. Ibid., 41.

stepping into the public life of Israel when that community's distinctive identity as light unto the nations was in danger of being compromised.

As we have seen, critical to the prophetic task, according to Brueggemann, is an appreciation for the communicative power of symbol and of heightened poetic speech. A cursory glance at the prophets confirms Brueggemann's claims. Hosea marries Gomer the prostitute in a dramatic sign-act of Israel's unfaithfulness to God (Hos. 1:2–3). Jeremiah dons the yoke as a sign of the judgment that awaits the community for its sin (Jer. 27–28). Later he buys a vineyard to signal God's forgiving and faithful intent in spite of that sin (Jer. 32). Equally important to the prophetic arsenal is the power of poetry. According to Isaiah, for example, where once God turned the sea into dry land in order to destroy Egypt's horse and rider, Isaiah promises a "new thing" wherein God "will make a way in the wilderness and rivers in the desert" in order to bring home the people exiled to Babylon (Isa. 43:19). In the first instance, water becomes dry land to accomplish death. In the second, dry land becomes water to restore life. Such is the juxtapositional power of symbolic action and poetic speech. It breaks the power of speech and action that serve to maintain the status quo by enabling persons to see themselves and their situations in a new light. Poetry also speaks to the heart. It carries the power to move persons to new ways of seeing, acting, and being. Brueggemann asserts the need to "nurture people in an openness to this alternative imagination" as a critical means to hear prophets, to heed prophets, and to cultivate their own prophetic imaginations.[121]

This brief discussion of the pedagogies of the prophets places in appropriate context Hauerwas's own pedagogical practices. Whether intuitively or deliberately chosen, as with John the Baptist, Hauerwas's simple manner of dress assists him in not merely symbolizing, but actually embodying his prophetic convictions. In addition, his poetic hyperbole, as with the introductory comments to our students, comes straight out of the prophets' playbook. His speech confounds and even breaks ordinary patterns of thought and expectation. It causes disruption to Christian conventional wisdom.

---

121. Brueggemann, *The Creative Word*, 47.

Significantly, students spend considerable energy discussing Hauer-was's pedagogies in addition to the content he offers them. They don't use that word necessarily, but they wonder aloud at the nature of his speech. They ask, "Is he exaggerating for effect or does he really believe what he's saying?" This question goes directly to the relation-ship between heightened speech and telling the truth. By using the mode of prophetic speech, Hauerwas introduces students to a way of picturing the world that resists domestication. His speech is often radically different from the languages they learn to value in school. Nonetheless, as I argued in the chapter on formation through the arts, learning to hear and perhaps even use this language is critical for forming youth capable of resisting the Canaanites' gods.

On the relation of theology to critical reflection

The questions of what constitutes education and how best to educate have always been complex ones. For example, consider these images: is education best imagined as the process of pouring into students knowledge they would not otherwise possess, or is it best imagined as drawing out (the Latin root *educare* means "to draw out of") knowledge already resident (if dormant) within students by way of their experiences of life in the world?

DYA attempts to do theology with youth by maintaining a ten-sion between "pouring in" and "drawing out." One the one hand, it seeks to transmit to students the content of the Christian tradition: the biblical stories and their liturgical enactment, the legacy of their theological interpretations, and their corresponding doctrinal claims. We do not, however, advocate passive acceptance of this tradition. Our stance with regard to Christian theological tradition is sympa-thetic but not uncritical. With the ethicist Alasdair MacIntyre, DYA views tradition as "an historically extended, socially embodied ar-gument" about what comprises the tradition.[122] Thus, our view of tradition is anything but static. We understand it as ever changing,

---

122. Alasdair MacIntyre, *After Virtue: A Study in Moral Theory* (Notre Dame, IN: University of Notre Dame Press, 1984), 222.

rather than for all time, and as inclusive of diverse voices, not a narrow party line. We do "pour in" the tradition to youth at times in part because, as Christian Smith notes, most Christian youth are bereft of that tradition.[123] But we also "draw out" by teaching students that tradition is an argument that they must learn to engage in light of their social locations, their sufferings and hopes, and their unfolding lives with God. This points to the importance of teaching youth how to think critically about their lives.

My own reflections on the task of educating youth theologically and for critical thinking are deeply influenced by the work of the Roman Catholic Christian educator Michael Warren. Warren was among the first North Americans to appropriate the Brazilian liberative educator Paulo Freire's pedagogical methods for youth ministry. Freire's landmark work, *Pedagogy of the Oppressed*, claims that the purpose of education is to assist oppressed peoples in coming to critical consciousness of their oppressive conditions so that they may act to overcome them. Freire employs a "drawing out" methodology, one that teaches the poor, for example, to recognize their poverty as historically constructed and therefore not fated for all eternity. He is deeply suspicious of "pouring in" methods because he believes them to be tools for maintaining oppression by way of upholding the status quo.[124] Education controlled by oppressors, for example, pours into the oppressed the claim that they must obey their masters. Naturally, it also avoids teaching critical thinking.

Michael Warren, following Freire, asserts that youth are also an oppressed group.[125] Thus he advocates for youth ministry practices that assist them in recognizing how their voices are silenced and their agency thwarted by principalities and powers. One consequence of youthful oppression, says Warren, is that youth are consistently duped into fighting our wars for us or into becoming the drones for our economic engine. Thus, for Warren, education for critical thinking is crucial in order to assist students in finding their voices and

---

123. Smith, *Soul Searching.*
124. Paulo Freire, *Pedagogy of the Oppressed* (New York: Continuum, 1992).
125. Michael Warren, *Youth, Gospel, Liberation* (Dublin: Veritas, 1998). See especially chapter 2.

discerning their proper Christian vocations for peace and justice in the world.

Warren uses Freirean critical methodology to assist youth in uncovering how they are subject to an otherwise unnamed cultural agenda of oppression. What Warren does not do, however, is the deep theological work of naming how exactly the pursuit of peace and justice are consistent with Christian alternative vocation. Apparently, he assumes this theological work to be self-evident or otherwise already present.

Freire and Warren have influenced me deeply and therefore have influenced the youth academy's approach to ministry and to teaching theology. But I must confess that the youth academy does not begin out of a context that is self-evidently relevant to youth by attempting to locate itself in their immediate everyday experiences, i.e., their contexts of oppression. It is not our first priority to invite youth's critical reflection on their powerlessness, their muteness, their objectification as consumers, their utilization as economic worker bees, or their exploitation as naive warriors for the military-industrial complex. Instead, in a trajectory that seems decidedly un-Freire-friendly, we impose on them the pattern and context of the ancient *ordo*. We transmit and enact the Christian tradition. We also dictate the academy's theological educational agenda by way of theological exploration of the baptismal alliterative Cs. Critics might suggest that we practice the "pouring in" model of education that Freire insists perpetuates oppression!

I have reflected and ruminated on this problem more than any other single issue related to the shape of the youth academy. Here is my explanation: First, critical analysis is necessary to the process of theological education, but it is not sufficient by itself. Critique requires and sanctions separation and disengagement. Such separation is sometimes necessary for discovery. The prophets and many Christians ancient and contemporary use critique. But Christian faith must finally be characterized by engagement and not by separation. Teaching youth critical reflection exclusively may make them clever, but it risks making them cynical and it does not encourage the cultivation of trusting relationships with God and neighbor. Moreover, sometimes Christian educators and youth workers make the mistake of assuming that pedagogies teaching critical reflection are automatically identical with doing Christian theology. After all, isn't sniffing out injustice a prophetic task? But even responsible deployment of pedagogies like Warren's risks mistakenly assuming that youth are already in possession of the theological resources to name or construct distinctly Christian alternatives to the sin and oppression that critical pedagogies unmask.

Teaching skills for critical reflection is not identical to teaching theology, but teaching skills for critical reflection can assist theology in its work. Further, theology itself is an essentially self-critical enterprise and always will be so long as its object (faithful life before God) is at least partly a mystery and the church is willing to admit that it remains tainted by sin. Readers may have noticed the irony of my own exercise of a certain amount of critical analysis in my critique of critical analysis.

What alternative does the youth academy offer? In the following paragraphs I attempt to demonstrate an alternative approach, one that uses elements of pouring in and drawing out, that includes offerings from the Christian theological tradition and critical reflection on that tradition for the purpose of challenging students to more faithful Christian life. It does so by way of exploring Stanley Hauerwas's presentation to students on the relationship of Jesus' death to Christian peacemaking.

Many academy students are familiar with (or regularly use) the phrase "Jesus died for my sins." In fact, if you asked them to boil their convictions down to one sentence, "Jesus died for my sins" may be their number-one creed. So on the surface, it would appear that one dimension of Christian theology that nearly all students already recognize and appreciate is the significance of Jesus' death. They appear to know this part of the story and understand its meaning.

Almost none of them, however, perceive that when reciting this creed, "Jesus died for my sins," they are giving voice to one of several possible theological accounts of atonement — interpretations of Christ's saving work — in this case, Anselm's divine satisfaction theory. And no student (to date at least) has ever expressed how problematic aspects of this account, or at least narrow interpretations of it, may be for Christians. They have not noticed how a nearly exclusive focus on Jesus' death renders less significant his earthly ministry or his resurrection or the gift of the Holy Spirit to the church. They have not perceived how their version of Anselm's theory construes sin and redemption in individualistic rather than communal terms ("for my sins"). They do not recognize how it renders human beings as passive recipients instead of graced participants in God's gift of redemption. Finally, they have not considered how an account requiring the appeasement of an angry God through Jesus' violent death may be theologically and ethically problematic for Christians. What does it mean to imply that God is vindictive and Jesus is nice? And what about the Trinity? Aren't Father, Son, and Spirit supposed to be three coequal expressions of divine unity rather than separate actors in a cosmic courtroom battle?[126]

We return to Stanley Hauerwas and the content of his session. Recall that Hauerwas is an avowed pacifist. His subject is Jesus' passion, a subcategory of "Christ" on the list of alliterative Cs. Readers should know that I am making some assumptions with regard to the theology that Hauerwas offers in this session. Though the subject is Jesus' death, Hauerwas's primary mission is to teach the students why they should be Christian pacifists. Significantly, he does not merely attempt to turn them into culture critics. Instead, he proceeds by way of critical and constructive engagement with their largely unreflective inner Anselms to a reexamination of Jesus' death. In other words, his primary approach is theological.

Hauerwas's central claim is this: In Jesus' death, God was not vouchsafing the violence of the cross as a means to appease God's righteous anger and dishonored sense of justice (as with Anselm), but God was vouchsafing precisely *non*violence. In other words, Jesus' death on the cross means that God, by refusing to answer in kind to this world's violence, rejects violence as having any place in the method or content of God's salvation of this world. The theological contrast with divine satisfaction could not be more stark. Hauerwas

---

126. For helpful alternative views on the significance of Jesus' passion, see Robert W. Jenson and Leanne Van Dyk, "How Does Jesus Make a Difference? The Person and Work of Jesus Christ," in *Essentials of Christian Theology*, ed. William C. Placher (Louisville: Westminster John Knox, 2003), 183.

claims that God did not kill Jesus for our sin; we human sinners killed Jesus. The violence of the cross is our doing, not God's. Moreover, Jesus, rather than summoning the heavenly host to crush the world's violence with his own superior forces, submits to this death, empties himself, and takes the form of obedient servant. There is no need for appeasement in this scenario. Jesus, as God, acts consistent with the peaceful divine nature. In addition, says Hauerwas, Jesus, through his refusal to participate in the world's violence, establishes the way for his followers to live faithfully by way of their similar refusals of violence through the power of the Spirit.

Notice in this case how Hauerwas's teaching compares and contrasts with my descriptions of Michael Warren's work. Both scholars are pacifists and both desire deeply to form young Christians in the practices and attitudes of pacifism. But they ground their pacifism differently. Warren depends on the work of critical cultural reflection: "Look how the culture is trying to put one over on us, youth." Hauerwas's approach, though it contains elements of cultural critique, is more explicitly theological: "The God we follow is a God of peace, and here is why." Both scholars get to the place youth live: Warren starts there, while Hauerwas ends there.

I am committed to helping young Christians discover not merely culturally critical but distinctly theological reasons for resisting violence and war. Critical methodologies can assist in this task, but they are not automatically identical with or a replacement for the work of theology. Theology, for its part, has much to learn from methodologies that teach critical reflection and, indeed, I think Hauerwas's excavation of Anselm demonstrates how theology goes about its work in a responsibly critical-constructive manner.

The ordo *as context for theological critique and construction*

A case for Christian pacifism by way of critical constructive theological reflection upon Christ's passion may seem impossibly deep and wide for high school students to understand. There is no denying the bar is raised very high. Yet as with every practice or set of practices described so far, the teaching and learning of theology occurs in a context of rich interdependence with complementary practices of community life. Students who participate in the *ordo*'s prayerful patterning of time and in practices born out of its book, bath, and table are also acquiring ample formational and interpretive resources to call upon as they step into the rigors of academic theology.

Consider again youth's creed, "Jesus died for my sins." I have borrowed from Hauerwas's teaching plenary to show how he makes a theological case for this creed's distortion of the Gospel. At root, however, the creed is distortive not because it is completely wrong but because it is inadequate to the full significance of Jesus' death and life. It does not testify to the significance of his ministry or his resurrection or his place in the Trinity. Enter the *ordo* as an essential resource for teaching and learning theology.

Students immersed in a community that practices the *ordo* are regularly invited to ritualize around a baptismal font imagined as tomb but also as womb. They learn through Romans 6 that they share in Christ's death *and* resurrection hope.[127] They share daily in a Eucharistic meal that is both memorial of death and foretaste of the Reign of God. They discover through other encounters with the book (especially 2 Cor. 5) and daily practices of servant ministry in the Durham community that they are called to share in Christ's ongoing ministry of reconciliation with the world. Through this deep grounding in the *ordo*'s full range of the enactment of not only Christ's death but also his ministry and resurrection life, students acquire essential practices, language, and sensibilities for constructive critical theological engagement with their inner Anselms. Specifically, when it comes time for Hauerwas's plenary, they have at their disposal a wider range of imaginative and practical resources to call upon. They are better

---

127. Romans 6:3–5: "Do you not know that all of us who have been baptized into Christ Jesus were baptized into his death? Therefore we have been buried with him by baptism into death, so that, just as Christ was raised form the dead by the glory of the Father, so we too might walk in newness of life. For if we have been united with him in a death like his, we will certainly be united with him in a resurrection like his."

equipped to consider theologically the limitations of "Jesus died for my sins." They may also call upon the rich ritual and symbolic action of the *ordo* and the practices of Christian living that flow from it as ways of not merely accepting but of participating in Christ's ministry and sharing in his resurrection hope, including his Reign of peace. Indeed, DYA's two weeks partly embodies this peaceful Reign.

Teaching and learning theology at DYA never occur in a vacuum, nor is theology done for the sake of learning theology. Instead, it is practiced in the context of a Christian community to enable students to make sense of this rich life they are living together. The goal is for theology to become *habitus*, disciplined thoughtful reflection in service of faithful life. Failure to intentionally link theology to the wider life of the community and to the church's life before God and for the world would mean reducing it to the arcane angel-counting science Edward Farley warns against. At the same time, however, teaching theology well in this setting includes vigorous and compelling practices of the *ordo*. For DYA to attempt to teach theology while spending two weeks at Wally World instead of two weeks in disciplined Christian community would just as readily torpedo the task of theological education. Such a context simply could not generate the *gravitas* sufficient to theology's high calling. How many variations can you make on "life is like a roller coaster..."? The intentional weaving of theology together with the daily practices of the *ordo*-grounded community is essential.

There is another intent behind teaching theology in light of the *ordo*. It is serious about helping students to consider the liturgically grounded lived faith of the church as theology's generative source. The *ordo* manifests the church's identity for the world and the mode of this disclosure: Jesus Christ through holy things. Understanding this central story and its mode of disclosure are two of theology's central tasks. Such theological understanding also constitutes one component of youth's vocation before God

If this claim is true — Jesus Christ is manifest through holy things — then our explorations must continue. The next chapter explores in detail the *ordo*'s patterning of time, or, to put the subject a bit more creatively, how rising sun reveals the Son who is risen.

Six

Believing in time

Forming youth through prayerful temporal rhythms

Tempus fugit! Carpe diem! A stitch in time saves nine! Time waits for no one. Time is money! I got, got, got, got no time!

Time matters. Many North American youth and their parents have little to spare. They rush hither and yon from one fulfilling experience to the next, scarfing fast food and catching up with text messaging along the way. "There's not enough time in the day," they complain, so at night they gulp super-caffeinated energy drinks to steal time which was once devoted to sleep. The lack of time is a peculiarly North American condition. Said a relaxed Irish pub dweller to a harried American tourist one evening over shared pints, "You Americans are rich in many things, but we Irish are rich in time." Ironic, isn't it, how so much stuff leaves us with so little time?

This chapter explores the significance of time, showing how a culture's patterning of time shapes its members' imaginations. It suggests that to be immersed in a particular temporal rhythm is to be formed bodily to act upon and interpret the world in culturally specific ways. The chapter also describes how the church's patterning of time embodies its own bedrock theological convictions. Who knew that racing to church on Sunday morning with two just barely not comatose teens in the back seat could be a profoundly theological gesture? Through the church's liturgy, however, time becomes another holy thing — a human convention, yes, but also a medium for incarnation. Like book, bath, and table, Christian timekeeping bears transforming grace for those with eyes to see. As the theologian and educator Dorothy Bass suggests, the giftedness of time derives from the recognition that ultimately time is not a human invention, nor are we its masters. Rather, time is God's gift, and we its grateful recipients.[128]

Prayer is the church's principal practice of receiving the gift of God's good time. Thus, in addition to exploring the richness of Christian timekeeping, this chapter teaches youth workers how the prayerful patterning of time may assist their youth in communing with God more deeply and identifying God more profoundly. Consistent with the practice of youth ministry rooted in the church and its liturgy, this chapter advocates for reclaiming liturgical "daily offices" as a normative practice of prayer in the church, including youth ministry.

Patterns of time, patterns of meaning

Charles Foster, one of his generation's most influential Christian educators as well as a mentor and friend to me, once invited a class full of students to consider the implications of a variety of timepieces representing different historical epochs. Foster included on his list a sun dial, a clock tower, and a digital wristwatch. Like any self-respecting mentee, I have borrowed and expanded upon Foster's exercise. To the considerable amusement of my own students, I attempt to draw these timepieces while they shout out guesses. No, Brian, the correct answer still is not "Jesus." And to Foster's list I have added the image of Albert Einstein streaking away from the clock tower while riding on a beam of light and checking his wristwatch. More about that below. The point, of course, is to stimulate students' reflections on the cultural significance of the various patterns of time that these implements and images represent. Over the years, I've learned a great deal from my students' insights.

The sun dial, for example, suggests an organically ordered worldview. Civilizations that employed it knew that the sun could be counted on to appear daily. It guided their waking and their sleeping. It displayed the "natural" times, confirmed in persons' own bodies,

---

128. Dorothy C. Bass, *Receiving the Day: Christian Practices for Opening the Gift of Time* (San Francisco: Jossey-Bass, 2000).

for activity and for rest. Time "stopped" when the sun went down, only to resume with the next day's dawn. This form of patterning time was also self-evidently tied to cosmic powers. Egyptians, Greeks, and Romans, industrious as they were, readily conceded that they were not in charge of the sun, or of the rhythms of darkness to daylight, or the annual round. For these cultures, there was a givenness to time, and this givenness was interpreted as expressing transcendent power and not human construction, a natural or divine ordering into which human beings naturally fit.

Emblematic of a different era and a different culture, a clock tower located in the village square, though still indebted to the sun's daily round, proposes an altogether different pattern of time. First, we note its mechanical nature. In contrast to previous interpretations of time as natural or transcendent, a machine for patterning time fits well with a Newtonian view of the universe as mechanical system. And while it is still possible to imagine a God who created this machine, the door is also open to imagining human beings as the "keepers" of time (Who, after all, built the clock tower?), although those same humans are also increasingly the ones "kept" by it. Ticking on even after sunset, tolling its bells to mark the hours, such clocks introduce the notion that time marches on even when the sun goes down. It is no accident, therefore, that the invention of the clock tower parallels the invention of the industrial revolution. Two twelve-hour shifts and seven-day work weeks require clocks for laborers to punch.

Enter the digital wristwatch. Gone are the sweeping hands of time binding past to present and future. One sees only momentary pulses of light flashing isolated fragments in time. Precision is the order of the day. "Half past" and "quarter 'til" no longer suffice. Thanks to the watch, I know I am exactly seven minutes and forty-three seconds late to my next meeting. And fifty-seven days ahead of a manuscript deadline. "Deadline." Sounds ominous, doesn't it? And unlike the clock tower, my accountability to time is personalized, almost interiorized. Do I "watch" time or does time "watch" me? No need for Ebenezer Scrooge or the village clock tower; my own wrist holds me accountable, as close to me as my pulse.

More worrisome, time has become a scarce commodity. If I don't spend it well, I'll lose it forever. The fragmentation and scarcification of time mirror and heighten our own sense of communal fragmentation and personal lack. Not surprisingly, making time has become a growth industry. We pay others to walk our dogs, shuttle our children, fertilize our roses — all on time, at the right time, but without the benefits of social cohesion that we would enjoy had we the time to do these tasks in the company of neighbors. Buying time demonstrates how the entire capitalist system is premised on the scarcity of time. For if time is not money, then what's the rush?

Blessing to some, threat to others, Albert Einstein's theory of relativity holds the potential to "un-wrist" us from our watches and our servitude to modern conceptions of time. Einstein is reported to have done some of his best theorizing by imagining himself traveling on a light beam. Light, of course, generally travels at the speed of light. For our own purposes, say that our man Albert arranges to catch up with, then hitch a ride on, a beam of light departing from the village clock tower at noon. Allow that he is also wearing a digital watch synchronized with the tower clock to 12:00. Relativity suggests that as Einstein races off from the clock tower to catch that light beam — accelerating toward the speed of light in the process — were he to glance over his shoulder, the hands on the tower's clock will appear to him first to slow down then to stop altogether while the watch on his wrist pulses as "normal." The appearance of the hands of the clock tower slowing then stopping is the result of our friend Al's acceleration to light speed. As he flies away from earth at the speed of light, no trailing light beams reporting the subsequent movement of the hands on the clock tower can catch up with him. In other words, traveling at or near light speed has the effect of warping time. Einstein demonstrates the theoretical plausibility of what students have known in their hearts forever: last period on Friday really is the longest hour of the week. Relativity means that time is not constant, and is therefore no longer universally quantifiable by the means we moderns rely upon to do just that. And if it is not easily quantified, neither is time as neatly commodified.

Admittedly, relativity has not yet caused us to throw away our watches, but more chinks appear in the armor of the modernist worldview each day. Some Christians feel threatened by relativity. If nothing is dependably constant, they argue, then the foundations for belief in God are undermined. And they are right... to a point. The rationale for belief in God, to the extent that these rationales are constructed out of the philosophical foundations of modernity, are less defensible.

But what relativity takes away on the one hand it gives with the other. Take Christian timekeeping for example. The church celebrates Easter and Christmas each year. More than a bit of whimsy memorializing Christ's birth and resurrection, it celebrates those occasions as present realities. Christ's birth, death, and resurrection are re-presented. We've already noted that the first line of Wesley's hymn is "Christ the Lord is risen *today*," not "Jesus Christ rose approximately two millennia ago." Through the philosophical lenses of modernity, such a faith claim is dismissed as fantastic: the resurrection cannot be both past event and present experience. But with relativity, this is not a problem. This emerging worldview also helps find room for claims that the Reign of God is here now but also not yet. In other words, relativity allows for the possibility that Christians are not merely pretending at Easter or Christmas or, for that matter, every Sunday they gather for worship. That the glory of Christ's resurrection is re-presented and the future Reign is re-anticipated through the Christian patterning of time is entirely consistent with theories of relativity.

Of course, the church does not require the approval of physicists to authenticate its faith. It is interesting, however, and more than a little ironic that modernity, which seemed intent on replacing the church, presently finds its own foundations crumbling.

In addition to encouraging sympathetic reevaluations of Christian timekeeping, relativity challenges modern capitalist portrayals of time as a scarce commodity. Why do we, in fact, labor under the assumption that a moment wasted is gone forever, never to return? One answer is that it is in the interests of our economic system for us to perceive time this way. For if time is scarce, then time may also become money. But relativity suggests that time may be bent in ways that allow us to catch up with what we thought we missed. A recent physics experiment slowed light down to a leisurely 38 miles per hour. At those speeds you could hop on a Vespa and catch up to the end of your daughter's soccer match!

The intent here is more than the shattering of conventional wisdom. If time turns out to be available to us in ways that modernity could not allow us to perceive and in which relativity is only now opening to us — if only in mind-bending ways at present — then scarcity is not the last word on time. And if scarcity is not the last word, then the door is also reopened to the Christian conviction that time is a gift. As Dorothy Bass suggests, the task for Christians is to "receive the day" God has given with delight and gratitude. God, who is the creator of time, gives creation ample time for work, for blessing, and for rest. The operative description for time as God's good gift is abundance, not scarcity. God provides more than enough time for God's people to live a good life. Relativity implies that Christian claims for the abundance of time are not only metaphorically true or morally true, but actually true. Quite the theological wormhole, isn't it?

Insights into the patterning of time

At least three general insights follow from this introductory exploration of the patterning of time. First, similar to the water of the bath, the bread and wine of the table, and the words of the book, time functions as a symbol in human understanding and social intercourse. It holds together multiple and even competing meanings (time as scarcity, time as abundance); it evokes a range of affective valences (worn down by the clock, transfigured in a moment of joy); and accumulates around itself moral significance (the early bird gets the worm; eat, drink, and be merry, for tomorrow we die). This symbolic character of time makes it an excellent candidate for the status of holy thing which, as we shall see in more detail below, is exactly how the church regards it.

Second, the patterning of time is closely associated with a culture's ways of making meaning. Timekeeping is closely related to a society's metanarratives, stories about why things are the ways they are. As we have seen, the ancients regarded time as the expression of cosmic or transcendent power; for moderns, time corresponded to the machinelike orderliness of the world; and for physicists and other postmoderns, time confounds our efforts to master it, thereby upsetting convention but also creating interesting new possibilities for imagining the future — including imagining the future as an unfolding gift from God.

Third, not only is the patterning of time linked to cultural meaning-making, it sometimes frames the boundaries of cultural imagining. Time as scarce commodity is a case in point. For generations, North Americans have accepted this assumption as axiomatic of the universe. Thus, they find themselves unable to even conceive of an alternative to productive motion every moment of the day. Our teens are swept up in this whirlwind. Like their parents, they work from dawn late into the night because they have been formed unquestioningly into the myth of time's scarcity. Fortunately, the physicists provide us with the means to reflect on the matter in which we were previously immersed. In the process, Christian understandings of time, long ago discarded as anachronistic, reappear with renewed meaning and vitality.

Patterning time, forming identity, and embodying theological conviction

The Jews patterned time. "For six days shall you labor," says the Lord, "but the seventh day is a sabbath" (Exod. 20:9–10). Such was the covenant command from the creator of the world to the people of Israel. This command was not arbitrary, not "random," as today's adolescents like to say. It was in keeping with the very rhythms of God's own creation work. Human beings participate in this pattern of work and rest as part of their sharing in the *imago Dei,* the image of God.

The seven-day week bears additional theological significance. It turns out that God has far more to say about the seventh day, the Sabbath day, than the prior six. This day is to be unlike the others; rest and not relentless striving is the order of this day. In part, keeping Sabbath is intended to remind Israel of God's creative activity and of their own creaturely status. Moreover, since creation is clearly a gift from God, practicing Sabbath becomes the means for Israel to practice doxology before God and thanksgiving as well. To keep Sabbath is to practice gratitude for the gifts of life, work, and rest.

Practicing the weekly rhythm of work and Sabbath rest also serves as a reminder to Israel that these are not the bad old days. Once upon a time "we were slaves in Egypt" with Pharaoh in no mood to grant a Sabbath for resting. In the present, therefore, to keep Sabbath is to mark Israel's deliverance from slavery and into the promise of God's covenant blessing.

As with the other holy things, another way to frame the significance of the seven-day week for Israel is to suggest that to practice it is to be inserted into the narrative sweep of God's salvation. To practice the week is to become a character in the story of God's creation, redemption, and ongoing care for the world. Thus, the seven-day week "characterizes" those who practice it. By keeping Sabbath, Jews embody their stories and their theological convictions as well. Living in light of the seven-days forms their identity as a people in covenant with the God who is their creator, liberator, and the provider of their daily bread.

I am speaking here more than just figuratively. To pattern time is literally, actually, to pattern bodies. Most of us recognize this to be true, at least intuitively. Many North Americans work a pattern of five "week" days on with the two "weekend" days off. Occasionally, however, work requires us to labor straight through the weekend. Whether the cause is tax season or Christmas season or annual inventorying, persons accustomed to weekly rest report fatigue, irritability, and a loss of rhythm when forced to forgo their habitual temporal patterns. Simply put, their bodies don't feel right. Unfortunately, my own students report the opposite is also true. Toward the end of the semester students become accustomed to working seven day weeks in order to complete end-of-term papers and to prepare for final exams. Whatever dis-ease they experienced initially is replaced by a sense of the normalcy of this frantic way of patterning time. Then, after the final bit of work is at last completed, instead of restful restorative indulgence, they report an inability to sit still or otherwise take it easy. Their bodies have become patterned to breakneck productivity. In either case, the point holds: our deepest convictions and our pressing priorities are often housed in bodily habits, and those habits are shaped, in large measure, by patterns of time.

Since many of the first Christians were Jews themselves, they naturally inherited the Jewish temporal pattern. Quickly, however, their unique convictions about Jesus as the long-anticipated messiah came to be expressed through liturgical patterns of time that built upon but also transformed the traditional ones they inherited. Initially, the Christians, like all good Jews, kept Sabbath with their brothers and sisters. Soon, however, as the scriptures report, in addition to keeping Sabbath they began to worship together on the day of Jesus' resurrection, the "first day of the week." This day is also described in early Christian writings as the "Lord's Day" and, even more suggestively for our purposes, the "Eighth Day."

Why "Eighth Day?" The liturgical theologian Alexander Schmemann unlocks the mystery. He correctly asserts that the Christian eighth day only makes sense in light of Israel's prior seven. He argues that through their liturgical celebration of Jesus' resurrection on the eighth day, the Christians were transforming Jewish patterns of time as the means to enact their own theological convictions about Jesus. He describes the relationship between Israel's seven-day week and the Christian eighth day as one of contrasting conjunction. The eighth day is unintelligible without the seven. They are necessarily *conjoined*. Yet, for the Christians, the eighth day speaks to and enacts dimensions of God's new revelation in Jesus Christ. The eighth day, the day of resurrection, becomes for them the first day of the new creation as inaugurated by Jesus.[129] Herein lies the *contrast*. Similarly, the seven-day week embodies Israel's sense of covenantal relationship

---

129. Schmemann, *Introduction to Liturgical Theology*, 77–78.

with God from the very beginning of time. Israel works and creates in the style of God's own creativity, but also rests in order to bless the Creator whose loving care makes daily life possible. As with the reinterpretation of creation, the Christian eighth day does not cancel this covenant sensibility — it requires it for its own intelligibility — but at the same time the eighth day marks Christians' convictions about the institution of a new covenant delivered through the life, death, and resurrection of Jesus. The Lutheran liturgical theologian Gordon Lathrop describes this relationship as another example of liturgical juxtaposition. By liturgically "breaking together" Israel's week with the church's eighth day, the church "speaks" the Gospel into the world.[130]

Schmemann and Lathrop also attend to the temporal relationship between Israel's yearly celebration of Passover and the Christian Paschal celebration (the annual liturgical marking of Jesus' death and resurrection, the predecessor of the church's Holy Week, including Easter). Both scholars claim that it is no accident that these celebrations fall in close proximity to one another on the calendar. According to some Gospel accounts, Jesus was arrested, crucified, and resurrected near the time of the Passover. But notice especially the theological generativity enacted by the juxtaposition of the church's Paschal events with Passover. By dint of this temporal juxtaposition, Jesus becomes the new sacrificial lamb whose blood is poured out to deliver his followers from death. Jesus is the new Moses who frees his people from slavery. Through baptism into Jesus at the paschal celebration, Christians pass through the waters of chaos and slavery and death into the Promised Land of God's new reign. As was the case with the conjoining of the eighth day with the seven-day week, by intentionally juxtaposing on the calendar its own Paschal celebration to Israel's Passover, the church establishes a related but also radically distinctive temporal pattern for forming its people into distinctively Christian identity. It evokes all the theological themes rehearsed at the Passover but transposes them to speak this new word: "Jesus

---

130. Lathrop, *Holy Things*, 36–43.

Christ." Similar to our consideration of typology in the scriptures, this patterning is evidence of the *ordo*'s typologizing of time.

The relationship of time to other holy things

What is the relationship between the church's time and its book, bath, and table? The patterning of time "temporalizes" the central stories and their attending theological convictions later recorded in the book. Using the language of contrasting conjunction and juxtaposition, we may also note occasions where time is conjoined (or juxtaposed) with bath or table. The church of antiquity, for example, baptized new converts at Easter dawn only after they had fasted and kept vigil for two days beforehand. The power of this experience, the luminescent convergence of this holy time with the ritualized baptismal entry into Jesus' passion (descending beneath the waters) and resurrection (emerging as new creation from the waters) made for an unforgettable experience that early church fathers could only describe as "awesome."[131] The power of juxtaposition is also evident, for example, at the time of Holy Thursday and the church's gathering at Eucharistic table, or at the time of Jesus' "setting his face toward Jerusalem" and the Lenten imposition of ashes of mortality on the heads of his followers. Linking the practice of the other holy things to the holy patterning of time intensifies the potential for experiencing God's presence and better identifying who this God is.

To summarize, first the Jews and then the Christians patterned time. This practice alone distinguishes them from other religious traditions that seek escape from time. Israel and the church pattern time as a response to their convictions that God creates, enters into, and redeems time, thus also sanctifying time as a gift for God's people to receive. I have also suggested that part of the church's inspiration was to transpose temporal patterns inherited from Israel. Thus, the church patterns time in order to form its people into awareness of

---

131. This time see Theodore of Mopsuestia, *The Awe-Inspiring Rites of Initiation*; quoted in Finn, *Early Christian Baptism and the Catechumenate*, 84.

God's distinctive *identity* as incarnated in the life, death, and resurrection of Jesus. Equally important for our purposes, I suggested that to be inserted into this temporal pattern — the seven-day week with worship on the eighth day, and the yearly round as marked by Easter, and also Pentecost, Christmas, Epiphany — is also to be invited to *experience* and share in the life of this God who enters our time. For persons, including Christian youth, to keep time in this way is to join ourselves bodily to the rhythms of the Body of Christ, which is the partial enactment of Christian vocation.

Youth, youth ministry, and the patterning of time

How are our youth keeping time? Who really has time to contemplate time? Youth workers express frustration about the perceived lack of time to minister with youth. "How do we compete with the traveling sports teams, Sunday soccer tournaments, and SAT prep courses?" they ask with growing desperation. Some search for more convenient meeting times to accommodate busy students. How about "5:30 Prayer Breakfast"? Others opt to sponsor their own sports teams and SAT prep courses, saying, in effect, "We agree not to call into question your busyness so long as you stay busy here at the church." There's no use pretending that youth aren't busy. They are. But in the midst of its well-intended accommodation to their schedules, the church risks losing faith that it has something distinctive to offer precisely in the midst of such busyness: time as a holy thing, a gift of grace from the loving creator of time — a gift, that, if fully received into our lives, is capable of forming us into greater likeness of the giver.

Let me be clear. To ask, "How can we find time to fit church into youths' lives?" is to ask the wrong question. It is far better to ask, "How can we offer youth the gift of time that God has created, redeemed, and continues to sanctify daily through Jesus Christ?" More is at stake in these opposing questions than word games or semantics. They go to the heart of our capacities to imagine our way off the temporal treadmill that runs the culture and especially our youth and our ministries at present. Part of the solution is to reclaim our

own theological awareness of the grace and transformative power of
the church's patterning of time in light of God's salvation. Put simply,
that means relearning and practicing with vigor the church's patterns
of time and the theology resident within them. Practicing the eighth
day in relation to the seven, attending to the Christological pattern
of the annual round — these are essential dimensions of God's self-
giving that are pivotal to Christian formation. Such renewed practice
may then open the door to heretofore unimagined yet exceedingly
hopeful possibilities.

Here is a small but significant example. After a good deal of ed-
itorializing in our local paper about the importance of more high
schools offering more Advanced Placement (AP) courses to provide
qualifying students college credit, Chip Denton, the headmaster of
Trinity School of Durham, NC, wrote his own op-ed piece in which
he explained why his school will not offer AP classes. I imagined eyes
rolling all over my community as our gaggle of educational intellec-
tuals read his argument. He stated that a central tenet of the school's
mission is the pursuit of an "unhurried education." He further noted
that in his experience as an educator and a parent, a schedule full
of AP courses is anything but unhurried.[132] Though he did not say
so, I sensed that his vision for an "unhurried education" is the result of faith in God, who provides the gift of time. As such, like
manna for the Israelites, there is always enough time. In addition,
his stance demonstrates trust that God will work out God's good
purposes — including God's good purposes in and through the lives
of the students at his school — all in God's good time. He and his
school will likely face fallout from this decision in the form of a
shrunken applicant pool. But he will also provide students who do
attend, and community members inclined to notice, with a witness
to God's Reign.

Here is a second example out of DYA's experience. On the middle
Sunday of our two weeks, we practice Sabbath rest. After working
incredibly hard for six days, we refrain from work on the seventh.

---

132. Chip Denton, "A Case for Schools That Pass on Advanced Placement,"
Durham Herald-Sun, May 15, 2006, sec. A, 6.

The community sleeps in, attends late morning worship, then rests until evening. Parameters for rest include activity or inactivity that students judge to be personally restorative and pleasing to God. Some students nap, some read, some play music together. Keeping Sabbath elicits strong responses from students. Many confess that they never, ever rest in this way. They express gratitude without prompting.

Daily prayer and the patterning of time

So far I've provided little overt reference to prayer. But prayer is the church's principal practice of patterning time. So we have to expand the definition of prayer along with the estimate of what qualifies as the practice of prayer in order to propose a strategy for overcoming perceived deficits in the prayer lives of youth.

Through years of listening to youths' own reflections on prayer, I've gleaned at least four bits of information. First, most youth I've listened to do not pray regularly. Second, those who do tend to understand prayer as a form of transacting business with the deity: "This is what I need, God, and the sooner the better." Third, most youth have not yet been invited to consider how other practices of their lives — writing, reading, dancing, making music, and more — may themselves become prayerful. Finally, when asked "When and where do you pray?" very few mention Sunday morning at 11:00. I suspect the fact that so few name worship as a context for prayer is the result of their perception of prayer as a private conversation between individuals and God (or more likely a monologue addressed to God) rather than by groups in community. In support of this hunch, youth sometimes characterize prayers in worship as "rote" and note their preference for the freedom and spontaneity — and thus the perceived greater authenticity — of personal prayer.

Though some youth do perceive worship as offering a context for praying, absent here is any insight that to gather in community on a certain day or at a certain time is to be inserted into the church's unending prayer. Neither do youth voice awareness that the entire landscape of the liturgy is itself prayerful. For Don Saliers, however, to gather as a community for worship is to join with Christ through

Christ's Body the Church in the "ongoing prayer of Jesus" by offering praise, gratitude, intercession, and lament before God.[133] To that
end, all the practices of worship — the singing, testifying, Scripture
reading, preaching, offering, Eucharist sharing, and yes, the praying,
too — constitute the assembly's prayer. To paraphrase what Saliers
is fond of saying about liturgy, prayer is the setting where "human
pathos" meets the "divine ethos."[134]

In addition to broadening awareness of the community's liturgical life (its *ordo* of holy things, including its patterning of time) as
fundamentally prayerful, Saliers is also attempting to overcome what
he considers to be an artificial distinction between Christian praying
and Christian living. Instead, the whole of the church's life together —
worshiping, missions, evangelizing, studying, caring, and more — all
are envisioned as forms of prayer. Saliers's insight assists greatly in
dismantling our too-narrow view of prayer as the cloistered activity
of a private few. Broadening the perception of prayer from devotional
act to communal way of living can assist youth in tearing down the
partition between spirituality and the rest of their lives. With this
helpful interpretive lens, the ordinary stuff of teen life — studying,
working, creating, chilling, exercising, or befriending — all may be
reimagined as prayerful self-offering.

By broadening youthful estimations of prayer, however, I do not
wish to dismiss the expectation for prayer as a disciplined spiritual
practice with concrete form. To the contrary, the regular practice of
prayer is essential for experiencing God and identifying that God. It
also goes to the very heart of the Christian's vocation to love God
and neighbor. For this reason, it is important to assist youth in laying claim to the liturgical patterning of time — the weekly assembly
on the eighth day and the rhythms of the annual round — as fundamentally prayerful. Moreover, the church in its inspiration also offers
youth and all its people a prayerful pattern for each day. This pattern
is sometimes called "praying the hours" or "divine offices."

---

133. Saliers, *Soul in Paraphrase,* 87–98.
134. Saliers, *Worship as Theology,* chapter 1.

Patterns for daily prayer

A quick survey of the churches of antiquity suggests there was no single pattern for or constellation of practices included in daily prayer. One early source prescribes the Lord's Prayer three times daily. Others recommend praying the Psalms. In terms of schedule, still others suggest prayer at the third, sixth, and ninth hours of the day in order to attend closely to Jesus' passion — the time of his hanging on the cross, the midday sun turning to night, and, finally, the hour of his death. Along these lines others added the less convenient prayer times of midnight and "cock crow." Over time, gathering for prayer in the early morning and again in the evening became the most typical practice in most congregations.[135]

Why morning and evening? As we saw in the case of the Christian week and its year, by marking the hours of the day the church provided its people with specific Christological interpretation. Morning prayer rehearsed the following themes: the blessedness of creation ("New every morning is your creation, great God of light"), new creation through the resurrection of Jesus Christ (the congregation prayed facing east, the direction of the rising sun), and the propriety of gratitude to welcome the gift of the day ("O Lord, open our lips.... And we shall declare your praise!"). Morning prayer also included intercessions for faithful living throughout the day. Evening prayer gathered its own theological themes. In addition to gratitude for God's providential care through the daylight hours, Christians lamented the sins of that day and beseeched God to see them through the gathering dusk. Of special significance was the lighting of a lamp in the worship space, a sign of Christ's light overcoming darkness. Evening prayers also illumined themes of eschatological watchfulness for the one who promises to come "like a thief in the night." Christians prayed to be ready. Thus, as we've seen in the church's patterning of week and year, to pray daily at

---

135. Gregory W. Woolfenden, *Daily Liturgical Prayer: Origins and Theology* (Burlington, VT: Ashgate, 2004).

these hours is to be inserted into the stories and the theology of Jesus Christ.

Practices of daily prayer

In general, what are the practices that make up morning and evening prayer? In addition to the prayers and litanies with scriptural bases like those in the previous paragraphs, daily prayer includes the public reading of scripture. Typically, such readings come from a lectionary. Lectionaries for daily prayer usually follow closely the lectionary for Sunday worship. Keeping pace with the appointed scripture readings for daily prayer reinforces the rhythm of the annual round. Advent readings prophesy the messiah's birth; Lenten readings forecast his crucifixion; Easter readings testify to his resurrection life; and Pentecost readings detail the life of Christ's Body, the church, as empowered by the Spirit.

It may not be immediately clear how the public reading of scriptures qualifies as prayer. One key is in the listening. Christians believe that their book is Spirit-inspired. They trust that the Word of God speaks through the words of the book. Thus, the reading is for the sake of listening to what God may be saying. Prayer book rubrics prescribing periods of silence following scripture readings support this practice of prayerful listening. Perhaps this is so remedial as to appear insulting. Conversations (and relationships) are reciprocal. When one party speaks, the other listens. Yet in churches and youth ministries, silence often becomes the forgotten curriculum. Our prayers are noisy, wordy, and long. We talk much and listen little. One dimension of recovering the prayerful reading of scripture is learning to keep silent and listen for God to speak.

Certainly the Psalms should be included under the heading of prayerful reading of scripture. Yet the Psalms, sometimes described as the prayer book for Israel and the church, deserve special consideration. Countless Christian exemplars testify to their regular practice of praying the Psalms. Jesus, Augustine, Luther, Wesley, Teresa of Calcutta — this is just a short list. Roberta Bondi reminds us that the Psalms were also important to the desert mothers and fathers of the fourth through sixth centuries. Without them, they believed, "we would often be at a loss for words in prayer."[136] It is true that the Psalms have provided a language for conversation with God that pervades our imagining, our hymnody, and even our ways of addressing God and one another in the church. We tend not to notice this language only because its influence is so pervasive.

To pray the Psalms is to enter into a practice of forming the self before God. Consider these phrases: "O Lord, our Sovereign, how majestic is thy name in all the earth!" (Ps. 8:1). Or, "I love you, O Lord, my strength. The Lord is my rock, my fortress, and my deliverer, my God, my rock in whom I take refuge, my shield, and the horn of my salvation, my stronghold" (Ps. 18:1–2). In each case, these Psalms provide a language for naming God, and at the same time they insert those who pray these words into a grammar for praising God. Consequently, to address God through the Psalms is to be invited to practice gratitude before God, for it is only natural for us to praise what we delight in and for that praise to overflow into thanksgiving. Put simply, one formative effect of praying the Psalms is to teach us how to be grateful people.

Another way of describing this process is to suggest that praying the Psalms assists with the formation of "affections" in the hearts of believers. Affections are deep and enduring dispositions, "habits of the heart," inclusive of emotions but not wholly dependent on short-lived momentary feelings. Take gratitude, for example. While it is unrealistic to imagine that Mother Teresa bounced out of bed each morning feeling all perky and excited at the prospect of walking next door to love lepers, on a deep dispositional level, her ministry depended upon her cultivation of the affection of gratitude — an enduring heartfelt sense that her days on this earth were daily gifts from God and her ministry a grateful response to these gifts. No doubt, praying the Psalms was central to forming that affection within her, along with its ally, hope.

---

136. Roberta Bondi, *To Pray and to Love: Conversations on Prayer with the Early Church* (Minneapolis: Fortress, 1991), 50.

Christian holy men and women have long testified that praying the Psalms offers this kind of schooling for their hearts, one that shapes their capacities to receive each day with gratitude and hope. At the same time, as even casual readers of the Psalms quickly notice, these prayers are hardly sugar-coated. "You have made us like sheep for the slaughter, and have scattered us among the nations," the writer of Psalm 44 complains bitterly to God. It is true. In addition to ascending to the heights of praise and adoration, the Psalms regularly express the depths of human despair, frustration, anger, and lust for vengeance against enemies. Some interpreters of the Psalms suggest that these "enemies" are actually sinful passions (the opposite of affections) that reside within all human beings. Such a claim is most likely historically false, yet theologically and psychologically justified. Whether or not we have experienced the exact forms of oppression the Psalmist bewails, all of us do at times feel bitterness or despair because the world seemingly is lined up against us while God is nowhere to be found. Thus, to pray the Psalms is also to be invited to name honestly the struggles of being human and remaining faithful. Even so, whatever the doubt or anger expressed in an individual Psalm, the overall tenor of the Psalter is faithfulness. Discovering this to be the case requires regular and repeated praying of the Psalms, however, as the daily offices prescribe.

Augustine famously said that the person who sings "prays twice."[137] He was simply pointing out what we already know, at least intuitively. Music can add to the prayerfulness of our prayers. That is why we so often find the Psalms put to music and ourselves singing them. Psalms regularly appear in the church's musical resources as hymns, choir anthems, and praise songs. A distinctive musical form that fits the Psalms exceedingly well is chanting. We were surprised to discover how readily students at the youth academy took to this practice. In our case, we use a denominational hymnal that "points" the Psalm texts. The community learns to sing at a constant pitch through a line of a Psalm until arriving at a "point" or dot above a word that signals a rise

---

137. Augustine wrote of the virtues of song in his *Commentary on Psalm 73*. His words have been condensed to this often-used phrase.

or descent in pitch. Though it may sound complicated in description, it is really quite simple in practice. Agreeing with Augustine, students claim that singing the Psalms helps them to better pray them.

Of course, in addition to prayerful readings and singings of the scriptures, including the Psalms, the liturgies of morning and evening prayer prescribe the praying of prayers. Chief among these is the Lord's Prayer. Thousands of commentaries tout the significance of the Lord's Prayer for Christian life.[138] I cannot do it justice in a sentence or two. I simply note that its significance begins with the fact that it is the prayer Jesus gives his disciples to pray. In addition, its contents set the standard for all subsequent Christian prayer. It includes doxology ("hallowed be thy name"), intercession and petition to God for the sake of the world ("thy kingdom come"), confession of and repentance from sin ("forgive us"), and concludes with more doxology ("for thine is the kingdom, the power, and the glory"). As with praying the Psalms, when young Christians join in this prayer they engage in a practice shared with every Christian in every era of the church. They also join with the unending prayer of Christ and all the saints for the consummation of God's Reign.

Another prayer form common to the daily offices is variously called the "prayers of the people" or "prayers of intercession." Typically these prayers offer a bidding: "Let us pray for those who are troubled," for example, with the opportunity for the community to offer intercessions — voiced or silent — in response. Sometimes the prayer biddings begin with those closest to us then gradually expand our attention to the wider community we live in and eventually to the entire world. At other times the biddings begin globally and move to our local situations. Besides the obvious — we pray for *God's* grace, peace, healing, or transformation for specific persons or situations in the world — these prayers have a way of focusing and broadening *our* attention. One summer an adult leader at the youth academy had just returned from Uganda. Each day at morning prayer he prayed

---

138. Two recommended commentaries are Roberta C. Bondi, *A Place to Pray: Reflections on the Lord's Prayer* (Nashville: Abingdon, 1998) and William H. Willimon and Stanley Hauerwas with Scott C. Saye, *Lord, Teach Us: The Lord's Prayer and the Christian Life* (Nashville: Abingdon, 1996).

aloud for the church of northern Uganda and its people. Eventually students and other adults asked him about it. He reported what he had seen: religious conflict and persecution, work toward reconciliation, great suffering, and also heroic faithfulness. His simple gesture of prayerful intercession formed our community into a heightened awareness of God's saving action in the world.

Prayer and the vital experience of God's presence

Prayerfully reading the scriptures, keeping silence, praying or singing the Psalms, reciting the Lord's Prayer, joining in the prayers of the people, keeping watch for the sun and the Son, or lighting the evening lamp that casts out all darkness — these are some but not all of the practices that constitute the prayerful patterning of time that we call morning or evening prayer. As with each of the holy things of the *ordo*, the prayerful patterning of time may be trusted to bring worshipers into the loving presence of God. Prayer, after all, is straightforwardly intended to foster this communion. But what has it to do with religious experience, especially the present-day religious experiences of youth?

Experience itself is a norm for authenticity with youth these days; in fact, the more powerful the experience, the more likely it is to be considered authentic. This is the premise underlying every Mountain Dew ad ever produced. Not surprisingly, the maxim "experience equals authenticity" has found its way into youth ministry. It underwrites skiing, day trips to Wally World, white-water rafting, all night lock-ins, fun skits, and silly games. It also influences attitudes toward prayer. The prayer that is youth worship "pops" with amped musical instruments, razzle-dazzle staging and lighting effects, professional video and more, all intended to ensure that youth experience powerfully the presence of God.

In addition, in the explicitly prayerful moments of youth worship and youth ministry, I've also become intrigued with the repeated use of the word "just" in relation to religious experience. Here is an example: "We just thank you, Lord, that you are just such an awesome

God and we just want to praise your holy name...." "Just" functions in at least three ways in contemporary prayer. First, it conveys the pray-ers' appropriate humility before a God who is indeed awesome and praiseworthy. Second, "just" seems intended to intensify the other words of the prayer and, therefore, to heighten the experience of God for those who enter into that prayer. Despite the tendencies of some (my old less-redeemed self included) to stereotype pray-ers of the J word, this intent (if I read it correctly) is laudable. It shares the same intent with the stylized language of the Psalms. Youth need to know it is God they're talking to! Third, praying with "just" also signals implicitly that this prayer is an extemporaneous one, prompted in the moment by the Spirit in order to lift up the specific joys, needs, or concerns of this specific gathering of people. Aside from the fact that extemporaneous prayers often sound oddly similar to one another, I find much to commend them. Those willing to offer a people's joys and sufferings prayerfully before God at a moment's notice are wonderful gifts to their communities.

The question remains, however, whether the presence of God depends upon a particular kind of heightened or intensified religious experience. Present youth ministry practice suggests the answer is "yes." Many successful youth ministries feel resoundingly upbeat, fast-paced, energetic, and fun. The prayer that is youth worship and the prayers contained in that worship echo this aesthetic. They are self-consciously styled as hip alternatives to the stodgy church of generations past. Teens are encouraged to discover just how great following Jesus can be.[139] Tacitly, these ingredients suggest that authentic encounter with God is associated with or even requires a certain kind of experiential aesthetic. I have no deep investment in arguing against the claim that God may be encountered through cutting-edge means often associated with youth culture. Cultural innovation on the part of youth is one source of their prophetic ministry. I do protest, however, the assumption that authentic encounter with God is available only or exclusively through innovation aimed

---

139. See Chanon Ross, "Jesus Isn't Cool: Challenging Youth Ministry," *Christian Century*, September 6, 2005, 22.

at ever-heightened experience. I am suspicious, first, because experiential buzz is exactly what the marketplace is interested in selling at present, and second, because the content of the church's tradition points to a much wider experiential range, including, paradoxically, the absence of experience as linked to God's presence.

Consider the present-day criticism of "rote prayers," one often articulated by well-intended youth workers. The argument goes like this: Rote prayers (those printed in books or otherwise uttered to the heavens at least once prior) are bad. They are not sufficiently innovative, imaginative, or attentive to the present situation. They lack the "pop" youth require. Worse, they turn their pray-ers into mindless legalists who fail to attend to the immediacies of the Spirit's present promptings. Those who pray rote prayers come to rely on a table of contents more than the whisperings of the Spirit in their hearts. Worse still, they are boring. Since they are not the pray-ers' own language, they fail to capture their interest; therefore, they do not meet the requirement for heightened religious experience assumed to be essential for encountering God's presence.

Since much of what I advocate teaching youth to pray may be construed as "rote," I have an obvious stake in countering this argument. More than simply rescuing prayer books, however, I wish to challenge the too-narrow views of religious experience underlying this account. We simply cannot settle any longer for the therapeutic assumption that if it feels good for teens then it must be God. It is far better for youth to learn how God may be present to and therefore discerned through the breadth of their experience and not exclusively within its intensified expressions.

Predictably, I look to the church's prayer tradition for assistance. We need to travel no further than the Psalter to notice that feeling good all the time is not the aim of every Psalm. As often as they declare praise and thanksgiving, they also evince the psalmist's anger and frustration with God. At times, he or she even accuses God of taking time off, or worse, of forgetting to be God! This is to say that the Psalmist's prayers, instead of assuming God's comfortable loving presence, sometimes bewail God's apparent absence. Put differently, to pray these prayers is to learn to express a profound honesty about the struggle to remain faithful in a world full of suffering and trial. Conversely, *not* to pray and be formed by these prayers is to risk defaulting to a sugar-coated spirituality incapable of coming to terms with hardship. Praying the prayers of the tradition provides one means to form youth into broader and deeper awareness of the breadth of religious experience. God may be experienced in times of desert trial as readily as in times of abundance.

The related question of boredom also deserves attention. Youth workers fear boring their youth more than they fear the Last Judgment. And there's no denying that daily prayer, as with any regular practice, can become routine and, yes, even boring. Instead of adopting knee-jerk anti-boredom campaigns, however, I suggest we ponder the mysteries behind our teens' and our own boredom.

First, boredom with prayer or any spiritual practice may arise when expectations for close spiritual encounters of the upbeat kind are not met. These expectations are sinful and unrealistic, imbibed as they are from a culture that markets feeling happy as its principal end. Limiting the experience of God to these sorts of experiences also fails to open youth to the myriad and often surprising other dimensions of God's presence.

Second, we tend to associate boredom with the lack of progress, including the lack of spiritual progress. This assumption fails to notice, first, that God may work in us even when we cannot sense this grace-filled activity, and second, that prayerful discipline, though attended by grace, is also a form of *work,* as opposed to restful bliss. A story from the monastic tradition illustrates these claims. A young monk complains to his superior, "I sit in my cell [a tiny space sometimes hewn out of the side of a mountain] all day praying the Psalms and weaving my ropes [his source of income], and still I make no progress." Replies the old man, "Go, sit in your cell, and your cell will teach you everything."[140]

On the face of it, it is difficult to conceive of a less helpful response. Consider the youth's point of view. His deep faith and idealism likely

---

140. *The Sayings of the Desert Fathers: The Alphabetical Collection,* trans. Benedicta Ward, SLG (Kalamazoo: Cistercian, 1975), 139.

propelled him away from home and into this desert community. Expecting enlightenment ecstasies, he found instead relentless, unceasing boredom — praying and weaving on the floor of a bare cell from dawn to dusk, day after day. As he grows ever more restless, the old demons from home — lust and impatience to name two candidates — find him out. In desperation, he seeks the old man's counsel only to be sent right back to the place he most desires to escape. Hardly the most pastoral of interventions!

Yet the old man speaks wisely. Perhaps our fear of boredom masks a deeper fear, that of having to confront ourselves and our finitude honestly while in God's presence. Sometimes boredom becomes the excuse for our own unwillingness to do this work. It shields us from deeper pain. But the wise monk of the story trusts that God most desires to heal those places of deep internal suffering. Facing down the boredom is risky and difficult. It exposes our struggle and perhaps our sin. But to risk this prayerful work is to be met by grace.

Youth often express such boredom with prayer and liturgies of prayer through the phrase "I didn't get anything out of it." Again, this phrase reflects the expectation of a certain form of heightened religious experience as the exclusive means for encountering God's presence. It also implies that heightened experience itself is the primary goal of prayer. Further, it betrays a spirituality infected by therapy, since the self and not God is at the center of concern. But, as Roberta Bondi notes, "To love is the final goal of the life of prayer, and loving and learning how to love are the daily pleasure of prayer."[141] Bondi wisely sets things in their proper order. Prayer is directed to forming persons for love of God and neighbor and not merely to receiving that peaceful easy feeling from God. Thus, she is right to ask, "How can we love God if we only approach God [through prayer] in terms of what God can or will give us?"[142]

Love is another example of a deep disposition, an affection of Christian character, formed by grace over time in the heart of the believer. It does not exclude palpable experience of God's presence

---

141. Bondi, *To Pray and to Love*, 28.
142. Ibid., 54.

but is not entirely dependent upon it either. Since love is formed over time, over a lifetime in fact, it invites and requires believers to cultivate a lifetime of prayerful discipline.

Bondi offers a further wonderful analogy that speaks to a broadened range of encounter with God through prayer. Likening the relationship with God to marriage, she contrasts the intensely experienced love of newlyweds to the love shared in the "precious ordinary time" of long-term marriages. She suggests that love of God cultivated through prayer may undergo a similar transformation over time. In other words, not every occasion for prayer requires the fireworks of a first or second honeymoon. Indeed, such an expectation is unrealistic. "Ordinary" prayer on "ordinary" days offered out of "ordinary" habit may yet cause us to love God and neighbor more deeply, especially if, as we have seen, God is the giver and sanctifier of this "ordinary" time.

In summary, the church has consistently patterned time and the life of its members through prayer. It has regarded prayer as a trustworthy means to enter into God's presence and to be formed over time in God's love. It has resisted, however, requiring a certain kind of heightened religious experience as proof of authentic prayer or authentic encounter. Indeed, demanding that those who pray feel a certain way or experience something that they ordinarily do not experience opposes the fundamental notion that the purpose of prayer is to teach love for God and neighbor. Such a view is also contrary to the prayerful resources of the tradition that seem to invite all sorts of experience and even emptiness into the context of prayer.

I've traveled down this winding road partly out of need to say more about the relationship of religious experience to the presence of God and partly out of pastoral concern for youth. In both cases, I am trying to walk a fine line. While I want to emphasize how important it is for youth to encounter God's living presence in order to bring about their own formation and transformation — and the importance of the holy things of the *ordo* to help those encounters — I want to resist conceiving these encounters too narrowly, as if they required some extraordinary spiritual aesthetic. "Rote" prayers offered at "ordinary" times offer the means to show youth how God may be present to them in ways and at times that they may otherwise fail to notice or expect.

Members of a youth group once described how much they enjoyed an annual youth gathering sponsored by their denomination in the fall of each year. "We always get real close, and then we cry," they reported. I have no doubt that their weekend retreat offered an extraordinary loving encounter with God and each other. But the other 363 days are equally gifted and equally sanctified. Failing to form youth into this awareness risks turning them into "atheists of the ordinary." One remedy is teaching them to attend to the blessing and the struggle of faithfulness in the everyday through the rhythm (dare I say "routine"?) of daily prayer. The doxology, blessing, lament, and beseeching contained in the prayers of the tradition attend honestly to the suffering and the hope that characterize daily human life before God.

Prayer, community, and the practice of youth ministry

Most youth regard personal prayer as the norm, and communal prayer as the exception. This is precisely backwards. Private prayer makes sense only as it is understood to be joining with Christ's unending prayer through the church. Private prayer properly takes its cue from the corporate prayer that is the liturgy. Aside from the theology, corporate prayer simply makes more sense for remediating youthful lives of prayer. Youth who do not pray or do not know how to pray need to learn in community from those who do. In addition, as athletes teach us, it is easier to maintain discipline by working out together than alone.

Since its inception, the days of the youth academy have been bookended by morning and evening prayer. Communal prayer is the first practice of the day and the last practice before bed. Morning and evening prayer contain the prayerful practices described in this chapter: prayerful litanies, prayerful reading of scripture, silence, singing of Psalms, intercessions, the Lord's Prayer, and more. Initially,

daily prayers are led by adults, but leadership is shared ever more
frequently with students as the academy progresses.

Some community members react strongly — both positively and
negatively — to their first encounters with daily prayer. To some it
feels intuitively "right"; to others it could not be more foreign. We
are together long enough, two weeks, for these extremes of opinion
to moderate. Some who are initially enthused find themselves coming to terms with the routine and repetition of daily prayers. Many
who react negatively at first come around later. This is evidenced by
audibly heightened participation. Psalms are sung with more gusto,
the voiced prayers of intercession grow in number and length, and
students ask to take leadership roles. Heightened participation may
be a function of growing familiarity. In other words, participants are
being formed through this daily practice. In their evaluations, many
also speak to the fittingness of beginning and concluding every day
focused upon God. Using my own language, I would say that these
persons are assisted through the prayerful patterning of time to recognize the giftedness of time and the goodness of time's creator. In
the interest of "fair and balanced" reporting, I have to add that some
participants confess their struggles with sleepiness, especially during
morning prayer. They plead for more peppiness or a later hour. Their
evaluations have led to a later start time for the day. A few report,
"I didn't get anything out of it." Student and adult graduates of the
youth academy report that they are far more likely to practice morning or evening prayer and to use some of the prayer forms they learned
than they were prior to coming to the youth academy.

Implications for congregational prayer practices with youth

What do our own practices and findings mean for the practice of
youth ministry in churches? One of the abiding insights of Kenda
Dean and Ron Foster's *The Godbearing Life* is that youth ministry,
rather than being conceived as something done to teens, is best understood as inviting youth into the living of Christian life together with

adult companions.[143] In this case, it means that in addition to praying for youth and exhorting youth to pray, youth ministers will teach them how to pray and pray with them. The youth academy teaches prayer through the practice of the liturgy, including its gatherings for morning and evening prayer. We are blessed with exemplary practitioners, persons whose lives witness to Christian formation through a lifetime of prayer. The academy adds to the teaching of prayer the reflective theological piece: an appreciation for how prayer is deep participation in the church's liturgical patterning of time, how all of Christian life may be construed as prayerful, why it is valuable to learn to pray the prayers of the tradition, how these prayers may expand our sense of what constitutes religious experience, and that the aim of prayer is formation of attentiveness to God along with such Christian affections as gratitude, hope, and love. None of this is esoteric spiritual mystery available only to the elect. Further, just as with our approach to the other holy things, we follow the approach of preparation, participation, and reflection around the prayerful patterning of time.

Local communities may readily adapt some of these strategies to their own situations. But more than excellent strategies, such formation will most of all require leaders' commitments to slowing down sufficiently themselves to receive the gift of time. That way we may also hope to cultivate the patience to wait for God to do God's grace-filled formative work in youth — all in God's good time.

---

143. Kenda Creasy Dean and Ron Foster, *The Godbearing Life: The Art of Soul Tending for Youth Ministry* (Nashville: Upper Room Books, 1998).

Seven

Ordo-*nary practice:*
Youth living liturgically in the world

So far this book has advanced several claims. First, I have argued that since corporate worship is the orienting center of faithful Christian life, worship grounded in book, bath, table, and time offers youth reliable encounters with God's presence, keys to God's identity, and opportunities to practice Christian vocation before God and for the world. Put simply, youth who worship God through holy things may also expect themselves to be formed through grace and, perhaps, transformed through this worship.

One further dimension of this formation is the capacity for framing a liturgical vision of life in the world. Over time, youth formed through the *ordo* may come to imagine and interpret their lives in light of the manifold ways holy things "speak" Jesus Christ for them and for the world. Encounters with the font speak brotherhood and sisterhood in the one Body, sharing at table proclaims enough for all, and timely rest from labor enacts dependence upon God over self-idolatry.

Such vision is never merely theoretical ("I understand the meaning of baptism now") or merely practical ("See how ably I read the scriptures in the church"). Instead, liturgical vision consists of imagination born out of practice that consequently deepens practice — of liturgy and of living liturgically beyond the sanctuary walls. An example may assist in clarifying my meaning. After a youth academy experience that included two weeks of engaging in ritual around the font, one DYA alumna testified that she was better able to cope with her father's life-threatening illness in light of his and her own prior baptismal "deaths with Christ." She also suggested that the font should be front and center at funerals. Such insight exemplifies a liturgical vision of life. It demonstrates this student's deep insight into baptismal theology, her appropriation of that insight in light of her family's current suffering, and her ability even to offer sage advice for future congregational liturgical practice. Creating the conditions for fostering such liturgical vision in youth requires both strong practice of the *ordo*, where holy things are graciously and gratefully enacted, and also sustained opportunities for theological teaching and reflection on them in light of youths' lives.

Second, I have argued that the holy things of the *ordo* exist in ecological relationship with one another. The *ordo* as ecology suggests that holy things practiced together draw worshipers into an interpretive web of liturgical life. Bath, book, table, and time are "thickened" through this relationship and offer one another interpretive counterpoint. In addition, following Gordon Lathrop, I think that sometimes the interdependence of holy things does more than thicken or interpret; it "breaks" these things so that they are made to speak or enact something entirely new, a revelatory possibility not previously grasped.[144] In this chapter, for example, I attempt to show how holy things are presently being broken together and apart to offer a new vision and response to our planet's ecological crisis. But the inverse must also be acknowledged. If interdependent elements in an ecology sustain and are sustained by that ecology, then removal of one or more of those elements inevitably weakens or destroys the whole. For this reason, I have also attempted to show how forgetfulness about the *ordo* as ecology presently threatens youthful corporate and personal Christian identity. If youth do not know who they are as Christians or what Christian life is, it may be because holy things are endangered species in many congregations' worship. Or it may be that youth ministry itself is not conceived as situated within this interdependent ecology and is therefore free to absent itself from the *ordo*. Such freedom is illusory because book, bath, table, and time are as critical to Christian life as food, drink, story, and life constrained by earthly temporal rhythms are to human life. The church speaks

---

144. Lathrop, *Holy Things*.

Jesus Christ through ordinary holy things. I have, therefore, consistently sought to demonstrate how holy things conceived ecologically may strengthen and interpret one another while simultaneously creating the conditions for youth's faithful practice of them and faithful imagination by way of them.

After all this, some readers may still find themselves asking with Peggy Lee, "Is that all there is?" Is my proposal entirely about teaching congregations to worship better? Isn't there more to Christian life than worship? Or, hasn't this account so far focused on liturgy as forming persons into awareness of God's presence and knowledge of God's storied identity to the detriment of practicing vocation before God and for the world?

The answer depends on how you define "worship" and also "vocation." Because definitions of *ordo* range from the very pragmatic (*ordo* as liturgical "how-to" manual), to the partly pragmatic, partly visionary (*ordo* as presenting a liturgical pattern that funds a broader pattern of ecclesial life), to the cosmic (the church at worship as the sacramental sign and vehicle of God's redemption and sanctification of the world), I find each of these renderings helpful. With respect to vocation, clearly the church's offering of itself to God through worship, and God's gift of the church as sacrament of life for the world through Jesus Christ, are consistent with the primary calling to love God and neighbor. For some, including myself, however, this cosmic account may nonetheless risk allowing an overly spiritualized faith. It may seem to imply that there is no need to actually love one's neighbor through concrete practices of care and compassion beyond the sanctuary, for example.

I find it helpful to conceive of the liturgy of the *ordo* as a generative source for and an overlapping practice with a wider liturgy of living beyond the sanctuary. When imaginatively and ecologically engaged by way of practical liturgical wisdom, the *ordo*'s holy things may inform what I playfully call "*ordo*-nary" practices of Christian life. For example, hospitality is essential to the practice of the *ordo*; the hospitality that the *ordo* offers is real — as, for example, in welcoming persons to Christ's table — yet the liturgical practice of hospitality does not exhaust the church's gift and responsibility for welcoming others in the name of Jesus Christ. Similarly, Christian liturgy requires the proper stewardship of holy mysteries. This stewardship is real, yet the practice of Christian stewardship extends outward from the worshiping community to the whole of creation. Equally important from the standpoint of this chapter, these practices have everything to do with the concrete embodiment and enactment of Christian vocation before God and for the world.

The two practices to be explored here are housekeeping and gardening. Choosing practices at once ordinary and metaphoric allows us to align them conceptually and imaginatively with bathing, eating, storytelling, and timekeeping. Just as the church's practices of the *ordo*'s holy things depend in part on analogous practices of ordinary life for their revelatory and formative power, so do church practices that extend beyond the sanctuary. The church has no monopoly on the practices basic to sustaining human life or promoting human flourishing. Its inspiration and gift to the world is its practice of these things ecologically and in light of its story of salvation. Yet the church has often forgotten that its practices also belong, at least in part, to the world. Fortunately, the recovery of this insight has helped the church to see again that baptism is far more a bath than a few drops and that Eucharist is intended as a feast, not a strange snack.

Housekeeping and gardening also partake of this dialectic of inspiration. They are at root ordinary human practices, but, practiced by Christians, they may also enact and embody Christian story, Christian vocation, and God's Reign. But these ordinary practices also find themselves in creative association with the holy things of the *ordo*. Hospitality, one specific form of Christian housekeeping, looks both to the world of ordinary human practice and to the *ordo*, especially its book and its table, for the creative "thickening" in the recipe of faithful practice. Similarly, ecological stewardship, one specific form of Christian gardening, looks to both *ordo*, including its table of abundance and its Sabbath time of "enoughness," and also to the broader culture for inspiration. These practices participate in a three-way conversation. Practice and reflection upon housekeeping and gardening go on in mutually critical dialogue with the world's creative practices on the one hand and the church's creative practices of the *ordo* on the other. In this way, the liturgy of the church's worship engenders and informs the liturgy of the church's life before God and for the world, while the need to live faithfully before God and for the world may also mean that insights from the world may cause the church to rethink the depth and proper practices of its holy things.

Christian hospitality as a form of housekeeping and ecological stewardship as a form of gardening are not the only possible *ordo*-nary Christian practices. I could just as easily have chosen to focus upon others — forgiveness, reconciliation, caring for the body, or more.[145] But first, these are two practices that have gained real traction at DYA in light of the *ordo*, so I'm able to speak from experience, and, second, they are practices through which I am best able to demonstrate at present how the ecology of the *ordo* may extend youths' Christian vocations into the world. Third, Christian hospitality and ecological stewardship are themselves ecologically interdependent with one another. Our care for neighbors is tied up with our care for the planet. Finally, both hospitality and ecological stewardship paradoxically literalize and transform the metaphor of "ecology" as I am using it.

The chapter proceeds as follows. First, storytelling. I attempt to describe in detail how practices of hospitality and stewardship have emerged and been refined since the youth academy's inception. The story is not meant for simple application in each and every youth ministry context. There is no one-size-fits-all approach to youth ministry. Instead, it is intended to portray how youth ministry may unfold by way of imagination and discernment, including the use of liturgical vision. Next, after a thorough description of what goes on in such practices of hospitality and stewardship and why, I draw upon the theological tradition for insights into both practices. This move from practice to theory parallels our actual attempts over the years to deepen and put more flesh on our practices at DYA. We have

---

145. See Dorothy Bass, ed., *Practicing Our Faith* (San Francisco: Jossey-Bass, 1997); Dorothy Bass and Don C. Richter, eds., *Way to Live: Christian Practices for Teens* (Nashville: Upper Room Books, 1992); and Miroslav Volf and Dorothy C. Bass, eds., *Practicing Theology: Beliefs and Practices in Christian Life* (Grand Rapids: Eerdmans, 2002).

tended to practice first mostly on intuition, or maybe even inspiration, then reflect on what we have been up to in order to enliven that practice. In the process of learning from the tradition, I also hope to show better the ecological relationship and need for conversation between these *ordo*-nary practices and ordinary human practice as well as practices of holy things through the *ordo*. Attention to this ecology also helps to demonstrate how, through the *ordo*, youthful worshipers may actually keep God's house and tend God's garden.

DYA's story of hospitable housekeeping

Hospitality in measures large and small is crucial to the youth academy. It is practiced most explicitly in two forms. First, members of our community prepare meals for, and then dine with, guests and residents of various community ministries and agencies. Second, through what have come to be called "hospitality meals," students and adults in our community learn to receive the hospitality offered by outsiders with gratitude and thanks.

The first form of practicing hospitality is likely a familiar one to youth workers. The community is divided into teams based on the number of people required for different forms of ministry in the community. Hospitality ministries regularly include cleaning house, preparing a meal for, and dining with, guests of the Ronald Mc-Donald House, the community homeless shelter, and a residential HIV/AIDS community, with different teams serving in different settings. Though schedules do not always allow for DYA participants to dine with the persons for whom they have prepared meals, we try our best to make this happen.

The second practice of hospitality, the "hospitality meals," works as follows. Members of the academy community gather for lunch with youth and adults from an area congregation which has spent the morning preparing the meal in exchange for a small youth ministry grant to their community. A litany of gathering is spoken and grace is offered. Members of each group — academy and congregation — then sit down at tables together. The tables are set with real cloths, china, tableware, and glasses made out of glass. No plastic or Styrofoam allowed! Often they are decorated with fresh local flowers. Food is served family style at the tables: people pass bowls and platters around, serving one another in the process. Hospitality meals feature fresh, healthy foods with plenty of seconds and dessert to boot. Each table uses "conversation starters," sets of questions that help strangers introduce themselves to one another and begin to become acquainted. Examples include, "What is your favorite holiday?" or "Describe an interesting place you've visited recently." Mostly, however, we depend on the simple dynamics of sharing food at table in community to turn strangers into friends. Diners are encouraged to relax and linger over their food. A full hour is devoted to the meal. Toward the end of the hour, members of the community that prepared the meal are introduced to the entire DYA community. They describe their local church and their youth ministry. They also share what they plan to do with the small ministry grant they receive for preparing the meal.

Even this bare-bones description should make clear that our shared hospitality meals hardly represent cutting-edge youth ministry innovation. Instead, they are an attempt to retrieve well-worn practices of welcoming strangers by breaking bread together. That this practice may seem unusual is testimony to North America's present forgetfulness, not to DYA's innovation.

Some things we've learned along the way through our table hospitality

The youth academy leadership is committed to the same reflective practice that we demand from students and staff. Thus, our understanding and practice of hospitality has deepened and, we think, improved over the years. Below I offer a collection of unsystematic insights derived from six years of reflective practice.

With respect to offering hospitality in area community ministries, we have learned the importance of our community members not only preparing meals but also eating together with those being served.

We do so in an attempt to level the hierarchy that even "servant" ministry may create. If I prepare a meal for a needy neighbor then leave without meeting her, I imagine that I am the sole giver of gifts. If, however, I sit down with that neighbor at table, I am invited to recognize in that neighbor the image of God and the gifts she offers me with her presence, wisdom, or humor. Thus, this neighbor may deepen my own understanding and love for God in part by chastening my unreflective presumption of superiority. Actually sitting down with others may be difficult at first. Christine Pohl points out, "We are familiar with roles as helpers but are less certain about being equals eating together."[146] Gently (we hope) forcing the issue with our students and staff, combined with reflective conversation before and after, may help ease youth's uncertainty. It may also become a generative context for cultivating virtues of compassion and courage.

With respect to the intercommunal "hospitality meals," I should note, first, that they were born out of necessity as much as any inspired vision. In the summer, Duke food services feeds hundreds of teen campers every day. Wrestlers, soccer players, basketball players, golfers, and students attending Duke's Talent Identification Program all file through one central dining hall three times daily. The sheer number of campers places a premium on speed and efficiency. Our community of nearly one hundred is allotted thirty minutes to pass through the food line, sit down and eat, then clear out to make room for the next group. The hall itself is cramped and loud. Even without a full-blown vision of a hospitable alternative, we recognized that a Christian community needed to eat together differently. This recognition also testified to our awareness that the whole life of a faith community is formative, even if only implicitly so.

Out of this context, the vision for hospitality meals was born. But this vision immediately bumped up against other institutional realities. What spaces were available for these meals? Who would prepare

---

146. Christine Pohl, *Making Room: Recovering Hospitality as a Christian Tradition* (Grand Rapids: Eerdmans, 1999), 74.

the meals and where would they be prepared? How would we satisfy the university's strict catering requirements? Where would we find tables, real dishes, and the like? Our attempts to answer these questions revealed that the university was configured in such a way that it actively militated against hospitality as a practice of human flourishing. (My experience with numerous Christian camps and retreat centers is similar.) At least in terms of Christian meal sharing, Duke was not a hospitable place. The solution was to take hospitality meals off campus to a welcoming local congregation that understood our vision and "made room" for us by offering the use of their fellowship hall, kitchen, and the gifts of their staff. These gifts came at no small cost to their human and monetary resources.

Second, we learned that with respect to hospitality meals, the phrase "if you build it, they will come" is only partly true. We had begun to conceive of hospitality as a way of welcoming strangers in the spirit of Christ's own welcome of outsiders into God's household. We intuited that welcome could be communicated through shared meals. Providing the context for hospitality, however, is a necessary but not sufficient condition for actually giving or receiving it. For instance, we noticed early on that, despite our exhortations to the contrary, students and staff tended to sit down to eat with persons they knew rather than with strangers. Similarly, our hosts or guests from local churches tended to hide in the kitchen making busy with dirty pots rather than sitting down to eat together with *their* guests or hosts. The solution was to assign and then enforce seating by number. We also noticed that many members of our community simply did not know the basics of hospitable table etiquette. Though at first tempted to declare them all boors, we came to understand that these skills are rare precisely because family meals where such skills are learned are increasingly rare. Through role-playing and demonstration we set out to teach "good table manners." This teaching is offered in good humor, but we nonetheless instruct persons in the art of holding dishes for others, passing dishes on, in complimenting the hosts, in using napkins, in waiting for all to be served before beginning one's own meal, and so on. We also practice the art of table conversation. Our community learns about and practices skills for self-introductions, asking hospitable questions, and listening. These little practices comprise the wider practice of offering and receiving table hospitality in our culture.

As I will suggest in more detail below, Christian hospitality operates from the premise that it is best exemplified when shared between strangers. Thus DYA strives to share meals with persons from a wide variety of faith communities. These communities represent many ethnicities. Their distinctive traditions and contexts also tend to engage them in distinctive or creative ministries. A Mennonite community shared its commitment to simple living along with food from its members' gardens. A Hispanic community described its ministries with new immigrants and introduced our students and staff to authentic Latin food. A United Methodist community with a Russian-speaking youth group shared its story of how a mission trip to Eastern Europe turned into an ongoing ministry sheltering children from the radioactive fallout of the Chernobyl nuclear reactor by opening their homes to them each summer.

At least two outcomes are drawn from these hospitality meals. First, DYA community members are repeatedly exposed to and pressed to engage with strangers. Judging by increasingly comfortable energy levels at tables, most members of the community experience strangers as less strange over the course of two weeks. Said one student, "I came to see our oneness." Second, some persons also discover that receiving the stranger's gift of hospitality is precisely tied to welcoming her or his "strangeness." Structured encounters with persons of various ethnicities bearing foods representative of their own tables and with fascinating church stories make possible deeper understanding and practice of "one faith, one Lord, one baptism." It becomes possible to celebrate difference in the unity of Christ. Thus, community members may learn that receiving the fullness of God's abundant life requires, in part, learning to value and receive what is most distinctive about the other. These lessons may be learned only through practiced hospitable engagement with other human beings.

DYA *tending the garden*

In addition to housekeeping, a second constellation of practices in
DYA's ecology may be described as tending or stewarding the earthly
garden. These practices include gleaning of crops on commercial
farms and the recently added opportunity to labor in a nearby church/
community vegetable garden.

Gleaning with Ruth

The practice of gleaning is rooted in the scriptures.[147] Ruth and her
mother-in-law, Naomi, ward off starvation because Boaz obeys the
Levitical injunction not to harvest a small percentage of his crop,
thereby making available food for the poor to glean for themselves.[148]
In the present day, DYA gleans through the Society of St. Andrew, a
ministry devoted to delivering excess agricultural produce that otherwise might go to waste to hungry or food-insecure individuals and
families. Typically, the academy community travels on a summer
Saturday to an area farm and harvests whatever is in season and
whatever a generous farmer has offered to the cause. In past years
we have harvested tons of cantaloupes, bushels of blueberries, and
truckloads of collard greens.

Most of our students and adults have never been on a farm before, much less harvested from one. The sights, the smells, the feel
of earth and vegetation are completely new to them. Other than
those few who live on farms, neither have community members ever
really engaged in significant amounts of manual labor. Most are unaccustomed to lifting loads, sweating, getting dirty, or smelling like
overripe produce. Yet, after some initial stumbling and grumbling,
folks start to get into a rhythm of things and even begin to enjoy themselves! They chat and joke as they work through the field, they turn
reverent Taizé chants into ribald or just plain silly harvest songs,[149]

---

147. Ruth 2:2–23, among others.
148. The injunction to leave a portion of the field unharvested is found in Leviticus
19:9 and 23:22, as well as Deuteronomy 24:21.
149. Example: "Po-ta-to in the bag, po-ta-to in the bag, fill it, knot it, al-le-lu-
ia . . . "; lyrics by Philip Mumford, Durham, NC, 2003. Sung to the tune of "Laudate
Dominum" (J. Berthier, . . . Ateliers et Presses de Taizé, F-71250 Taizé Communauté).

and they laugh when they trip over rows and fall on their faces. Could it be that they are sensing something inherently natural and good about tending God's earthly garden together?

One year as we picked cantaloupe, a group of immigrant laborers harvested the field next to ours. Though they numbered less than a third of our group, by the end of the day they'd harvested a much larger quantity of melons than we. When finished, they retired to a clump of shoddy trailers clinging to the top of the hill. This juxtaposition injected an interesting counterpoint into community members' reflections on that day. How could a practice that seemed life-giving and even fun to some become otherwise for others? Gleaning always raises questions for students about the inequities and injustices built into the North American food industry. On that particular day, however, the questions were even more personal and poignant.

Tending Jeremiah's garden

The scriptures tell the story of Jerusalem's final days before its destruction and the exile of the people. In the midst of this chaos, the prophet Jeremiah, instead of inveighing further against corruption or shouting, "I told you so," decided to buy a garden (Jer. 32). Admittedly, it was a buyers' market, yet investing in real estate on the eve of exile reeks of economic folly. Jeremiah, of course, knew what he was doing. Purchasing the little farm at Anathoth was a sign of future restoration. In the darkest of days, Jeremiah was signaling that God would one day redeem God's people by returning them to this land.

This story has animated the story and the life of a little faith community in the countryside west of Durham.[150] In brief, the church's own story goes like this: A man was murdered in this quiet farming community where murder previously had been unheard of. The murder, which some believed to have been racially motivated, elevated racial tensions in the community. The church set to praying and discerning how it could best practice reconciliation in response to this crisis. Others were doing the same. Though I'm skipping details at

---

150. See Fred Bahnson, "The Salvation of the City: Community Gardens in The Great Northern Feedlot," in *Places of God: Theological Conversations with Wendell Berry*, ed. Joel Shuman (forthcoming). See also *www.anathothgarden.org*.

this point, two gestures combined to bear fruit. A wealthy African American landowner prayed about the situation, received a vision, then donated two acres of agricultural land to the mostly Caucasian church. At the same time, the church had been keeping company with the *ordo*'s lectionary which, in that season, was winding through the sections of Jeremiah that chronicled his purchase of the garden at Anathoth as a sign of God's promised reconciliation. Inspired by the scripture and the gift, the church decided to turn this land into a garden, a sign to its own community of God's continuing promise of reconciliation.

The first gift members of DYA receive when they travel to work in this garden is the hearing of this remarkable tale. It testifies eloquently to Christian communal life shaped through participation in the *ordo* while simultaneously keeping eyes wide open to the realities of life beyond the walls of the sanctuary. Indeed, it demonstrates beautifully how a church's ministry grows out of this matrix of liturgical imagination employed in response to the world's sufferings.

DYA guest laborers also receive informal teaching on the ecology of farming. They learn that the garden uses only organic materials for fertilizing and hand tools for cultivating, and that garden members work together cooperatively in the garden. Anyone, not just church members, may become a member of the garden. Members agree to work several hours a month in exchange for sharing in the harvest. On a given Saturday, the garden welcomes all kinds of people — rich, poor, male, female, Christian and not — who work together weeding, picking, building up beds, turning soil, and whatever else needs doing. Not unlike with our own experiences of gleaning, these gardeners find themselves talking, laughing, and singing as they work. In the garden, strangers who might not normally cross paths with one another become friends. They practice hospitality, reconciliation, and ecological stewardship. Anathoth Garden is a sign of God's peace and promised restoration.

Our own students and staff discover this grace-filled dynamic as they work in the garden. After listening to the stories, they weed, transplant, and pick what's ready. They also chat, bend over, get their hands dirty, sweat, straighten up to wipe their brows and pause to admire the countryside. It is time well spent. To our great delight, members of this community and the church's youth group also graciously share with DYA in a hospitality meal. This meal features fresh vegetables from the garden in salads and casseroles and free-range poultry from members' farms. Students and staff of the DYA community take special joy in sharing in a meal that they played a small role in nurturing toward the table.

Theologies of housekeeping, garden tending, and the interrelationship of practices

The serendipity of DYA's relationship with Anathoth Garden and sharing at table with youth and adults from its sponsoring church has engendered new ways of conceiving our practices. It has helped us to better understand, for example, how Christian faith is not only metaphorically but also literally ecological. Through our practices, community members are immersed in a fertile context where they are better able to name the reciprocity between hospitable meal sharing and the appropriate stewarding of God's creation. In the paragraphs that follow, I briefly engage in further theological examination of Christian hospitality and stewardship. I flesh out these practices in light of the biblical and wider tradition and show their organic relationship with one another, including their shared participation in Christian justice. How might these practices be helpfully informed by both the *ordo* and by insights, crises, or opportunities emerging in human life today?

Hospitality

Hospitality has deep roots in biblical culture. In a region where food and water could be scarce commodities, travelers often depended for their very lives on the willingness of strangers to shelter and feed them.[151] Practices of hospitality also received theological interpre-

---

151. See Matt. 10:5ff., where Jesus sends out his disciples and tells them to take nothing with them and instead to rely upon others (and God) to provide for their needs.

tation in Israel and later in the church. Abraham and Sarah make welcome three unexpected visitors by offering to wash their feet and by preparing a feast for them. Abraham comes to recognize that he has actually encountered God through these three guests (Gen. 18:1–15). Much later, Jesus suggests that when the poor, sick, and imprisoned are made welcome, he himself is welcomed (Matt. 25:31–46). The writer of the letter to the Hebrews claims that in providing hospitality we are entertaining angels "without knowing it" (Heb. 13:2). Two points follow from these texts. First, hospitality is an expression of love to and from God. Second, hospitality is best directed toward persons on the margins of human life, because these are the persons in whom Christ dwells with deepest compassion.

Members of churches described in the New Testament displayed hospitality by regularly receiving one another as guests at communal meals. In contrast to most Roman and Greek cultural practices, Christian hospitality was notable for blending together persons of unequal social status. Rich and poor, male and female, Greek and Jew all sat at table together. Jesus' parables suggest that the best possible display of God's new Reign was this form of Christian fellowship. Traditions of offering hospitality were sustained for a time by the church's monastic tradition, but were gradually lost to the West's privatizing and individualizing tendencies. Notable exceptions include the Underground Railroad and the more recent church Sanctuary Movement.[152]

With respect to Christian justice, the practice of hospitality reclaims the significance of moral agency in relation to the articulation of moral principles. Offering a stranger food to eat and a place to stay may not exhaust Christian requirements for justice, but, as Christine Pohl puts it, "The practice of hospitality forces abstract commitments to loving the neighbor, stranger, and enemy into practical and personal expressions of respect and care for actual neighbors,

---

152. The Sanctuary Movement was an ecumenical religious and political movement among several hundred American congregations to help Central American refugees by protecting them from U.S. Immigration and Naturalization Service authorities in the 1980s.

strangers, and enemies."[153] Related to this point, Pohl quotes a Christian provider of hospitality: "Without supper, without love, without table companionship, justice can become a program that we *do* to other people."[154]

Hospitality is a practice of justice in another way, as well. As Pohl suggests, it contributes to the proper "recognition" of those dwelling on the margins of community life who would otherwise remain invisible.[155] This recognition takes at least two forms. First, youth at DYA, by sitting down together at table with persons who find themselves in need, learn that these persons also bear the image of God. John Calvin insisted that "as long as we are human creatures, we must contemplate as in a mirror our face in those who are poor, despised, exhausted, who groan under their burdens. . . . "[156] Only through encounters with human suffering may youth be prompted to respond with compassion to the needy neighbor as a person of sacred worth just like themselves. Second, practicing hospitality may elicit a different form of awareness equally important to justice. Sharing table with persons at the margins of North American life may also awaken them to the structural injustices that make persons hungry, homeless, or ill.

The ordo *and hospitality*

The churches in the New Testament recognized the organic relationship between their Eucharistic table fellowship and other practices of hospitality. As noted, one of Jesus' principal images of the Reign of God is the messianic banquet where the poor are made welcome at the master's table. Paul makes a related point, albeit negatively and in the form of a serious scolding, in his first letter to the Corinthians (1 Cor. 11:17–34). Having received word that wealthy members of

---

153. Pohl, *Making Room*, 75.

154. Ibid., 74.

155. Ibid., chapter 4.

156. John Calvin in *Corpus Reformatorum: Joannis Calvini Opera Quae Supersunt Omnia*, ed. Guilielmus Baum, Eduardus Cunitz, and Eduardux Reuss (Brunswick: C. A. Schwetschke et Filium, 1863–1897), vol. 51, column 105; quoted in John H. Leith, *John Calvin's Doctrine of the Christian Life* (Louisville: Westminster/John Knox Press, 1989), 186; quoted in Pohl, *Making Room*, 65.

the community are overindulging in food and drink and refusing to share what they have with poorer members at the parish supper, he assures them that such behavior definitely is *not* the Lord's Supper. In fact, by neglecting their poor brothers and sisters, these wealthy Corinthians are "eating and drinking judgment against themselves" (1 Cor. 11:29).

The most telling, if subtle, New Testament connections between Eucharist, justice, and hospitality are made by Luke in his account of Jesus' appearance to the disciples on the road to Emmaus (Luke 24). In this episode, after their extended conversation, the disciples invite Jesus to dine with them and spend the night. Here they are simply following customary hospitable practice of the day. In a complete reversal of convention, however, Jesus, framed in the story as the stranger who rightly merits the gift of hospitality, instead presides over the meal and makes the disciples welcome in their own home. The guest becomes the host.

Luke's theologizing through this account is paradoxical. That Jesus is regarded first as stranger strengthens Jesus' own identification with those on the margins of social life. The Gospels repeatedly place Jesus in solidarity with the social outsiders of Israel. Matthew 25 goes further in holding that the poor *are* Jesus or, at least, are linked with Jesus by more than just his advocacy for them.[157] On the other hand, Jesus' surprising assumption of the duties of host in the Emmaus story characterizes him as the consummate *insider*. This would seem to suggest that at Emmaus, not he but the disciples and, by extension, we ourselves are the true outsiders in need of Christ's graceful welcome. Only through Christ do any of us outsiders find our way into God's household and to a seat at God's banquet table. Gordon Lathrop offers this supporting insight: "At least part of me, the outsider and unbeliever, comes along with the freshest newcomer. We are beggars here together. God's grace will surprise us both. We will together be outsiders brought into Israel's promises."[158] Thus, as Lathrop notes, a dialectical tension exists in our worshiping life. If Jesus is identified

---

157. Matthew 25:40: "...Truly I tell you, just as you did it to one of the least of these who are members of my family, you did it to me."

158. Lathrop, *Holy Things*, 121.

as both outsider and insider, guest and host of our worship, including our Eucharistic meal, then our proper encounter with him involves attention to both the feast and those outsiders, including ourselves, hoping to find a seat at the table. Thus, Eucharist, by definition, is at once a practice of hospitality that requires further practices of hospitality. Jesus' identification as guest and host means that Christians will constantly be seeking to attend to his presence through the sacramental body and blood *and* to his incarnation in the person of the stranger. He welcomes us so that we may welcome him.

This form of tension, and its requirements for attention and intention, was understood and practiced by many early Christian communities. Lathrop proposes that a common practice of these communities was to distribute both food and monetary collections from the common meal and Eucharistic feast to the poor and sick.[159] Thus, the already essentially hospitable practice of Eucharist is extended beyond the liturgical gathering. Lathrop eloquently captures this movement:

> Eucharist is not an economy, but it is an economic proposal: founded upon the astonishing presence of God with the limits of human flesh, it is a sharing of food within limits, enough for everyone and for sending into the streets to the absent and the hungry, blowing a hole in our usual patterns of supply and consumption, our buffets of "all you can eat."[160]

The ordo *and ecological stewardship*

Less well understood is the relationship between Christian worship and practices of stewardship. Mostly, the church thinks first of money in relationship to stewardship. This assumption may be necessary in the North American money-based economy. By no means, however, does it exhaust the meaning of the term "stewardship." Fortunately, the growing ecological movement has prodded the church toward deepened understanding and practice of stewardship. The paragraphs

---

159. Ibid., 45–46.
160. Lathrop, *Holy Ground*, 17.

below lay out some of that growing awareness, especially insights into the relationship between *ordo* and stewardship.

Environmentalists have previously criticized the church's stance — or the absence of such — on the issue of caring for our planetary home. With some justification, they have pointed to Christian tendencies to spiritualize their faith, to construe the Reign of God in otherworldly terms, to emphasize personal salvation over communal pilgrimage, and to exercise dominance while forgetting about care. These critics find evidence to support their claims simply by pointing to the supposedly Christian West and its rapacious, industrializing practices carried out in the name of lifestyle. Clearly, the burden is on the church to demonstrate that these critics miss the mark. Demonstrating that he has comprehended this criticism, the theological ethicist Larry Rasmussen sounds this alarm:

> It's sinking in: A beautiful world is being lost, and the drumbeat is really about ourselves. We are enemies, structured enemies, massively structured enemies of much of the rest of life. Biodiversity is the name science gives a fierce "ontology of communion" and an intimacy of all life. But human and other-than-human life, invariably together, is at enmity, an enmity at the hands of those who, without wincing still dare to name themselves creation's stewards.[161]

Theological redress to this crisis and for the church's role in creating the crisis proceeds across several related fronts. First is the concern to reclaim the unqualified goodness of creation by way of reasserting the earth as *oikos*, "a vast world house."[162] Second, theologies of the human being (called "theological anthropologies") are reclaiming the essential earthly materiality of human beings, while also noting their special status and responsibility as stewards over the rest of creation. Third, one stream of the church, the Christian agrarian movement, is

---

161. Larry Rasmussen, "Eco-Justice: Church and Community Together," in *Earth Habitat: Eco-Injustice and the Church's Response*, ed. Dieter Hessel and Larry Rasmussen (Minneapolis: Fortress, 2001), 4.

162. Larry Rasmussen, *Earth Community Earth Ethics* (Maryknoll, NY: Orbis Books, 1996), 103.

attempting to practice a sustainable way of life in relation to the earth consistent with these theological insights. My own conviction is that the practice of the liturgy may also provide a generative context for earth-friendly theologies. Practicing the *ordo* in self-conscious relationship with practices of ecological stewardship may also strengthen the character and vocation of Christian youth as God's stewards.

The earth as oikos *(household)*

That God's creation is good is an undisputed truth of the Jewish and Christian traditions. Genesis 1 echoes resoundingly with the conviction that God is the creator of all and that this creation is good. Yet for a long period in history, until either the industrial revolution or the detonation of the atomic bomb over Hiroshima, depending upon whom you ask, the goodness of creation was not a pressing issue. The earth seemed a womb of limitless fertility. Less charitably, it was also considered a great big apple available for human picking. Presently, we live in an era unknown to our forebears. Not only have we discovered that the earth and its fruits are finite, we now hold the power either through sins of commission or omission to destroy it. Thus, there is a new urgency to reassert the doctrine of creation: the earth is God's, not ours; we are contingent creatures, not our own creators; and this world in which we exist as creatures is good.

Another crucial theological insight to an ecological account of creation theology is registering creation's essential interrelatedness. Says the theologian Kosuke Koyama, "The webbedness of all things is a basic image of ecology. The word 'ecology' derives from the Greek word *oikos,* house. All things in this planetary-house make good sense in their interacting and interdependent relationships."[163] Or as Rasmussen puts it, " 'Comm-unity' is nature's way. All that exists, coexists."[164]

Christian claims for Jesus as *Logos* — creative Word existent with God and as God from the very beginning — and as incarnation — this eternal Word taking on flesh and becoming part of the created order

---

163. Kosuke Koyama, "The Eucharist: Ecumenical and Ecological," *Ecumenical Review* 44 (1992): 85.
164. Rasmussen, *Earth Community,* 324.

of things — also contribute essential insights to an ecological theology of creation. As the theologian Ralph McMichael Jr. proposes, since all creation (and not merely human beings) is rightly understood as inaugurated by Jesus Christ, all creation, therefore, will find redemption in Jesus Christ. He comments further, "In the incarnation Jesus became part of the created order, and in the resurrection creation was ordered toward God as its source of redemption. In other words, God redeems creation from the inside out."[165]

The human as oikunomos (steward)

Already implicit in an ecological theology of creation are implications for a theology of the human being. Simply put, human beings are called to be stewards, caretakers of God's household and tenders of God's earthly garden. A steward is both servant and supervisor: one that "holds in trust what is of value to God, or in the divine ordering of life."[166] A steward, according to Wendell Berry, obeys "the divine mandate to use the world justly and charitably...."[167] As creatures uniquely capable of imagination, creativity, and reflection, this vocation falls to humanity as gift and responsibility.

Yet we human beings, as a result of our sinfulness, have tended to forget or reject our stewardly vocations. Instead, we have fancied ourselves as our own creators, or as standing above or over against nature and thereby validating our exploitation of creation as an object, rather than receiving creation as a gift.

Larry Rasmussen uses a poet-prophet's way with words in an effort to restore the right relationship:

"Humans," as all things of earth, are of "humus," that organic residue of roots, bone, carrion, feces, leaves, and other

---

165. Ralph N. McMichael Jr., "The Redemption of Creation: A Liturgical Theology," in *Creation and Liturgy: Studies in Honor of H. Boone Porter*, ed. Ralph N. McMichael Jr. (Washington, DC: Pastoral Press, 1993), 153.

166. Nathan Wright, "Liturgy, Stewardship, and Creation," in *Creation and Liturgy*, 191.

167. Wendell Berry, "The Gift of Good Land," in *The Art of the Commonplace: The Agrarian Essays of Wendell Berry*, ed. Norman Wirzba (Emeryville, CA: Shoemaker and Hoard, 2002), 299.

debris mixed with minerals and organized as community for life. We ought, then, to be humble and look upon ourselves with some "humor." "Humility" means never trying to outgrow our "humanity" and escape or transcend our earthiness. It means accepting ourselves for what we are — spirit-animated nature.[168]

More concretely, he says that this sort of recognition of human dependence upon creation should make clear that "justice for people and for the rest of the planet are knotted together."[169]

The practice of ecological stewardship

Wendell Berry cautions that the right theological reclamation of stewardship cannot substitute for the actual practice of stewardship. He says, " . . . stewardship is hopeless and meaningless unless it involves long-term courage, perseverance, devotion, and skill. This skill is not to be confused with any accomplishment or grace of spirit or of intellect. It has to do with everyday proprieties in the practical use and care of created things — with 'right livelihood.' "[170] Thus, Berry has become the informal champion of and spokesperson for the Christian agrarian movement. This movement repudiates present practices of industrial farming as unconscionably wasteful and destructive to the earth's ecology. Christian agrarians argue that Christian stewardship must reclaim proper care for the land as the means to sustain the world God has created. It also argues for urban dwellers to reclaim some of their own dependence on the earthly garden by eating foods produced in sustainable and humane ways.

Berry's deeper insight also points to the relationship between human flourishing and the flourishing of the natural world. He suggests that the "agribusiness" is the principal destroyer of rural and, indirectly, urban human communities. He says, "in the loss of skill [for caring for the land] we lose stewardship; in the loss of stewardship we lose fellowship; we become outcasts from the great

---

168. Rasmussen, *Earth Community*, 275.
169. Ibid., 103.
170. Berry, "The Gift of Good Land," 299.

neighborhood of creation."[171] He argues, therefore, that right care for the land is part of the same ecology that will enable human communities to flourish. Youth have the most at stake in this conversation, for they and their children are the inheritors of our ecological legacy.

Anathoth Garden clearly embodies Berry's vision for Christian ecological stewardship. The garden was a church's response to a human crisis — murder in the community. Yet the church's insight was that the invitation to tend the earthly garden could be integral to the reconciliation and deepening of their human community. Like gardening itself, the nurture of human community takes patience and time. Setbacks are inevitable, but the results may be extraordinary.

Recently, those of us who thought we'd lost the capacity to be shocked were shocked once again by the murders of some Amish schoolgirls.[172] Many people were also shocked by that community's forgiveness of the murderer, their care for the gunman's family, and their attendance at his funeral. My guess is that Berry and other agrarians were shocked by the murders but not by the Amish community's response. He might argue, in fact, that generations of reconciling practices with the land, of working with nature rather than trying to subdue it, of gently stewarding God's gift, have contributed to the formation of a similar human ecology. Being reconciled with the land and being reconciled with one's human neighbors are woven together into the common cloth of the community.[173]

---

171. Ibid., 303.

172. See David Kocieniewski and Gary Gately, "Man Shoots 11, Killing 5 Girls, in Amish School," the *New York Times*, October 3, 2006, sec. A, 1.

173. The Amish are a case in point of a certain form of liturgical iconoclasm mentioned earlier. Paradoxically, they often exemplify *ordo*-nary living. Nevertheless, I do not believe that the correct conclusion to draw from the Amish is to form non-Amish Christian youth as liturgical iconoclasts. The primary purpose of the liturgical *ordo* is to promote worship of God; graced formation flows from this worship secondarily as a gift. I would prefer, therefore, to consider the Amish as exemplifying the practical force of the *ordo*'s generative theological vision rather than its irrelevance. Moreover, most youth do not presently live in disciplined sectarian communities, as do the Amish. Today's youth require stronger ecologies, more substantive visions and practices, and more theologically generative touchstones, not fewer.

Stewarding God's mysteries

Paul, who seems to be speaking to ministers in Corinth, says, "Think of us in this way, as servants of Christ and stewards of God's mysteries" (1 Cor. 4:1). Presumably, he means that he and his kind are entrusted with God's holy things: book, bath, table, and time. Once again, these are ordinary things, components of ordinary human practices. They involve the materiality of everyday human existence. We drink of the waters, we eat of the fruits of the earth, we pattern our days by the sun's progression, and we relish our roles as planetary storytellers. Through our labors, grain becomes bread and grapes become wine. These are good things, but they remain ordinary things. When set next to one another in the *ordo* and offered up to God, however, these ordinary things also become holy things. God receives these ordinary things and transforms them into the gift of Jesus Christ for the renewal of all creation. That is why Paul calls these things "mysteries," and urges the proper stewardship of them.

But there is a further conclusion to draw. The church cares for earthly, ordinary things not only because they are gift but also because through them God offers redemption. This is the right answer to the question of incarnation. A God who would take on material form both intends and accomplishes the redemption of materiality. Thus, as Alexander Schmemann says, everywhere and always the Eucharist is connected with "the life of the world."[174] Gordon Lathrop provides a visual representation of Schmemann's claim. The liturgy, he suggests, "maps a line into the world that we ourselves may follow."[175]

Paul could not have understood at the time that proper stewardship of these mysteries requires more than abiding by proper baptismal procedures or right presiding at the Eucharistic table. But in light of twenty-first-century ecological consciousness and of Lathrop's por-

---

174. Alexander Schmemann, *For the Life of the World: Sacrament and Orthodoxy* (Crestwood, NY: St. Vladimir's Seminary Press, 1974), 25–26; quoted in Frank C. Senn, "The Care of the Earth as a Paradigm for the Treatment of the Eucharistic Elements," in *Creation and Liturgy: Studies in Honor of H. Boone Porter*, ed. McMichael, 246.

175. Lathrop, *Holy Ground*, 81.

trayal of liturgy as cosmic map, the line that we are invited to follow takes us toward care for the land that nourishes grain and grape, preservation of the great bodies of water so that they may retain their role as baptismal wombs of all life, attending to the earthly rhythms that pattern our lives rather than seeking to subdue them in the name of conquest, and sustaining a global ecology that will allow the planet's story to continue to unfold and our youth to survive in order to tell it. The *ordo* of the liturgy advocates ecological stewardship through the practice of holy things.

Issues of formation

Just as understanding the organic relationship between the *ordo*'s liturgical practices and extraliturgical practices is key to its theological generativity and revelatory power, so, too, grasping this thoroughly ecological understanding is key to appropriating the *ordo*'s formative benefits for youth ministry. The youth academy strives to create a practice-rich community in which the hospitality of our worshiping is purposefully linked with other practices of sharing and receiving hospitality such as those described above. Similarly, our eating at the *ordo*'s table and our Sabbath resting are strategically interwoven with extraliturgical ecological practices of stewardship. These practices are bolstered by teaching about the practices themselves and about the theology that is embedded in them. Teaching on themes of creation, Christology, ecclesiology, redemption, and eschatology is always conducted with an eye to the *ordo* and an eye to *ordo*-nary practices responding both to the *ordo* itself and to crises and opportunities in the world. As always the aim is that evocatively thick environment, one in which connections may readily be drawn between mutually supportive practices. Nor is that connection making left to chance. DYA students and staff reflect repeatedly on this theological and formational ecology.

Church ministries, including youth ministries, often engage in exemplary practice but fail to strategize across the ecology of practices. Youth may travel halfway around the world in mission, practice hospitality with a maturity and grace that belies their years, but fail to explore the book's stories of hospitality or to give and receive hospitality at the Eucharistic table. This failure does not mean that they have not done a good and redemptive thing or that God's Reign failed to appear. It does mean, however, that the opportunity for even deeper formation for these youth was lost. Neglecting to tell the book's stories of hospitality may leave youth in the dark about the identity — Jesus Christ — of those they are graciously receiving. Youth may also fail to recognize their own status as resident aliens in this world. Neglecting the table means that youth do not participate in the generative ground for and primary practice of Christian hospitality. Nor does the opportunity to reflect on the interwovenness of these practices present itself.

To frame this scenario positively, thinking ecologically about formation is likely to offer youth opportunities to experience God's presence, learn God's identity, and practice vocation before God and for the world. Practicing hospitality and stewardship in light of the practice of the *ordo* and in light of the world's need and blessedness assists youth in identifying God as at once creator of all that is and the homeless stranger at our doorstep. Thus youth may expect that the practices of welcoming strangers and caring for the earthly garden provide reliable means for experiencing God's living presence. These practices are fraught with vocational implications. If God is creator, creation is good, and the redemption of all creation is being accomplished through Jesus Christ, then the primary human vocation is, first, grateful worship — "Love the Lord your God. . . . " In addition, these practices display concrete examples of the second dimension of vocation: " . . . and love your neighbor as yourself." The concreteness is important. Left to their own devices, most youth (and adults) would prefer that neighbor love remain a comfortable abstraction. Formless neighbor love enables them to exclaim with a straight face that "smiling at people who are mean to me" actually counts as such. Only actual practices of extending welcome to persons who cannot return the favor or of living simply and sustainably within ecological limits can save youth from contentless and sentimentalized expressions of neighbor love.

Housekeeping and garden-tending may offer two examples of youthful vocation. But what does it mean to speak broadly of vocation for youth? And what is youth's vocation in the present and in their unfolding futures with God? What further vision does the *ordo* offer toward youth's discernment and practice of vocation? Why should youth workers care? We turn to those questions in the final chapter.

Eight

Plunging In

Baptismal vocation and youth's ministry

In a classic sketch, the comedian Bill Cosby gives voice to an imagined conversation between Noah and the Lord. According to Cosby, Noah lives in an ordinary suburb until one day he hears an unfamiliar voice call his name. After the voice speaks a second time, Noah says, "Who *is* that?" The voice replies, "It's the *Lord*, Noah." To which Noah responds, after a pause for comedic effect and with a voice dripping with sarcasm, *"Right!"* Later in the sketch, the Lord provides Noah the precise measurements for building an ark, then instructs Noah to collect a pair of each of the earth's animals and put them two by two into the ark. Having gone from skeptical to incredulous, Cosby's Noah blurts out, "Who is this *really?"*[176]

The sketch is hilarious yet also true. Christian youth often find themselves in Noah's boat, so to speak. It may not automatically occur to them that their relationship with God implies a distinctive way of life. This is not to say that Christian youth harbor no ideals. Many carry big dreams in their oversized backpacks. Like their peers, they are determined to make a difference, build a kingdom, be somebody, and marry (later but well). Somewhat surprising, however, for the Christian teens at least, is the absence of the language of vocation in their dreaming. They are far more inclined to ask: "Who am I becoming?" than "Who is God calling me to become?" and "What am *I* to do?" rather than *"Whom* am I to serve?" Perhaps, like Cosby's Noah, Christian youth find it nearly impossible to imagine the God of deep mystery calling *them* in the midst of their

176. Bill Cosby, "Noah," "Noah and the Neighbor," "Noah: Me and You Lord," on *Bill Cosby Is a Very Funny Fellow* (Warner Brothers, 1963).

ordinary lives and inadequacies. Perhaps they assume that vocational discernment is only possible by way of theophany — a dramatic personal encounter wherein God calls them, sometimes even audibly, to a specific life task — and since they've had no such encounters they conclude they must not be called. Or perhaps, like Cosby's Noah, for Christian youth to consider embodying faithful response to a call from God is the contemporary equivalent of building an ark in one's driveway. It's all just too weird for a world driven by a different story. What would the neighbors think?

This chapter recovers and clarifies the language of Christian vocation for youth. By building upon the baptismal theology introduced in chapter 5, it demonstrates how youth gifted with the life, death, and resurrection of Jesus Christ through Christ's baptismal waters are also called and commissioned to share in Christ's vocation for ministry with a broken world. Like we tell the students at DYA, the question for the baptized is not, "Will it be ministry for me?" but, "What form of ministry will it be?" Such an account will also require clarification of the term "ministry."[177] Only by clarifying the relationship between Christian baptism and a vocation for ministry can we hope to provide students adequate resources to faithfully imagine their present lives and unfolding futures with God. Next, working from this foundation, this chapter also pays attention to how the temporary Christian community at DYA is intentionally structured to become a fertile context to support youth's Christian vocational discernment. It points to practices that may heighten students' capacities for vocational discernment at the same time that they cultivate in youth the means to resist the "calling" of the stereotypical (but powerfully formative) culture of "success." Along the way, it addresses some of the serious questions youth ask: What is the relation between

---

177. Some denominations, prompted by a shortage of clergy, have begun to offer students programs and resources for considering a calling to *ordained* ministry in the church or to some other form of full-time Christian service. This effort is good so far as it goes, but it may unintentionally preserve the abiding misperception that ministry is the special domain of a few people who dress up in robes on Sundays. It is essential, therefore, to recover an understanding of ministry not as a job for a specialized few but as the vocation of the whole community of the baptized, including youth.

my baptismal vocation and my career? Will answering Christ's call burden me or free me? To what or whom may I turn to discern vocation? As with all the chapters in this book, this one is offered with the hope that congregations and youth workers will consider and implement their own contexts and practices to assist their own young people in taking up their baptismal ministries.

That there is a need for such contexts is more than mere assertion. Students admitted to DYA complete a presurvey which includes questions on vocation. Responses to the question "What expectations does your church have for you upon completion of high school?" are telling. A small minority of students describe a relationship between being Christian and the pathway toward their unfolding futures. Most, however, find little more to say in response to the question than "be a good Christian" or "be a success" or "none whatsoever." That professedly Christian students carry with them into adulthood either vague, secularized, or entirely absent notions of Christian vocation should trouble congregations. Clearly, what once might have been described as the "culture of the call," in which congregations invited students to explore the relationship of faith to vocation, no longer exists. The *broader* culture, however, readily fills this imaginal void with its own narratives. And students know *these* stories chapter and verse. They know that this version of the good life entails celebrity, stuff, beauty, empire, personal amusement, and freedom from any entangling relationships that may hint at responsibility. This story is ubiquitous. It is proclaimed to youth when they sit in their houses in front of their television screens, when they walk by the way to the mall, when they lie down and plug in, and when they rise alone in a house already emptied of its adult workers. The story of success as vocation is everywhere. Given its ubiquity, should we really be surprised when Christian youth "choose" it?

So the challenge of this chapter is actually twofold. While clarifying the sometimes confusing messages youth receive from the church about vocation, calling, and ministry, it must also take into account a cultural climate in which media literally sell youth a competing vision for their lives. Lest all this seem too daunting, recall that Noah said "yes" to God's strangest of calls. Consistent with the Spirit's work in our midst, and assisted by the wealth of stories, theological resources, nurturing communities, and practices of discernment our tradition may offer them, Christian youth may yet do the same today.

Christian baptism and Christian vocation: Issues of being and doing

Baptism is key to clarifying issues of Christian vocation. The church of antiquity recognized this centrality of baptism for vocation, but the contemporary church is only just beginning to remember what its forebears once knew. In the paragraphs that follow, I lay out some of the church's theological reflections on the relationship between baptism and *being* (how baptism conveys distinctive identity upon persons and what that identity is) and baptism and *doing* (how baptism forms persons into a distinctive way of life).[178] Baptismal *being*

---

178. The issue of identity (being) is a complex one. At its most basic level, "identity" is the answer persons provide to the question "Who am I?" or "Who are we?" Youth workers readily understand that these questions are often pressing ones for the youth they serve. They recognize also that teens' emerging capacities for introspection and self-reflection make possible this imaginative work. For example, "Joan," one of the teens chronicled in Patricia Hersch's *A Tribe Apart: A Journey into the Heart of American Adolescence* (New York: Ballantine Books, 1999), describes passing an early phase of her adolescence as a "wamma" (aggressive, violent, female person of color), only to be transformed for a time into a peace- and nature-loving, tie-dye wearing "environmentalist" before undergoing still another transformation in response to family reconciliation and to a powerful converting experience on a Christian retreat. Hersch implies that Joan's transformations are towards more authentic identity. Thus, one meaning for identity is that which points to core values or truths or stories that persons claim constitute the very center of themselves. In addition, Joan's story also helps us to see that identity possesses elements of both stability and change. While Joan testifies to shifting dimensions of identity, no one would dispute that it is this person *Joan* whose identity is shifting. Joan's case also reminds us that identity is always and everywhere embodied: it never exists outside or above the embodied self. The social and historic circumstances of teens' upbringings, their expressions of embodied capacities for reason or for feeling, the practices (study, family, work, and more) that fill their days — all these constitute the *corpus* of identity. Further, though we are accustomed to thinking about identity in terms of individual selves (*my* identity vs. *your* identity), teens remind us that identity is interrelational and interdependent. They know, for example, that there's no such thing as a solitary goth and that it takes a whole trumpet section to raise a band nerd.

and baptismal *doing* are integrally related. They are the flip sides of the coin of baptismal vocation. Though the logic may seem circular, in fact the Christian baptismal vocation is to embody and practice the fullness of Christian identity. In other words, Christians are called to become who they are through baptism!

Baptism and being

So who are the baptized? An excellent starting place for considering the question of Christian identity is Matthew's account of Jesus' baptism by John.[179] Given our stated interest, what stands out immediately in this story is that within the context of Jesus' baptism comes also the declaration of Jesus' identity. As Matthew puts it, a "voice from heaven" declares, "This is my Son, the Beloved, with whom I am well pleased" (Matt. 3:17). Like a congressional oversight committee, we could engage in endless speculation concerning "what Jesus knew and when he knew it" in relation to his own discernment of his identity as messiah. It is not unreasonable to assume that Jesus had a considerable degree of self-insight prior to this occasion. Yet Matthew significantly chooses to situate his clearest declaration on Jesus' identity at the occasion of Jesus' baptism.

Establishing additional links between baptism and identity requires that we remind ourselves of Matthew's interests in shaping his own Gospel "portrait" of Jesus. Recall that Matthew lived in and wrote for a community of Jewish converts to Christianity. His Jewish Christian brothers and sisters were intimately familiar with the Hebrew scriptures, so they recognized and understood Matthew's textual hints and allusions to the strong relationship between the biblical accounts of God's entire history of saving action with Israel (including creation, covenants, deliverance from slavery into the Promised Land, and more) and their experience of the significance of Jesus

---

Personal identity is woven through a web of relationships. Who I am is the blessing or burden of the relationships I share, because personal and corporate identity are mixed in the same bowl. This, then, is a bare-bones description of what I'm imagining when writing about identity. I offer it as a means to clarify what I will describe below as an essential relationship between baptism and Christian identity.

179. I am informed in this section by Stookey's *Baptism*, especially the chapter titled "But is it Biblical?"

as the fulfillment of all God's prior saving work. For example, in Matthew's Gospel, the central ingredients in Jesus' baptism by John (water, voice of God, Spirit of God) correlate exactly with the central ingredients in the story of creation (see Gen. 1:1–3). Thus, the members of Matthew's community would have recognized that Matthew is suggesting a relationship between God's initial work of creation, Jesus' baptism, and God's work of *new* creation in and through Jesus. Put differently, through his baptism Jesus is revealed as the embodiment of this new creation. Thus, Matthew provides a second hint of the relationship between Jesus' baptism and his identity. In addition, noting the Spirit's "descending like a dove,"[180] as opposed to, say, a turkey buzzard, Matthew is alluding to the story of God's deliverance, then covenant making with Noah and his family. Could it be that Matthew intends us to understand Jesus' identity in and through his baptism as the embodiment of God's new and lasting covenant? Finally, in addition to the manner of the Spirit's descent, Matthew reminds his readers that the Spirit's empowerment is precipitated by Jesus' baptism. To summarize, Matthew uses the story of Jesus' baptism to communicate Jesus' identity as *Christ*, as the embodiment of God's new creation, as the inaugurator of God's new and lasting covenant (God's profoundly loving relationship with God's people), and as the bearer of the Spirit of God.

Since Matthew lived and worshiped in a baptizing community, it is reasonable to suggest that in fashioning his Gospel portrait, he was not only theologizing on the significance of Jesus' baptism, but also reflecting on the theological significance of those practices of baptizing persons into Jesus that he witnessed at his church down the street. If we accept this assertion, we may say, first, that Matthew is claiming not only that Jesus is identified with the new creation, but that all those persons baptized into Jesus become themselves new creations. Paul makes this inference explicit in 2 Corinthians 5 (about which more below). In other words, for Matthew, as for Jesus himself, the theological relationship between baptism and identity of converts to Christ was equally clear if mostly implicit. To be baptized was to

---

180. Matt. 3:16. Compare to Genesis 8.

die to one's old self and to be born again as a little brother or sister of Christ, or, in other words, to become a new creation. In addition, the allusions to previous covenants imply that Matthew viewed baptism as incorporating persons into a new covenant and a new covenant community, one with a long history of shared love and obligation. Finally, through his baptismal story, Matthew implies that the Spirit empowers this new form of being.

The apostle Paul also reflects on the theological significance of practices of baptism in the communities he visits. In Romans 6, musing on their ritual practices of descending into then rising up out of the baptismal waters, Paul imagines that new converts are actually, if mystically, taken *into* Christ's death and the hope of Christ's resurrection.[181] Indeed, Paul repeatedly uses the phrase "in Christ" (*en Christo*) as code for "the baptized." And as Laurence Stookey observes, there is a critical difference for the issue of identity when persons are baptized not because Jesus was baptized or like Jesus was baptized but into Jesus.[182] And Paul reminds us that whatever features may have been central to their identities prior to baptism — Jew, Greek, slave, free, male, female — all these are now superseded for Christians by their baptismal union with Christ's life, death, and resurrection (Gal. 3:28). In my own case, by virtue of my baptism I am not first a middle-class, Anglo, Southern, (rapidly) aging male parent of teens; I am first a member of Christ's own Body. The other pieces of my identity remain, but their importance is relativized. In other words, the usual markers of identity, like race, class, gender, and age, neither procure me high status in the church (indeed, baptism washes me from that sinful presumption), nor do they retain the power to hold me down or keep me in the margins of community life as they may have in my old life (through baptism all God's children are made new).

---

181. Romans 6:1–11. Following Paul's lead, later church writers characterized the font as "tomb and womb." For example, see Cyril, third century bishop of Jerusalem, in Thomas Finn, *Early Christian Baptism and the Catechumenate: West and East Syria* (Collegeville, MN: Liturgical Press, 1992), 39.

182. Stookey, *Baptism*, 27.

The book of 1 Peter, often cited as a collection of teachings and exhortations for the newly baptized, also affirms and develops the relationship between baptism and Christian identity. It declares to the freshly washed: "You are a chosen race, a royal priesthood, a holy nation, God's own people.... Once you were not a people, but now you are God's people" (1 Pet. 2:9–10). The choice of language (race, priesthood, nation, God's people) displays the author's particular interest in the power of baptism to create a distinctive communal identity. To be baptized is not only to be in personal relationship with the mystery of Christ's salvation, but also to be in relationship with all other persons who also find themselves *in* Christ. In other words, Christian identity requires essentially Christian community. Baptism as covenant means that Christians are bound to one another as they are bound to Christ. Christian identity is always worked out in community. It does not exist in isolation. Later, by way of his own analogy with God's covenant with Noah, 1 Peter reiterates that baptism is God's pledge of covenantal relationship with and through this community (1 Pet. 3:20–22).

Another way to describe the relationship between baptism and identity is to employ the language of story. For example, we might say that Paul, by way of theologizing a connection between baptism and the life, death, and resurrection of Jesus, was in effect suggesting that to be baptized was to be gifted with a new story — the Gospel story — as the ground of personal or corporate identity. The ritual practices of the church of antiquity support and extend this way of imagining identity in light of the community's story. Ancient prayers over the baptismal font prior to baptisms, for example, became increasingly detailed storied accounts of God's past saving work on behalf of God's people.[183] The point of such prayers was more than

---

183. Here is my own condensed version of a prayer over the baptismal waters:

O God, we thank you for creating your world out of the chaos of the waters, for delivering Noah and his family safely through the flood, and for providing the rainbow as a sign of life and not judgment. We thank you that you delivered your people out of slavery and through the waters of the sea to freedom. You made water to flow from rocks to quench their thirst, and when the time was right, you again delivered them across the waters of the Jordan and into the

the clever association of biblical water stories with baptismal waters. The early church was convinced that through the gracious mystery of the Spirit, such ritual recitation of the stories of God's saving action re-presented them to the community in a powerful way. Further, those baptized were being "re-membered" into these stories. This active use of the language is consistent with the scriptures' and the church's conviction that God acted through baptism to recapitulate all God's saving activity and to convey storied identity upon the community's members.[184]

So far I've tried to offer an accounting of the relationship between Christian baptism and Christian identity by way of the scriptures and the baptismal practices of the early churches. According to the scriptures, baptism was the means by which persons died to the old self and were re-created and incorporated into Christ. Moreover, part and parcel of this re-creation was initiation into a covenant community,

---

Promised Land. When they failed you yet again, you sent Jesus, born out of the waters of his mother's womb, as our savior. He healed with water, calmed the storm-tossed seas, and turned water to wine. Water flowed from his side at his passion. Save us now through Christ's baptismal waters and transport us on the waters of the river of life toward the fullness of your heavenly city....

184. These claims may seem very abstract and foreign to our experience, but they really are not. Consider the Christmas Eve pageant. You know how it goes: Two teenagers are drafted to play Mary and Joseph. They dress in bathrobes, towels and sheets, borrow somebody's baby, and when cued process down to the chancel to "O Little Town of Bethlehem." There they find a manger and other youth dressed as barnyard animals trying to stifle their giggles. After a few more carols and a few more readings, all the children of the community, variously decked out as angels, shepherds, and wise people make their own pilgrimages to the manger. Then, while the congregation beams and the pastor manages crowd control so that nobody tramples the Holy Family, everyone sings together "Joy to the World, the Lord is Come!" Those famous words say it all for the re-presenting and re-membering significance of this event. The congregation does not sing, "Joy to the World, the Lord Came and Went." It uses the present tense. That is because in the midst of this gentle ritual action, this enactment of a story we know so well, it is the community's experience that the living Christ is re-presented to them, and they to him. They are not merely remembering a story now two millennia old, but being re-membered into it. Thus, the community's identity is made and remade through the ritual telling of this and other central stories. Such lively meaning and significance is what the scriptures and the church once imagined for baptism, though today we may have forgotten this was ever the case.

Christ's Body, with the implication that such a community would shape the course of its members' lives over time. In addition, in light of the church's ritual practices around baptism and its sensibilities for the ways they carried and conveyed meaning, baptism was regarded as providing the baptized with a radically new and different storied identity.

Baptism and doing

We turn to the doing side of the baptismal vocational coin and to Matthew's Gospel, as well. Immediately following Jesus' baptism and the voice's declaration of his identity ("This is my Son, the Beloved, with whom I am well pleased"), Jesus is driven to the wilderness to do battle with the devil (Matt. 4:1f.). His dialogue with the devil essentially serves to raise and answer the question "OK, what do I *do* about *being* the messiah?" Satan offers a variety of options — bread making, some miracle work, a bit of world dominion — each task worthy in its own right. Ultimately, however, Jesus decides that none of these vocational doings suits his messianic being. As Paul so eloquently explains to the Philippians, Jesus clearly understood that "though he was in the form of God," his ministry required self-emptying servanthood for the sake of the world.[185] Thus, disregarding the devil's career counseling, Jesus heals the sick, forgives sinners, welcomes outcasts, rejects violence, rebukes the powerful, and proclaims freedom from oppression and the advent of God's Reign. These practices of ministry demonstrate consistency between Jesus' being and Jesus' doing. Jesus has found his baptismal vocation. Later, however, in a moment of prescient foreboding, Jesus recognizes that there is still more to his baptismal vocation. In light of his encounter with John and in the context of commenting to overeager disciples, he alludes to the suffering he will endure this way: "Are you able . . . to be baptized with the baptism that I am baptized with?" (Mark 10:38). Through and through, what Jesus does is tied to who Jesus understands himself to be. Moreover, what Jesus does (the practices of his ministry, his self-giving passion, his teachings, and more) reveals more clearly who

---

185. Phil. 2:5–8, a section commonly known as the "Christ hymn."

Jesus is. Jesus' vocation, then, is the faithfully interwoven expression of his being and his doing.

Just as with the previous section, it is also fair to ask what Matthew may have intended for his own community members to glean from this account in relation to their own baptismal lives. We might say that Matthew, with the benefit of hindsight, was linking together the stories of Christ's baptism, temptation, and the commencement of his earthly ministry in order to offer a prototypical pattern for Christian life. For *all* the baptized, then, baptism becomes a sign of their commissioning into and spiritual empowerment for ministry. And *all* Christians will need to discern what shape their ministries will take in light of deeper investigation into the meaning of their identities as brothers and sisters of Christ. Perhaps Matthew also recognized that truthful discernment of vocation may require resisting difficult and dangerous temptations to opt for more comfortable alternatives. Then, finally, *all* Christians are called to take up forms of servant ministry that faithfully reflect their identities. In summary, Matthew's theological intent is once again clear, if implicit. Just as Jesus' baptism called him into ministry for the sake of God's Reign, so does Christian baptism call the baptized into kingdom ministry as members of Christ's Body.

Other New Testament writers offer further insight into the relationship between baptism and the Christian vocation for ministry. Paul deepens the connection between baptism and ministry in his second letter to the Corinthians. Using his baptismal code, he suggests that being "in Christ" conveys not only the status of new creation (2 Cor. 5:17), but the responsibility for sharing Christ's "ministry of reconciliation" (2 Cor. 5:18). Of the Colossians, he requires that those who have "died" and been "raised with Christ" (more baptismal imagery) "put on" a garment of virtues (a reference to the gift of new robes at baptism?) promoting loving relationship in the community (Col. 2:12–13, 3:12–14). 1 Peter calls those newly washed and newly named "God's own people" to be witnesses to "the wonderful deeds of [the One] who called you out of darkness into his marvelous light" (1 Pet. 2:9). Matthew's Jesus commissions the disciples to "go and make [more] disciples of all nations" by baptizing and teaching them (Matt. 28:19–20). Acts 2 reiterates these ministry practices and includes the practices of communal care for the common good and communal worship, including breaking bread.[186] Each of these ministry doings may be framed as either a specific expression of Jesus' general command to love God and neighbor, as imitations or the embodiment of Jesus' own ministry practices, and/or as grateful responses to God's revelation in Christ. Though I will take up the issue of individual giftedness below, most of these ministries named by Peter, Paul, Matthew, and Luke do not appear to be reserved for a few based on their unique giftedness or status. Instead, if anything, the writers direct them to attend the whole community of the baptized. Indeed, for Paul, the church, the community of the baptized, had become no less than Christ's postresurrection Body in the world by the power of the Spirit. That is how he could be so bold as to claim that the ministry of reconciliation once belonging to Christ alone had now become the responsibility of all persons baptized into Christ. In summary, those in Christ through baptism, a way of being, are also called to re-present Christ through ministry to the world in practices of doing. That is what it means to speak of Christian baptismal vocation for ministry.

Christians are not Borg, however.[187] While continually insisting on ministry as the practice of the collective, whole people of God, Paul also recognizes the varieties of gifts bestowed by the Spirit at baptism upon individual believers.[188] Through these passages, Paul reminds his hearers that though all of God's people are called to serve, different persons are differently gifted and will therefore need

---

186. The special character of the care for the common good to which the baptized are called is evident in the some of the practices of the catechumenate, a process of preparing converts for baptism prevalent in the third through fifth centuries. Throughout this process (one that sometimes lasted three years), catechumens were required to provide special care for orphans and widows. Typically, these persons lived on the margins of society, but the church's requirement that they be cared for brought them to the center of Christian life. Apparently, to love the poor was to love, encounter, and perhaps even *be* Christ.

187. *Star Trek* fans know that the Borg are those who have had their individual human identities erased for the sake of the collective. Their expression, spoken in robotic monotone, is "We are the Borg. You will be assimilated."

188. See especially 1 Cor. 12 and Rom. 12.

to work out their ministries in response to their unique giftedness. By way of extending the metaphor of the Body to imagine its multiple interdependent parts (hands, ears, feet, and more), Paul makes space for these varieties of gifts and therefore varieties of ministries within the body. Here also is the space for individual youth to discern how their particular gifts may contribute to the common good within the general call of the baptized to ministry. How, for example, may a young person's individual gifts contribute to Christ's ministries of reconciliation, healing, justice, covenant fidelity, hospitality, stewardship, and more? Herein we also find space to speak of ordained and lay ministries, but with the firm recognition that each form of ministry, though different, is an equally valid expression of baptismal vocation.

Implications for Youth

How does all this baptismal theologizing apply to youth? Below I suggest several possibilities.

Identity shaping

First, youth and those who minister with them should understand that baptismal life means participating in an identity-shaping process. Whether students are baptized at infancy then spend the rest of their lives learning to swim in baptismal waters, or whether, as in other traditions, they journey toward the font through childhood then "put on Christ" at adolescence or young adulthood, the baptismal curriculum remains the same. The purpose of baptismal life is to form and transform persons whom Christ is graciously re-creating through his baptismal gift. "Christing" or christening, the ancient church practice of "sealing" new believers — anointing them with oil, sometimes while making the sign of the cross — exemplifies this appreciation for the identity-forming intent of the baptismal rites. Through the waters and also the chrism, the baptized become Christ's . . . but also *Christs*, at least little christs, themselves. They are sealed into the identity of the one who saves them.

This baptismal invitation to youth to become who they are in Christ is an especially grace-filled and timely one, developmentally speaking. The literature of developmental psychology, increasingly supported by work in neuroscience, confirms the practical wisdom of persons who work with youth that not only are young people becoming qualitatively different selves, they are also developing self-reflective capacities to think about their own becoming. James Fowler characterizes teens' growing self-awareness with this couplet: "I see you seeing me. I see the me I think you see."[189] This clever phrase also points to the fundamentally relational character of identity construction. Teens look to others in order to peer inside themselves for answers to questions of identity. In addition to thinking more deeply, including thinking about their thinking, teens may also acquire emotional depth, the capacities to be moved toward others in love and to feel these emotions more acutely. These affective capacities provide the foundations for deepened relationship with others, including God, and for Christian affections and virtues, including compassion, justice, peaceableness, and love.[190] Put differently, these capacities for new thinking and new feeling, critical for pending adolescent life

189. James Fowler, *Stages of Faith: The Psychology of Human Development and the Quest for Meaning* (San Francisco: Harper & Row, 1981) is still required reading for youth ministry practitioners. See especially 151–73.

190. These agendas of deepened thinking (self-reflection) and deepened feeling (related to relationship) are also where the specter of sin arises. Serene Jones, paraphrasing R. Niebuhr and Karl Barth in "What's Wrong with Us?" in *Essentials of Christian Theology,* ed. William C. Placher (Louisville: Westminster John Knox Press, 2003), 148–50, suggests that sin is either the consequence of human beings thinking too much of themselves (prideful idolatry) or too little (slothful settling for a life constituted only by sensuality or raw passion or low self-expectation). My experience on a campus of undergraduates exemplifies both. When they arrive, Duke first-year students are reminded in public orientation addresses that they are the absolute zenith of the meritocratic elite, the alpha members of their tribe, and that they face no limits to achievement save their own limited ambition. On the other hand, when police arrived at a recent house party adjacent to campus, they discovered tubs filled with baby oil for wrestling contests, then witnessed oil-covered, bikini-clad students fleeing into the subfreezing night. The undergraduate host of the party turned out to be the son of high-level Duke officials. For Duke undergrads, it appears that both pride and sloth goeth before the fall, though it is not clear that school officials recognize their own rhetoric or their students' behaviors as exemplifying sin.

tasks including navigating complex social situations and parenting, also open the door to theological capacities for experiencing, imagining, and shaping identity radically centered in Christ. They make possible bodily affective experience and deepened consideration of mystical union with Christ, to be incorporated into Christ's life and to have Christ dwell within one's own life. They also make possible consideration of Christ's Body, the church, as a grace-filled web of identity-forming relationships where youth gain proper insights into themselves as Christ's own, and where they may cultivate distinctly Christian affections in relation to Christ and one another.

All this may still seem a bit abstract, so I offer a concrete example from my own experience. I am the parent of two teens, a sixteen-year-old son and a thirteen-year-old daughter. The sixteen-year-old has been entirely too easy so far, so perhaps it was inevitable that the thirteen-year-old should morph into a new (and not entirely welcome) creature in our house over the past year. Recently, after finally putting a fall semester to bed, I decreed to my children that on a given day the three of us would travel to the mall to find their mother's Christmas gift. My son mumbled assent. My daughter was enthused at the prospect of stretching her mother's fashion horizons. On the appointed morning, however, the phone began to ring early. The daughter asked if the shopping trip could be organized around a movie matinee with her friends. When it appeared that the schedules didn't jibe, she declared that she would opt for the movie with friends over finding a present for her mother. Of course, I was not pleased with such a declaration and delivered my own ultimatum that she would go in search of the gift with her brother and me. I also offered helpful parental insights, such as, "Life's not all about you, you know." My displeasure begat her displeasure, and she sulked in the back seat on the way to the mall. Still, I sensed she was coming to terms with the way things were and that we three could salvage a good day. Then my cell phone started ringing—for my daughter, of course. Apparently, the matinee plan was not dead. What I had imagined to be the final resolution was to this daughter and her group of eighth-grade friends merely a temporary setback that required a new strategy. After a series of phone conversations, she proposed a series of new schedules to accommodate me to her wishes. When I asked how she would get home from the movie, she named the mother of a friend, a friend later discovered (after still another phone call) not even to be in town on this particular day. Though thoroughly irritated with her self-centered agenda, I had to credit the way she spun stories and logic to support her cause, if not the truth. It was an impressive display of thinking on one's feet. She could never have pulled this off at age eleven. Somehow managing a loving tone, I chuckled and said, "You're making this up as you go along, aren't you?" Reading her face and expecting signs of another confrontation, instead, she paused, smiled, and said, "Yeah, I guess so." The rest of the gift-hunting trip was delightful, except for my son who bordered on anxiety disorder in women's clothing stores (another story for another day).

This daughter of mine, in addition to demonstrating lofty skills for reasoning and rhetoric, also demonstrated budding self-awareness in the end. With my prompting, she employed the perspective of external observer on herself (a process of self-reflection). She recognized she had, in fact, been building a house of cards, and when it all came tumbling down, she also demonstrated an emerging capacity to feel the right way about it (a mixture of humility and humor rather than angry denial) and to give her heart over to the agenda of enjoying searching for the right gift for her mom. Her story illustrates that this process of identity formation is very much a *process,* one that proceeds through fits and starts and trial and error. It can also be messy for youth to come to terms with all this new equipment for making sense of and being in relationship with self and world. Thus, her story also illustrates the importance of communities capable of holding teens in love (and with more than a little patience) as they journey toward identity. More about this below.

Youth are called, right now

A second implication of a theology of baptismal vocation for youth involves the "doing" part of the equation. Baptized youth are just as baptized as the rest of us; therefore, they, too, are called to share in the ministries of the baptized. This claim stands in contrast to rhetoric describing youth as "the church of the future." Such rhetoric ignores fundamental baptismal realities. Calling baptized youth "preparatory" church or "future" church is simply wrong. It is analogous to parents labeling their own children preparatory or future members of their families. Do we really wish to tell youth that their abundant life in Christ will kick in at age 21? Of course, youth have not yet accumulated life experience that may constitute wisdom, but a variety of biblical call stories suggest that wisdom is not an essential prerequisite for ministry. Indeed, it appears that youth's inexperience and, therefore, their willingness to challenge the status quo and to dream new dreams is precisely what God seeks. Perhaps that is why youth have quietly led churches I have served to renewed servant mission work with the poor. They didn't know any better!

If youth are called right now, the key to living into that call is practice. Practice is something teens understand immediately. They've been doing it all their lives. Times tables, cursive letters, dance moves, soccer drills, arpeggios — all of these require rigorous practice. Only recently, however, have Christians recovered the importance of practice for shaping baptismal life. Simply put, if persons who minister with youth hope for them to discern baptismal vocation, it is essential to provide them opportunities to practice that vocation. This means that youth themselves should practice ministries of reconciliation, witness, servant care for persons on the margins, hospitality, garden tending, and peacemaking. Such practices incarnate the identity Christ bestows upon the baptized. In other words, practice is the way youth learn to be who they are in Christ, to swim in baptismal waters, and to grow into their baptismal garments.

Renewed attention to the need to invite youth into the ministry practices of the baptized also reveals an unwitting bias in many youth ministry contexts. Especially in my own evangelical background, churches have sought to provide youth knowledge of Christ or powerfully felt "spiritual" experience of Christ before deeming them fit for ministry. In contrast, a practice-based approach assumes that persons may act their way to new modes of thought and feeling. Another example is in order. I read dozens of extensive interviews with churchgoing teens each year. Youth workers will not be surprised to learn how often teens cite their experiences on mission trips (short-term excursions away from home, often to serve in marginalized communities) as life changing. They report that opportunities afforded them in mission to apply all the practices of Christian life (worship, study, community, pilgrimage, servanthood, hospitality, witness, reconciliation, and more) in close proximity to one another make Christianity more real to them than a year of Sunday school classes or a powerful last-night-at-camp altar call. They suggest that these practices provide them fertile ground to think about and feel more deeply who they are as Christ's own. In short, they are saying that in the context of missions, their doings are integrally related to their becoming. One wonders what happens to the vocational aspirations of youth who are judged too young, too immature, or too inexperienced to share in ministries that are properly theirs by virtue of their baptisms.

Wading into the future

A third implication of a baptismal theology of vocation with youth involves their unfolding futures with God. Yes, youth are called right now, but it is also true that most North American youth do not yet possess complete adult responsibility for their own lives. They remain in a process of becoming, a process that increasingly extends into their twenties in contemporary North America. To be sure, experts offer a variety of compelling explanations for youth's delayed maturity: better relations with parents, housing costs or student loans that prevent stepping out, the sheer volume and array of choices concerning what one is to do with one's life. Thus, for most youth, the future still seems an open question.

Baptismal theology teaches youth to critique contemporary notions of choice. Specifically, youth must ask themselves whether their being in Christ is compatible with the idea of limitless unfettered choices for their personal futures. "Choice" in present-day North America is tied to the sinful myth of self-creation. Choice insists that I as fashioner of my own life have the right to become anything or anyone I wish to be. To be in Christ, however, is to recognize one's self as creature, not creator. And to be in Christ means being joined to nothing less than the life, death, and resurrection of Jesus Christ. So, in fact, for Christian youth, not just anything goes with regard to living into their futures with God. Empire and its many self-insulating trappings — personal fortune, exploitative power, privilege, coercion, violence, isolation — these do not go. Neither does the illusion that vocational choices are limitless for Christians. The church of fourth-century Rome excluded pimping, harlotry, and soldiering among others as vocations incompatible with being in Christ. It was also suspicious of academic types![191] It told potential members that it would not tolerate such inconsistency between their desire for baptismal being and their daily doings. Reclaiming the integrity of baptismal vocation suggests that churches rightly intervene with youth when it comes to helping them imagine how they will earn their livings and live their lives in the future. The contrast between the church's willingness to proscribe vocation in the fourth century and the present-day assumption that anything goes so long as you're happy also reveals how the church's vision for youth has been co-opted and domesticated. Youth academy participants report that their churches' dreams for them include prosperity, happiness, and success more often than participating in Christ's ministry of reconciliation.

Some may suggest that high school is too soon to contemplate, let alone make serious decisions about, one's future. Isn't the church engaging in manipulation, they say, by challenging youth to heed baptismal callings before they possess sufficient life experience to fully appreciate the nature of those calls? Shouldn't we let them grow up first so that they are free to make informed life decisions? In response, we should first note that neither the military-industrial complex nor the fashioners of our consumerist economy are deferring their "calls" to youth to paths of soldering and consumption.[192] By way of a more

---

191. Hippolytus, *Apostolic Constitutions*, book VIII.

192. While we're being suspicious, it is interesting to note how the military and fashion industries employ the rhetoric of freedom — the "all-volunteer" military, for example, or exhorting the purchase of fashion products as a means to demonstrate one's freedom from convention — while implicitly testifying to freedom's absence. Just how free are poor young persons with limited educational resources to seek meaningful work outside the military in the United States? And exactly how free is a slave to fashion? Bob Dylan didn't make a huge splash during his Christian phase, but he did offer keen insight into the contemporary illusion of freedom. "It

positive example, neither do parents wait to bring their children to church until after they are fully formed adults. This latter example points to the fact that the church operates out of a different understanding of freedom from that of the contemporary United States. Culture claims that persons have the right to existence as free, autonomous individuals. Freedom, in North America, is assumed to be the starting point. In contrast, Christians believe freedom is not a starting point but a destination to be sought through life in Christ. Thus, calling youth now to futures marked by ministry in Christ holds the promise of making them free — as opposed to giving them space to make up their own minds out of the misguided belief that they begin from a place of freedom. Of course, none of this means that youth won't be working out the specifics of their callings for years or over a lifetime. Still, the church rightly invites their practice within the parameters of a general call to the baptized and rightly teaches that within these parameters they may expect that God is opening future scenarios tied to the specifics of their personal contexts and gifts. By contrast, rejecting the possibility that youth may receive and respond to callings means that the church is missing a tremendous opportunity and obligation in the lives of its young while other societal forces are all too willing to step into the vacuum our negligence creates.

A related objection to calling the young is the claim that teens simply cannot adequately contemplate a life devoted to Christian ministry. For example, some would argue that youth cannot differentiate the love and acceptance they feel currently in their congregations from the tasks of leadership that may at times isolate or marginalize them from faith communities in the future. Adults know what youthful idealism sometimes prevents youth from knowing: life in faith communities is not all wine and roses. Thus, calling youth to baptismal vocations, especially to full-time ministries in faith communities, should be deferred until youth are less naïve, they say.

---

may be the devil or it may be the Lord," he sings, "but you're gonna have to serve somebody."

Aside from the fact that this is another veiled version of the modernist "freedom" argument, it rings hollow on other grounds as well. As a covenant reality, Christian baptism binds past, present, and *future*. Such binding, a gift of God's grace, includes the promise of God's providential care to the end of one's life and beyond. Thus, the church may trust that its efforts to bind its young to baptismal vocations are faithful even if youth themselves cannot anticipate all the scary details of that binding. In this regard, baptism is something like marriage. (Actually marriage is an expression of baptism.) When two twenty-five-year-olds stand at the altar to exchange vows, they have absolutely no idea of what these vows actually will entail for their future together — especially the "in sickness" and "or worse" parts. Yet the church, in its wisdom, offers them these vows trusting in their power to shape that shared future out of God's promise of abundance. In its efforts to bind the futures of its young through baptism and the call to take up baptismal vocations, the church demonstrates similar hope and trust in God's unfolding future and providential care.

The claims in this section are a bit abstract yet vitally important. I do not wish to reduce the mystery of God's call on youth's lives to some quantifiable formula, but make no mistake, I do wish to clear away some of the confusion. I contend that much current confusion over vocation is the result of the church failing to appreciate its own theology of vocation and thereby defaulting to un-Christian but pervasive notions around choice and freedom. That is why I've attempted to offer general parameters for Christian identity and baptismal vocation. Youth will be less confused about God's call on their lives when they understand (and practice) more clearly who Christians are and what Christians do. Eventually, they may come to understand how they lean into their futures in Christ as less about choosing and more about the organic expression of their Christian identities. Ideally, they will say about their lives, "I am simply doing who I am."

Yet popular culture is not the only entity sowing confusion around the issue of vocation. Sometimes churches needlessly mystify the notion of calling. Admittedly, God has called some folks to do some pretty strange stuff. Consider the aforementioned Noah, or Simon the Stylite who lived on top of a pole for decades.[193] But churches ought not declare the exception as the norm. A call does not have to be either extreme or spoken out of a whirlwind to qualify as authentic. Nor should churches continue to act as if calls come only to clerical types: the whole point of describing vocation in baptismal terms is to do away with the notion that only a few Christians are called, including those lucky few called to clerical vocations. All of God's children swim in Christ's waters. By teaching youth that the church's vision for their futures is distinctive from the world's, and by teaching our churches that callings are not as mysterious as all that, we cultivate in them more faithful vocational imaginations.

Discerning baptismal vocation

Baptismal theology lays out a broad vision of vocation. How may youth begin to discern more specific vocational possibilities for their own lives? Frederick Buechner's axiom for vocation provides a helpful guide. Buechner defines vocation as the place where one's deep joy and the world's deep hunger meet.[194] We should pay attention to corollaries of both sides of this equation. On the one hand, Buechner suggests that one's vocation brings joy. Presumably, joy in this context means something like deep and abiding gladness or enduring satisfaction and not merely temporary feelings of ecstasy. Eating dessert probably does not qualify as vocation under this definition of joy. Equally important, however, under these rules, the absence of joy equals the absence of vocation. One may work day and night on a cure for AIDS in response to the world's hunger, but, if one is miserable, driven into research by guilt or obligation, then one

193. Simon the Stylite was a fourth- and fifth-century monk who tired of life in monasteries (visitors were too distracting). He was convinced that the way to true happiness was through suffering, so he spent thirty-six of his sixty-nine years living on top of pillars. He stood most of the time, despite weather conditions or time of day, and almost never stopped praying. After his death, a great basilica was built on the spot of his last pillar in Syria; the ruins of the basilica and the pillar remain today.

194. Frederick Buechner, *Wishful Thinking* (New York: Harper & Row, 1973), 95.

is outside of one's vocation. The opposite corollary is equally true. One may rejoice at the prospect of selling pet rocks, but the question of whether marketing rocks as friends responds adequately to the world's hunger is a legitimate one. Authentic vocation must pass both the tests of joy and of hunger. Offering a slightly different but still complementary perspective, the Virginia Theological Seminary professor of theology Michael Battle quotes his teacher, Desmond Tutu, as saying, "Those who are God's friends are distinguished by the fact that they suffer."[195] Battle seems to suggest that solidarity with suffering is capable of transforming both our understanding of the world's deep hunger and our possibilities for discovering joy.

Youth discern baptismal vocation

The fact that baptismal vocation is not necessarily identical to the manner in which one earns a living adds complexity to the vocational discernment process for youth. Paul, after all, paid the tax bill through tent making, but his vocation was not tent making: it was apostling. This is not to say that tent making could not be a legitimate vocation for someone else. Certainly, the provision of shelter responds to a fundamental human need. For my part, I would plead that while acknowledging vocation and "job" may not be identical, neither should they ever be too conveniently separated from each other in the imaginations of the young. In an economy driven by world capitalism, jobs are not neutral. There are baptismal implications to our decisions about earning a living. That is why, for example, listening to Beyoncé rationalize the tensions between her Christian upbringing and her often sexually provocative dress and gesture on her music videos rings hollow. Less publicly visible but also problematic are jobs requiring the exploitation of workers, taking money from the poor, or the manufacture of weaponry. Jobs like

---

195. Desmond Tutu, "The Holy Spirit and South Africa," from his handwritten lecture notes; quoted in Michael Battle, "How Should We Live?" in *Essentials of Christian Theology*, ed. William C. Placher (Louisville: Westminster John Knox, 2003), 281.

these are incompatible with life in Christ and may not be easily rationalized by the disclaimer that "my real vocation is being nice to people." Let's be honest, however. In a fallen world, no job can completely escape entanglement in the web of sin. Still, admitting the reality of sin is not the same as allowing the rationalization of any job.

Such complexity extends particularly to young women for whom vocational discernment is much more complex than for young men. In the language of our culture, women are now nearly as "free to choose" their adult paths as men. Yet this "freedom" comes at a cost. Women are expected to take their place in the American workforce, yet they are also required, in most cases, to take primary responsibility for child-rearing. The result for many women is a catch-22, one that leaves them feeling unable to meet the demands of either role. Like their male counterparts, young women must learn to distinguish Christian vocation from the story of success. In addition, however, while resisting patriarchal tendencies to limit women's Christian vocational aspirations based on outdated gender stereotypes, the church should continue to affirm the care and nurture of children as a faithful vocational option. Care for its most vulnerable members remains at the heart of the church's counter-cultural vocation, so neither women nor men should have to apologize for raising children — nor can men abdicate their responsibility for doing so. So it is no surprise that in more than half of Christendom, women who experience calls to ordained ministry are told they must be mistaken. I personally find this situation lamentable but do not presume to offer a solution here. Instead, I simply note that in this regard, young women may require gender-specific pastoral and theological support for discernment as they mature.

Implications for ministry with youth

How might one practice ministry with youth in light of baptismal vocation? What can congregations and youth workers do to assist youth in understanding, practicing, and discerning baptismal vocation?

I do not advocate a new or different youth ministry program, or a dynamic, life-changing, and easy-to-teach baptismal vocation kit complete with CD of water sounds guaranteed to determine life paths or your money back. Instead, I advocate a way of being church gathered around the font that is fully inclusive of youth. I also suggest that a faith community faithful to the shared vocation of the baptized will be a fertile context within which youth may practice and discern their own. For youth workers, there is good news and bad news. The good news is this: the responsibility for assisting youth with baptismal vocation does not rest on your shoulders alone or lie with your individual programmatic genius. Here is the bad news: when is the last time you bumped into somebody else in the congregation who could talk coherently about baptismal vocation, much less live one out? To paraphrase Augustine's preaching to a group of newly baptized converts, "I am not so worried about your ability to resist the temptations of the world as I am about your encounters with the folks already here in the pews."[196]

Looking to the congregation as a broad context for youth ministry often amounts to a deal-breaker in the minds of youth workers. Accustomed to locating themselves at the bottom of the church staff power hierarchy and often lacking the keys to the sacristy that ordination might otherwise afford them, they see little practical advantage in advocating congregation-wide renewal or reform inclusive of baptismal liturgical reform. Their domain is youth; everyone else is not their business. Aside from the fact that youth ministry fiefdoms have begotten great youth groups but few adults taking up their baptismal vocations in the community of faith over the past two generations, for youth workers to remain silent on the issue of congregational obligation to youth (part of its own baptismal vocation) is to make peace with theological error. In multi-staff congregations, pastors and youth workers might covenant to read and discuss this chapter together as a means to begin the conversation about what congregation-centered youth ministries might look like in their setting.

---

196. Augustine, Sermon 376A.2, cited in William Harmless, *Augustine and the Catechumenate* (Collegeville, MN: Liturgical Press, 1995), 332. I encountered the reference in an unpublished essay by L. Gregory Jones titled "A Dramatic Journey into God's Dazzling Light: Baptismal Catechesis and the Shaping of Christian Practical Wisdom."

So what characterizes a congregation capable of inviting youth into the community-wide task of discerning and living out baptismal vocation? Below I offer several hints.

Robust ritualizing around the font

My claim that baptism is a central ritual symbolic gesture that bears all of Christian life through its life-giving waters is flatly contradicted in every faith community where baptismal practice is — to repeat my list — truncated, edited, minimized, condensed, overlooked, deleted, or otherwise ham-handedly engaged. I personally have served under pastoral regimes that preferred not "to take up time in worship" for baptisms, opting instead for more "convenient" times and places. The effect of such omission, of course, was the removal of baptism from the consciousness and theological imagination of an entire faith community. I've witnessed other pastors rush through baptisms in the first five minutes of worship ("so the baby doesn't fuss and upset folks") employing baptismal "fonts" the size of sherbet bowls with the apparent aim not to actually get anyone too wet. Again, the effect was to remove baptism to the periphery of congregational consciousness, in so doing inadvertently testifying to their pastoral ignorance of baptismal theology. I would hope that faith communities that practice full immersion or believers' baptism would at least avoid these mistakes of impoverished practice. Robust practice is critically important to deepened baptismal life.

Appropriately, we do not baptize at the youth academy because we are not a congregation. We do, however, intentionally ritualize around the font every chance we get. Students are regularly invited to touch the baptismal waters, listen to the waters, and consider their lives in light of these waters by way of scriptures, prayers, litanies, preaching, and others gestures that evoke baptismal themes including, of course, the theme of baptismal vocation. The youth academy also concludes with a service of baptismal renewal and remembering where persons dip their fingers into the font and are then "Christed" on their foreheads with oil. In addition, as noted in chapter 3, students' artistic practices through the Arts Village are intended, in part, to deepen their facility with aesthetic ways of knowing through which

God may communicate God's own grace-filled mystery, including by way of the baptismal waters. Thus, students explore the range of symbolic resonances for water, they create poetry that employs water imagery, they do pop art employing baptismal themes and multiple blue hues, and they learn the art of biblical storytelling in light of aquatic themes. Our hope is that upon returning home, students will possess many more touchstones for making theological sense of their lives in Christ linked to actual congregational practices around the font. By opening new channels for youth's apprehension of God's self-revelation, we hope they may better sense God's call on their lives.

Congregations, at least potentially if not actually, are in even better positions to invite youth into close proximity with the baptismal waters, since congregations are, by definition, communities constituted by baptism and whose ministry is baptism. Teens in many congregations are either preparing for baptism or preparing for reaffirmation of baptismal vows through confirmation. Presumably, these occasions offer tremendous opportunities to explore baptismal themes and consider afresh, or for the first time, baptismal vocation. Not too long ago, my own denomination tended to use confirmation classes to focus on institutional concerns — counting bishops and passing out offering envelopes and such. Lately, I'm delighted to note how renewed attention to baptism has begun to reframe the confirmation process as one of deepened incorporation into Christ. Beyond the milestones of baptism or confirmation, congregations should strive to bring youth into close proximity with the baptismal waters on multiple other occasions as well. Even though on a given baptismal Sunday perhaps only one or two persons are baptized, the practice nonetheless belongs to the whole faith community. At occasions of baptism, congregational members, including youth, are renewing their own baptismal vows and making covenant promises to the newly baptized to help them grow into their baptismal garments.

At Sunday night youth group, I often asked our students how they planned to uphold the promises they made to the babies baptized that morning at worship. One response was our youths' continuing faithful service as teachers and assistants in summer vacation Bible school. This was a small signal to me that they were making the connection between their own baptisms, a communal, covenantal baptismal way of life, and their call to take up baptismal ministries. They were, in other words, embodying a dimension of baptismal vocation.

Further still, youth and adults who take on identifiable ministries or leadership positions in a congregation ought to be commissioned and affirmed for those roles around the baptismal waters. What better way to register the significance of baptism as vocation for ministry than by commissioning a mission team in close proximity to the congregation's font? Yet further, students who return from such missions or from camp with powerful testimonies to transformed lives should also do so close to the font. Without diminishing youthful enthusiasm, such thoughtful ritualizing will help students understand, by way of linkage of testimony to font and by continuing thoughtful reflection, that even dramatic transforming moments are part of a wider life's journey upon Christ's baptismal waters.

Finally, the significance of being acolytes ought not to be overlooked. An invitation to youth from thoughtful and skilled worship leaders to assist with the care and handling of the church's holy things holds real promise for deepened appreciation and encounter with the incarnational aspects of Christian worship.

In all cases, close encounters with baptismal ritualizing must be accompanied by thoughtful and imaginative reflection. I have witnessed, and probably offered myself, far too many worship-related instructions to youth that focused on where to stand and what to say when, rather than acknowledging the possibility that through these symbols and ritually embodied gestures youth may find themselves washed in loving mystery. The point of such reflection is to continually remind youth that the font is a wellspring of their Christian identity, and to cultivate in youth ways of recognizing and receiving God's grace-filled self-communication, opening new channels for revelation so that they may hear and heed the Spirit's prompting in the task of discerning the specifics of vocation.

Sponsoring youth in practicing baptismal vocation

Congregations serious about assisting youth with discernment and embodiment of baptismal vocation will stop talking about Christian life to youth or playing at Christian life with youth and start living it. As with fifteen-year-old Martha Schwehn in *Way to Live*, I'm convinced that so many teens describe their experiences on mission trips or in other sorts of intentional Christian communities as profound because they practice baptismal life so intensely at those times.[197] Journeying from home, they pray, study, serve, worship, see themselves in the biblical stories, care for the common good, ponder, and imagine, often in the presence of adults who share their pilgrim spirit. The logic and abundance of Christian life are self-evident when these fundamental Christian practices are so thickly intertwined and this sort of community emerges.

Just as in the youth academy, youth groups can and should become contexts for practicing the whole ecology of Christian practices, and, therefore, for living into baptismal life. Youth may pray, visit the sick, care for the poor, and do justice as readily as the rest of us. But the broad inclusivity of baptismal covenant making means that congregations must also look beyond the youth group as the sole context for youth ministry. Youth's servant leadership should be invited and encouraged across congregational life. Youth may become part of worship leadership as lectors, ushers, or choir members, and their visible presence ought not to be limited to one Sunday a year. Youth should also be involved in planning for, participating in, and reflecting upon other congregation-wide events. This congregation-wide practice of youth ministry means that all adults in the congregation will consider themselves mentors in the baptismal life as well as stewards of a particular ministry role. Again, the point here is not to create more intergenerational programs but to shape the congregation as a community in which youth's baptismal gifts and callings are welcomed and cultivated.

Perhaps much of the confusion over baptismal vocation stems from a crisis of faith in congregations. Is the endless parade of ski trips and visits to Wally World implicit testimony that we don't believe our youth have ministry gifts to offer? Or, worse, that our own practices

---

197. Bass and Richter, eds., *Way to Live*, 1–4.

are not really life giving? Is it possible that much of youth's confusion and anxiety over present or future vocation will dissolve when congregations begin living out their own?

Teaching and reflection with youth on baptismal vocation

Over a period of two weeks, DYA students put in nearly as much class time in the study of theology as a college semester course. Students tell us they have never experienced anything like it in their congregations. I could devote several paragraphs to blame at this point, but I prefer to focus on remedies. Congregations and persons who work closely with youth would do well to find ways to acquire and then share theological vocabularies to assist youth in making sense of their lives. Youth workers also do well to recognize that moralizing to youth or entertaining them is no substitute for their learning the language and skills for theologizing. Certainly, teens capable of algebraic abstraction and solving chemical equations can learn to wrestle with the theological tradition. Perhaps adults perceive church youth as apathetic because we expect so little from them. Christian Smith claims that teens are paying more attention to us than we imagine.[198] What are they gleaning for their efforts? Moreover, DYA's choice of baptism as a central context for teaching theology is intended to signal to students, and, indirectly, to congregations, that the sources for theologizing are not limited to theology schools but actually exist as close as their own sanctuaries. But somebody needs to get a clue. Pastors need to wake up to the theological richness of baptism and, indeed, to the entire *ordo* as a constitutive and future-orienting practice of the church. Registering his own pastoral understanding, the former youth academy assistant director Brian Jones explained in a sermon to the community in the summer of 2004 that "we could have taken you snorkeling in the tropics and taught you some Bible verses, but instead we focused on practicing and understanding Christian baptismal life. Why? Because this water ain't goin' away."[199] In light of the language I've been using, Jones is affirming that holy things

---

198. Smith, *Soul Searching*, 260.
199. Brian Felker Jones preaching during evening worship at the Duke Youth Academy, July 23, 2004.

are what the church has been given to speak and live Jesus Christ. Unfortunately, Jones's assertion may at once be theologically true and empirically false in congregations where baptism, for example, is absent or ignored.

If there is no substitute for the focused, straightforward, creative, and effective teaching of theology to youth as a means toward vocational discernment, neither is there a substitute for multiple opportunities and quiet spaces for formal and informal reflection on baptismal teaching and living. Key to the process of faithful baptismal vocational discernment is repeatedly asking a set of questions as youth grow. At DYA they are variations on these:

- Where did you encounter Christ today?

- Where did Christ seem absent or hidden?

- How did you understand yourself as engaged in what Christ is doing?

- How do you know when you are engaged in Christian ministry?

- How will your participation in Christ's ministry with the world here at DYA shape your vocation for ministry at home?

- What gifts for ministry are you discovering or nurturing?

- How will taking seriously a baptismal vocation for ministry shape your unfolding future with God?

Sometimes these questions are food for conversation between adult mentors and students; sometimes they are the subjects of meditative prayer, journaling, or artistic creation. But in one form or another, they are always being made present to youth's imaginations.

Such questions presuppose at least two realities. The first is that the life of the community is rich enough that Christ's work in and through it may actually be glimpsed. The second reality is the presence of a significant number of adults (thirty or more in a community of fifty students) who are also engaged in the lifelong process of discerning and attempting to live faithfully into their own baptismal vocations.

Here, at the end of this chapter, I return to a theme common to nearly all of these chapters. Just as was the case with cultivating deepened appreciation for Eucharist, for the practice of the arts, for acquiring storied biblical literacy and learning to do theology, for practicing prayerful rhythms, for offering hospitality and stewarding the earthly garden, when it comes to calling youth to take up baptismal vocations, the key is not a single silver bullet but an ecology rich enough for them to do the necessary imaginative and practical work. The youth academy depends on a web of thick and mutually interdependent strands of practice to serve all its goals. So, as was the case with the others, baptismal vocation bubbles up through worship, study, service, and reflection *working in concert*, and not from any single one of them or from any targeted strategy. Thus, the challenge for the churches is the same — to build the same sort of thickly evocative web for their own youth. And I find this challenge to be good news. Good news, because in the end, churches are being called not to invent a new or better mousetrap for youth, but simply to be who they are and to do what they are *en Christo*.

Postscript

Three themes integral to renewing the practice of youth ministry run throughout this book:

First, youth ministry rightly conceives adolescents not only as objects of ministry but as agents of ministry. Youth ministry's past practices of either saving youth's souls or meeting their therapeutic needs have not surprisingly tended to produce needy adults with shallow theological convictions. We now better understand that salvation by way of incorporation into the life, death, and resurrection of Christ is a gift that also implies a certain kind of agency and a certain kind of life. Youth possess vocation, youth are to become disciples, youth may take up ministries. All these are also features of their redemption. Congregations that embrace this countercultural vision of adolescence as a season of active engagement with the Gospel rather than merely a time of passivity or indulgent liminality prior to adulthood are in the best position to invite teens to share in youth's own ministry for church and world.

Second, youth ministry rightly conceives of ministry in theological terms. Our past contentment with just giving youth Jesus or just giving the youth group a good time has begotten technique and market-driven ministry practices and domesticated spiritualities. My own account in this book has attempted to show how critical theology is to youth being able to discern authentic experience of God, to rightly identify God, and to practice present and future Christian vocation. Further, since these goals of youth ministry are themselves theologically grounded, they also imply a certain theology of ministry. In a word, youth workers become pilgrims with youth rather than programmers for youth. They patiently mentor teens over the long haul into a graceful way of life. Thus, congregations that envision youth ministry as relational, communal, oriented to bodies as well as minds and spirits, rooted in historic traditions and practices of Christian life (probably not including ski trips), and journeying toward God's unfolding Reign exemplify the hopeful possibilities of theologically grounded youth ministry.

Third, youth ministry rightly understands church as an ecological configuration. In the present historical epoch and in the contemporary North American cultural and social contexts that create fragmentation — youth displaced from families, youth ghettoized from children and adults, youth confined to the margins of congregations, congregations as separate programmatic fiefdoms, youth prohibited from creating in the name of consumption, youthful conversation digitized and disembodied, youth cut off from the natural world, youth with no sensed connection to the past or future — an ecological configuration of church as Body of Christ urges itself upon us. Youth ministry that understands teens as integral to that Body and congregations as interdependent constellations of ecologically interdependent ministries and, finally, the *ordo* as disclosing this ecology, are in the best position to build and sustain an ecology in which youth may come to thrive as disciples of Jesus.

Nothing in the preceding paragraphs is especially innovative. In fact, nothing in my entire account is novel. Nonetheless, I do hope it displays something of the hopeful possibility for disciplined, thoughtful, and effective youth ministry that springs confidently from the church and its Gospel. It is partly an exercise in retrieval, of remembering in such a way that youth themselves may be re-membered in the church and grafted into the Body that practices God's unfolding Reign.

Bibliography and Works Cited

Aristotle. *Nicomachean Ethics.* Translated by Terence Irwin. Indianapolis: Hackett, 1985.

Bahnson, Fred. "The Salvation of the City: Community Gardens in The Great Northern Feedlot." In *Places of God: Theological Conversations with Wendell Berry,* edited by Joel Shuman. Forthcoming.

Bass, Dorothy C. *Receiving the Day: Christian Practices for Opening the Gift of Time.* San Francisco: Jossey-Bass, 2000.

Bass, Dorothy C., ed. *Practicing Our Faith.* San Francisco: Jossey-Bass, 1997.

Bass, Dorothy C., and Don C. Richter, eds. *Way to Live: Christian Practices for Teens.* Nashville: Upper Room Books, 1992.

Battle, Michael. "How Should We Live?" In *Essentials of Christian Theology,* edited by William C. Placher, 280–96. Louisville: Westminster John Knox, 2003.

Benedict, Daniel T. "The Basic Pattern of Worship: Is Your Church 'Playing' at Home and Away?" In *Worship Arts* (November–December 2004): 8–12.

Berry, Wendell. "The Gift of Good Land." In *The Art of the Commonplace: The Agrarian Essays of Wendell Berry,* edited by Norman Wirzba. Emeryville, CA: Shoemaker and Hoard, 2002.

Bondi, Roberta C. *A Place to Pray: Reflections on the Lord's Prayer.* Nashville: Abingdon, 1998.

———. *To Pray and to Love: Conversations on Prayer with the Early Church.* Minneapolis: Fortress, 1991.

Brown, Frank Burch. *Good Taste, Bad Taste, and Christian Taste: Aesthetics in Religious Life.* Oxford: Oxford University Press, 2000.

Brueggemann, Walter. *The Creative Word: Canon as a Model for Biblical Education.* Philadelphia: Fortress, 1982.

Buechner, Frederick. *Wishful Thinking.* New York: Harper & Row, 1973.

Crites, Stephen. "The Narrative Quality of Experience." In *Why Narrative? Readings in Narrative Theology,* edited by Stanley Hauerwas and L. Gregory Jones, 65–88. Eugene, OR: Wipf and Stock, 1997.

Cushman, Philip. *Constructing the Self, Constructing America: A Cultural History of Psychotherapy.* Cambridge, MA: Da Capo, 1995.

Daley, Brian E., S.J. "Is Patristic Exegesis Still Usable?" In *The Art of Reading Scripture*, edited by Ellen F. Davis and Richard B. Hays, 69–88. Grand Rapids: Eerdmans, 2003.

Damasio, Antonio. *Descartes' Error: Emotion, Reason, and the Human Brain*. New York: Bard Avon Books, 1998.

Dean, Kenda Creasy. *Practicing Passion: Youth and the Quest for a Passionate Church*. Grand Rapids: Eerdmans, 2004.

Dean, Kenda Creasy, and Ron Foster. *The Godbearing Life: The Art of Soul Tending for Youth Ministry*. Nashville: Upper Room Books, 1998.

DeWaal, Frans. *Good Natured: The Origins of Right and Wrong in Humans and Other Animals*. Cambridge, MA: Harvard University Press, 1996.

Edie, Fred. "Cultivating Baptismal Spirituality in High School Youth." *Doxology* 19 (2002): 85–107.

———. "Uncovering Eucharistic Vitality in High School Youth: Who Knew?" *Doxology* 21 (2004): 92–110.

Eisner, Elliot W. *The Educational Imagination: On the Design and Evaluation of School Programs*. New York: Macmillan, 1979.

Farley, Edward. "Can Church Education Be Theological Education?" *Theology Today* 42 (1985): 158–71.

———. *Theologia: The Fragmentation and Unity of Theological Education*. Philadelphia: Fortress, 1983.

Finn, Thomas M. *Early Christian Baptism and the Catechumenate: West and East Syria*. Collegeville, MN: Liturgical Press, 1992.

Forest, Jim. "Through Icons: Word and Image Together." In *Beholding the Glory: Incarnation Through the Arts*, edited by Jeremy Begbie, 83–97. Grand Rapids: Baker, 2001.

Fowel, Stephen E., and L. Gregory Jones. *Reading in Communion: Scripture and Ethics in Christian Life*. Grand Rapids: Eerdmans, 1991.

Fowler, James W. *Stages of Faith: The Psychology of Human Development and the Quest for Meaning*. San Francisco: Harper, 1981.

Freire, Paulo. *Pedagogy of the Oppressed*. New York: Continuum, 1992.

Goleman, Daniel. *Emotional Intelligence*. New York: Bantam Books, 1995.

Guite, Malcolm. "Through Literature: Christ and the Redemption of Language." In *Beholding the Glory*, edited by Jeremy Begbie, 27–46. Grand Rapids: Baker, 2001.

Harmless, William. *Augustine and the Catechumenate*. Collegeville, MN: Liturgical Press, 1995.

Hauerwas, Stanley M. "Character, Narrative, and Growth in the Christian Life." In *A Community of Character: Toward a Constructive Christian Social Ethic*. Notre Dame, IN: University of Notre Dame Press, 1981.

———. *The Peaceable Kingdom: A Primer in Christian Ethics*. Notre Dame, IN: University of Notre Dame Press, 1983.

———. "Preaching as though We Had Enemies." *First Things* (May 1995).

———. *Unleashing the Scripture: Freeing the Bible from Captivity to America.* Nashville: Abingdon, 1993.

———. "Worship, Evangelism, Ethics: On Eliminating the 'And.'" In *Liturgy and the Moral Self: Humanity at Full Stretch Before God,* edited by E. Byron Anderson and Bruce T. Morrill, 95–107. Collegeville, MN: Liturgical Press, 1998.

Hays, Richard B. "Reading Scripture in Light of the Resurrection." In *The Art of Reading Scripture,* edited by Ellen F. Davis and Richard B. Hays, 216–38. Grand Rapids: Eerdmans, 2003.

Hersch, Patricia. *A Tribe Apart: A Journey into the Heart of American Adolescence.* New York: Ballantine Books, 1999.

Jenson, Robert J., and Leanne Van Dyk. "How Does Jesus Make a Difference? The Person and Work of Jesus Christ." In *Essentials of Christian Theology,* edited by William C. Placher, 183–220. Louisville: Westminster John Knox, 2003.

Jones, James W. *Contemporary Psychoanalysis and Religion: Transference and Transcendence.* New Haven: Yale University Press, 1991.

Jones, Serene. "What's Wrong with Us?" In *Essentials of Christian Theology,* edited by William C. Placher, 141–58. Louisville: Westminster John Knox Press, 2003.

Kavanagh, Aidan. *On Liturgical Theology.* Collegeville, MN: Liturgical Press, 1984.

Kegan, Robert. *In Over Our Heads: The Mental Demands of Modern Life.* Cambridge, MA: Harvard, 1994.

Knight, Henry. *The Presence of God in the Christian Life: John Wesley and the Means of Grace.* Metuchen, NJ: Scarecrow, 1992.

Koyama, Kosuke. "The Eucharist: Ecumenical and Ecological." *Ecumenical Review* 44 (1992): 80–90.

Lathrop, Gordon W. *Holy Ground: A Liturgical Cosmology.* Minneapolis: Fortress, 2003.

———. *Holy People: A Liturgical Ecclesiology.* Minneapolis: Fortress, 2006.

———. *Holy Things: A Liturgical Theology.* Minneapolis: Fortress, 1993.

LeDoux, Joseph. *The Emotional Brain: The Mysterious Underpinnings of Emotional Life.* New York: Touchstone, 1996.

Levertov, Denise. *The Stream and the Sapphire: Selected Poems on Religious Themes.* New York: W. W. Norton, 1997.

MacIntyre, Alasdair. *After Virtue: A Study in Moral Theory.* Notre Dame, IN: University of Notre Dame Press, 1984.

Maddox, Randy L. *Responsible Grace: John Wesley's Practical Theology.* Nashville: Kingswood, 1994.

McMichael, Ralph N., Jr. "The Redemption of Creation: A Liturgical Theology." In *Creation and Liturgy: Studies in Honor of H. Boone Porter*,
edited by Ralph N. McMichael, Jr. Washington, DC: Pastoral Press,
1993.

Palmer, Parker J. *To Know as We Are Known*. San Francisco: HarperCollins,
1993.

Phillips, L. Edward. "How Shall We Worship?" In *Worship Matters: A
United Methodist Guide to Worship*, edited by E. Byron Anderson,
23–29. Nashville: Discipleship Resources, 1999.

Pohl, Christine. *Making Room: Recovering Hospitality as a Christian
Tradition*. Grand Rapids: Eerdmans, 1999.

Postman, Neil. *Amusing Ourselves to Death: Public Discourse in the Age
of Show Business*. New York: Penguin, 1986.

Rasmussen, Larry. *Earth Community Earth Ethics*. Maryknoll, NY: Orbis
Books, 1996.

———. "Eco-Justice: Church and Community Together." In *Earth Habitat:
Eco-Injustice and the Church's Response*, edited by Dieter Hessel and
Larry Rasmussen. Minneapolis: Fortress, 2001.

Revolve 2007: The Complete New Testament, NCV. Nashville: Thomas
Nelson, 2007.

Rieff, Philip. *The Triumph of the Therapeutic: Uses of Faith after Freud*.
Chicago: University of Chicago Press, 1966.

Ross, Chanon. "Jesus Isn't Cool: Challenging Youth Ministry." *Christian
Century*, September 6, 2005, 22–25.

Saliers, Don. "Liturgy and Ethics: Some New Beginnings." In *Liturgy and
the Moral Self: Humanity at Full Stretch before God*, edited by E. Byran
Anderson and Bruce T. Morrill, 15–35. Collegeville, MN: Liturgical
Press, 1998.

———. *The Soul in Paraphrase: Prayer and the Religious Affections*. New
York: Seabury, 1980.

———. *Worship as Theology: Foretaste of Glory Divine*. Nashville: Abingdon, 1994.

The Sayings of the Desert Fathers: The Alphabetical Collection. Translated
by Benedicta Ward, SLG. Kalamazoo: Cistercian, 1975.

Schmemann, Alexander. *For the Life of the World: Sacraments and Orthodoxy*. Crestwood, NY: St. Vladimir's Seminary Press, 1973.

———. *Introduction to Liturgical Theology*. Crestwood, NY: St. Vladimir's
Seminary Press, 1986.

Senn, Frank C. "The Care of the Earth as a Paradigm for the Treatment of
the Eucharistic Elements." In *Creation and Liturgy: Studies in Honor of
H. Boone Porter*, edited by Ralph N. McMichael, Jr. Washington, DC:
Pastoral Press, 1993.

Smith, Christian. *Soul Searching: The Religious and Spiritual Lives of American Teens*. New York: Oxford University Press, 2005.

Stookey, Laurence Hull. *Baptism: Christ's Act in the Church*. Nashville: Abingdon, 1982.

————. *Eucharist: Christ's Feast with the Church*. Nashville: Abingdon, 1993.

Strauch, Barbara. *The Primal Teen: What the New Discoveries about the Teenage Brain Tell Us about Our Kids*. New York: Doubleday, 2003.

Volf, Miroslav and Dorothy C. Bass, eds. *Practicing Theology: Beliefs and Practices in Christian Life*. Grand Rapids: Eerdmans, 2002.

Warren, Michael. *Seeing Through the Media: A Religious View of Communications and Cultural Analysis*. Harrisburg: Trinity, 1997.

————. *Youth, Gospel, Liberation*. Dublin: Veritas, 1998.

White, David F. *Practicing Discernment with Youth: A Transformative Youth Ministry Approach*. Cleveland: Pilgrim, 2005.

White, James F. "Our Apostasy in Worship." *The Christian Century*, September 28, 1977, 842–45.

Willimon, William H. *Remember Who You Are: Baptism, a Model for Christian Life*. Nashville: Upper Room, 1980.

Willimon, William H., and Stanley M. Hauerwas with Scott C. Saye. *Lord, Teach Us: The Lord's Prayer and the Christian Life*. Nashville: Abingdon, 1996.

Woolfenden, Gregory W. *Daily Liturgical Prayer: Origins and Theology*. Burlington, VT: Ashgate, 2004.

Wright, Nathan. "Liturgy, Stewardship, and Creation." In *Creation and Liturgy: Studies in Honor of H. Boone Porter*, edited by Ralph N. McMichael, Jr. Washington, DC: Pastoral Press, 1993.

Yarnold, Edward, S.J. *The Awe-Inspiring Rites of Initiation: The Origins of the R.C.I.A.* Collegeville, MN: Liturgical Press, 1994.

Index